IMAGES
of America

THE CARO AREA

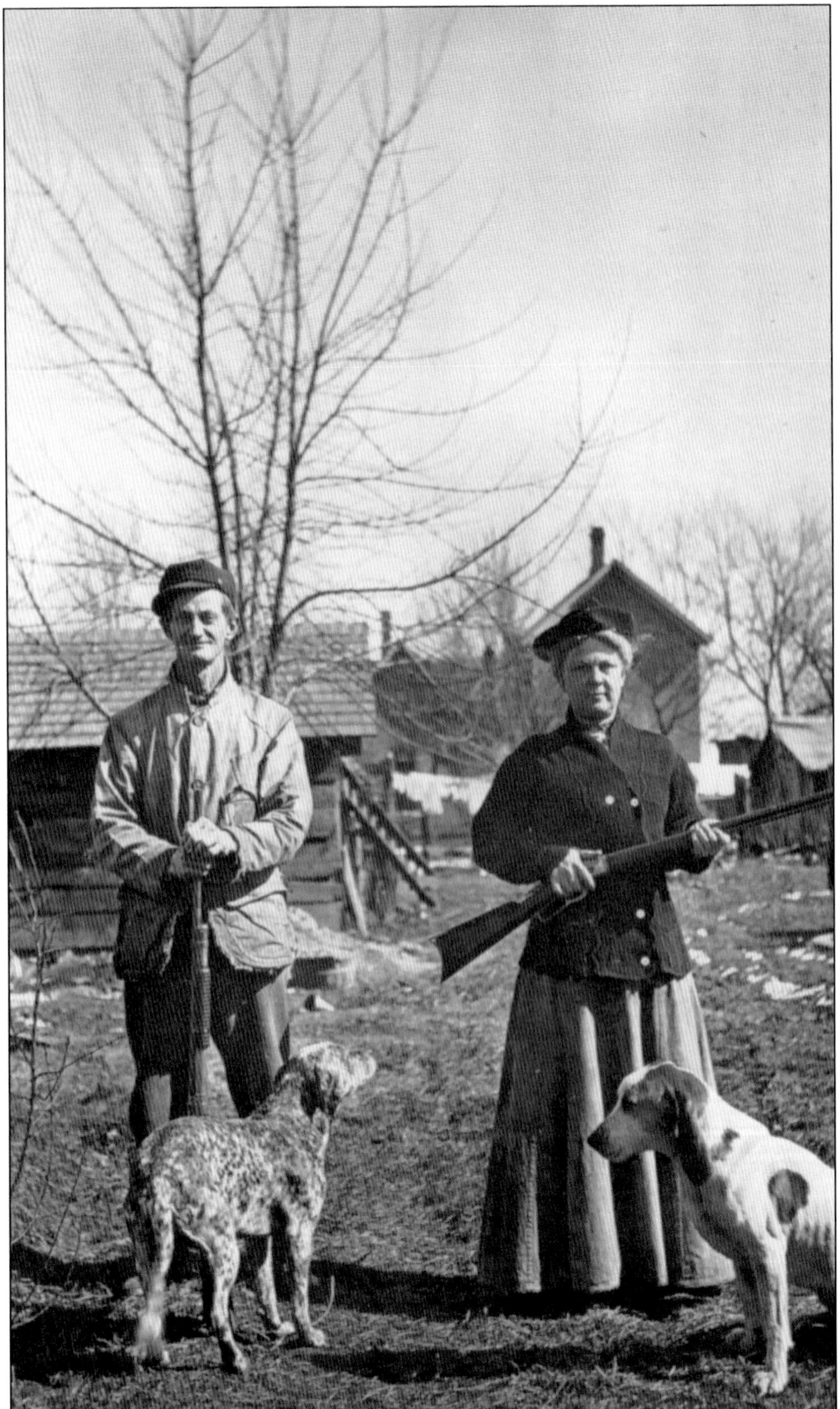

On the Cover: The Grays. This photograph from around 1910 shows George and Edna (possibly Edina) Gray of Indianfields Township. As befits an area only 58 years from first settlement, they appear quite self-sufficient. (Courtesy of Watrousville-Caro Historical Society.)

IMAGES
of America

The Caro Area

Marcia M. Dievendorf, Patricia E. Frazer, and Mark O. Keller
for the Caro Area District Library

ARCADIA
PUBLISHING

ISBN 978-0-7385-8362-4

Published by Arcadia Publishing
Charleston, South Carolina

Printed in the United States of America

Library of Congress Control Number: 2010931933

For all general information, please contact Arcadia Publishing:
Telephone 843-853-2070
Fax 843-853-0044
E-mail sales@arcadiapublishing.com
For customer service and orders:
Toll-Free 1-888-313-2665

Visit us on the Internet at www.arcadiapublishing.com

This book is dedicated to Peter DeWitt Bush, William A. Heartt, and Charles Montague, who spent their lives doing their best for their community.

Contents

Acknowledgments		6
Introduction		7
1.	Building a Village	9
2.	An Enterprising Caro	33
3.	Village Life	61
4.	A Walk through Caro	87
5.	Rural Life	111
Bibliography		127

Acknowledgments

Creating a book like this requires the talents, knowledge, and efforts of many people, past and present. From the past, Dorr Wiltse, Doug Gallery, and Harry Schubel, and from the present, Mark Keller, Mark Putnam, Rita Easlick, Gloria Hall, the Caro Historical Commission, and the Watrousville-Caro Historical Society provided invaluable personal recollections, information, and access to archives, compilations, and photographs. Their love for their community and their consequent need to find, preserve, and share the past shines through. The archives of the *Tuscola County Advertiser* were essential and are themselves an irreplaceable local treasure. The Caro Area District Library files were also an invaluable source of information. Above all else, we would not have this book of photographs without the great generosity of the Watrousville-Caro Historical Society; Tim Romain, custodian of the Cope collection; Gloria Hall; Norman Dorr Wiltse and the Dorr Wiltse collection; Laureen Joslin; Gail Lesoski; Dave and Jane Neese; Mark Putnam; Jerry Middaugh; and Almona Pierce Bradley. Terry Tomlinson was of great assistance in identifying and labeling photographs of local sites and the equipment pictured. Lenore Schultz, as a centenarian, added personal reminiscences that were unobtainable from anyone else. We also thank our families for their understanding and encouragement through this long process as well as our editors Anna Wilson and John Pearson at Arcadia Publishing. We celebrate all the photographs in this book that show the unique but also typical American life of the Caro area. It has been a pleasure to put this book together and to get to know our community as it once was.

Introduction

Huron, Sanilac, and Tuscola Counties comprise the Thumb of the Michigan Mitten. Tuscola County was set aside by the Michigan legislature in 1840 and organized in 1850. The first settler to live within the present site of Caro, in the township of Indian Fields, was Samuel P. Sherman in 1852. The Chippewa had long inhabited this area, having a village on the south bank of the Cass River where they raised corn and potatoes. This area became known as Indian Fields. The lure and opportunity of lumbering along the Cass brought the first settlers and among them was Samuel's son William E. Sherman, Peter DeWitt Bush, Melvin Gibbs, and William A. Heartt. In 1859, William Sherman built a hotel in the township named the Centerville House. Sherman felt that because this point was near the center of Tuscola County, it was a good place for a town that might become the county seat. From 1861 through 1865, many battles were waged over the final location of that county seat. By October 1865, Centerville had won the prize, and in December 1865, the village was established and platted by Peter Bush, Samuel Sherman, Melvin Gibbs, S.R. Cross, and Charles Austin. Previously, land had sold for $15 an acre. These village lots sold for $15 to $25 each.

The end of the Civil War brought many new settlers with the requisite new construction and enterprise. There were enough prospects to cause William Sherman to plat an addition of about 50 acres to the village. At that time, entrepreneur Charles Montague returned from his time in the army and began his long career in Caro. Many of the settlers in the area were originally from Ontario, New York, and New England, coming after a first stop in downstate Michigan or in Ohio.

In 1866, a post office named Tuscola Center was established in Centerville. This caused understandable confusion, and in December 1868, there was a vote to change the name of Centerville to Caro. Caro was an abbreviation of Cairo, Egypt, as suggested by William Sherman. In February 1869, this name change was established by an act of the state legislature and in June 1869, the post office name was changed to Caro as well. A post office was an important development in a village, putting the village on the map, allowing for easier communication, and serving as a money order office when no banks had as yet been established.

By February 1871, the village of Caro had been incorporated, and the first common council of the village of Caro began looking at needed local improvements. These improvements included streets and sidewalks as well as a pound for animals, such as cattle, which were running loose. At this time, the village had about 500 residents, a good variety of businesses, and many opportunities for new arrivals. Now the growth and prosperity of the Caro area really began, and by 1905, Caro was a thriving and cohesive center of business, industry, and middle-class life.

Vital to that growth and prosperity was the surrounding countryside. In the beginning, lumbering along the Cass River sent millions of feet of logs floating down the Cass each year until the supply of lumber was exhausted by around 1880. With the end of lumbering, farming became the driving economic engine. The great forest fires of 1871 and 1881, horrific as they were, cleared the land for farming. Wheat, corn, oats, grasses, stock including dairy, and later sugar beets were the farm products. The railroad became the highway for these products.

Churches and schools, a library, a hospital, clubs and cultural organizations, paved streets and sidewalks, and electric lights all appeared on the scene. Like so many small towns across America, most everything a resident could want was available locally. And so life in the Caro area progressed through individual effort and, more importantly, through the combined efforts of townsfolk or rural neighbors working together for the betterment of everyone.

One

Building a Village

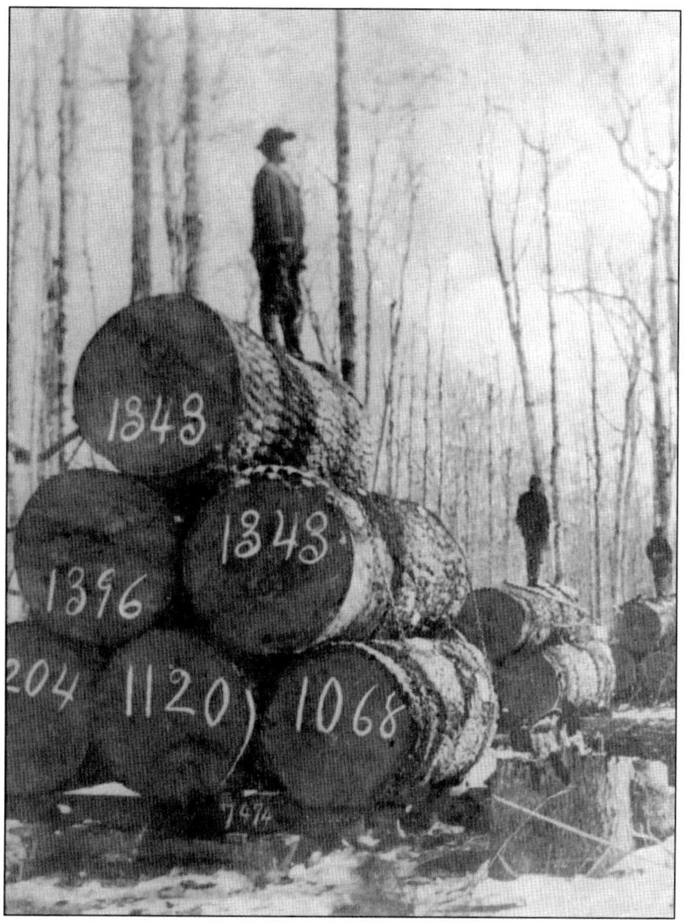

Logging on the Cass River. The opportunity for lumbering brought the first settlers to the Caro area. The forests along the Cass held cork pine of such quality that it was sold throughout the United States. The numbers painted on the logs indicated the estimated board feet each log would yield. The peak of lumbering in the area was reached in 1873, with 100,458,140 feet of logs. (Courtesy of Watrousville-Caro Historical Society.)

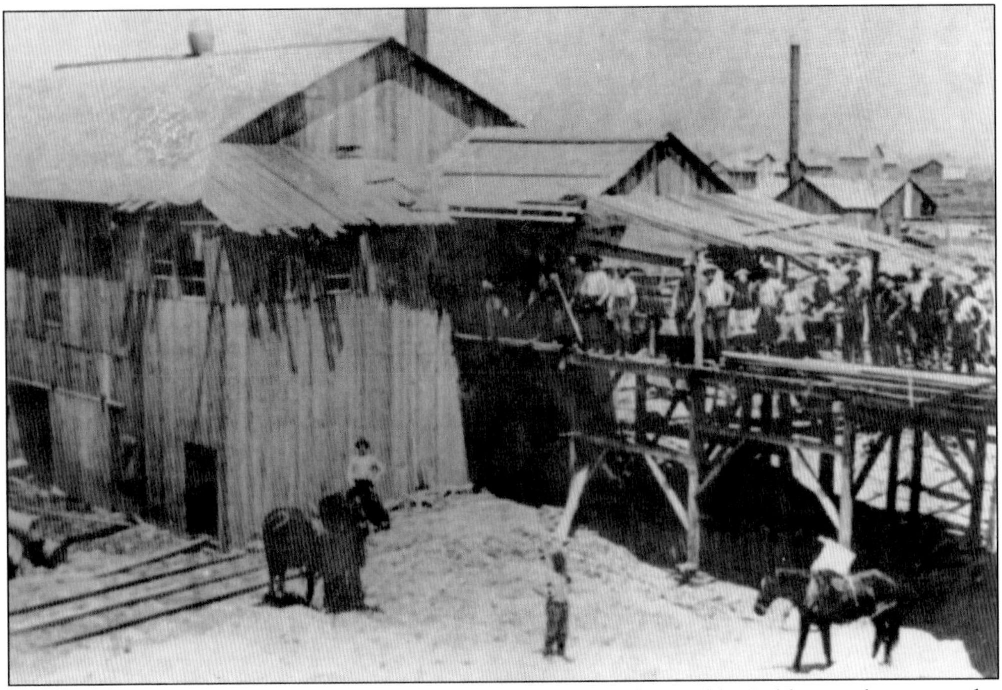

EARLY SAWMILL. A sawmill was built in Caro in 1867 by Joseph Gamble. Sold several times in the ensuing years, in 1876, it was bought by J.D. Wilsey & Company. The sawmill cut pine, hemlock, and all kinds of hardwoods that grew in the area. A circular saw was added in 1883 to increase the capacity of the sawmill. (Courtesy of Watrousville-Caro Historical Society.)

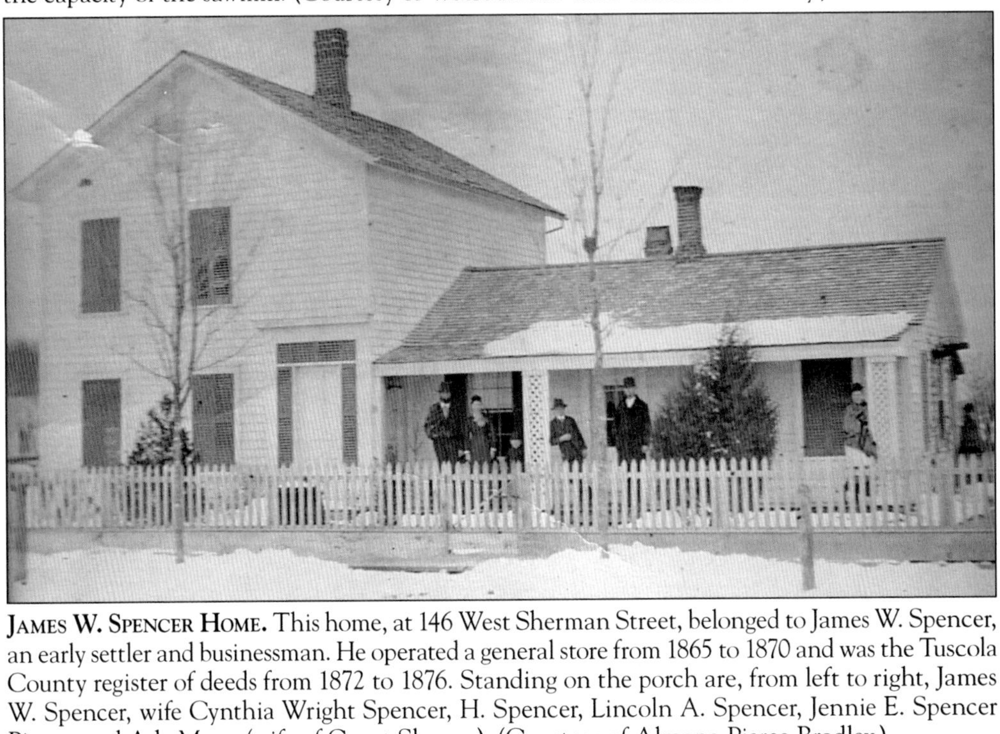

JAMES W. SPENCER HOME. This home, at 146 West Sherman Street, belonged to James W. Spencer, an early settler and businessman. He operated a general store from 1865 to 1870 and was the Tuscola County register of deeds from 1872 to 1876. Standing on the porch are, from left to right, James W. Spencer, wife Cynthia Wright Spencer, H. Spencer, Lincoln A. Spencer, Jennie E. Spencer Pierce, and Ada Mertz (wife of Grant Slocum). (Courtesy of Almona Pierce Bradley.)

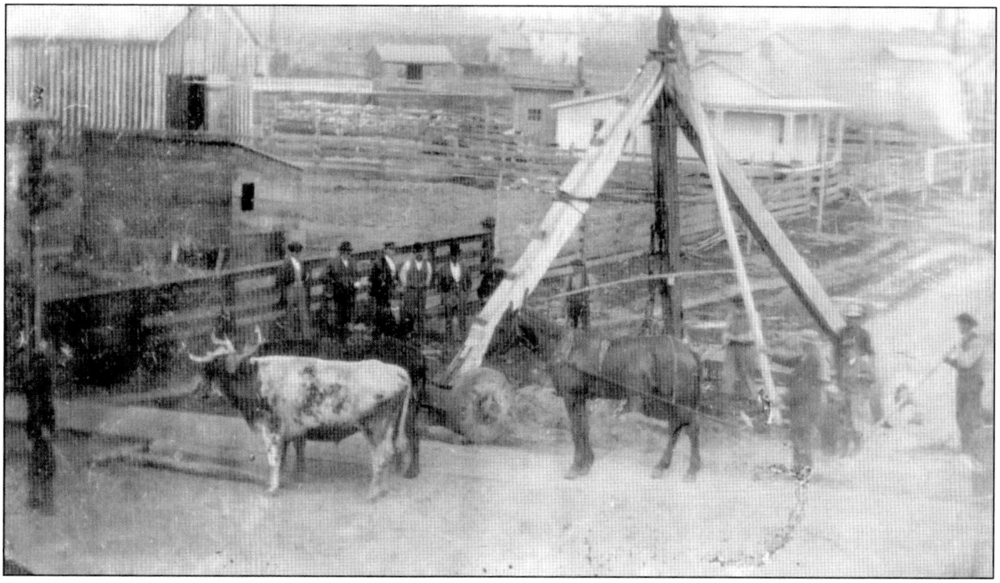

Stump Pulling, 1875. Stump pulling was a necessity in building the village. The area was heavily forested when settled, and stumps had to be pulled to have streets and roads and to open farmland. This stump pulling was taking place near Peter Bush's Lincoln Street home. (Courtesy of Watrousville-Caro Historical Society.)

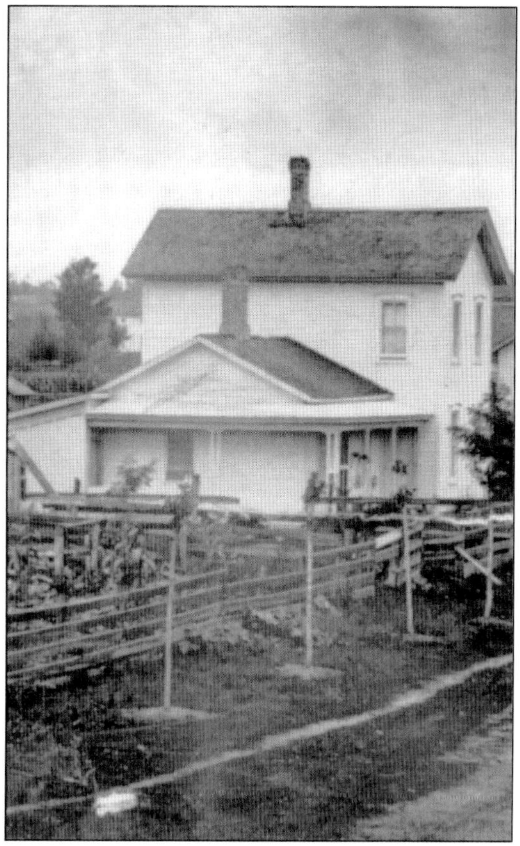

Peter DeWitt Bush Home, 1870s. This home was on West Lincoln Street and was later owned by Peter's son Dewitt Bush and his grandson Ervin Purdy. In the 20th century, this site was occupied for many years by Detroit Edison. Peter Bush was vital to the development of Caro, providing land (including the courthouse site), funds, and vision. (Courtesy of Watrousville-Caro Historical Society.)

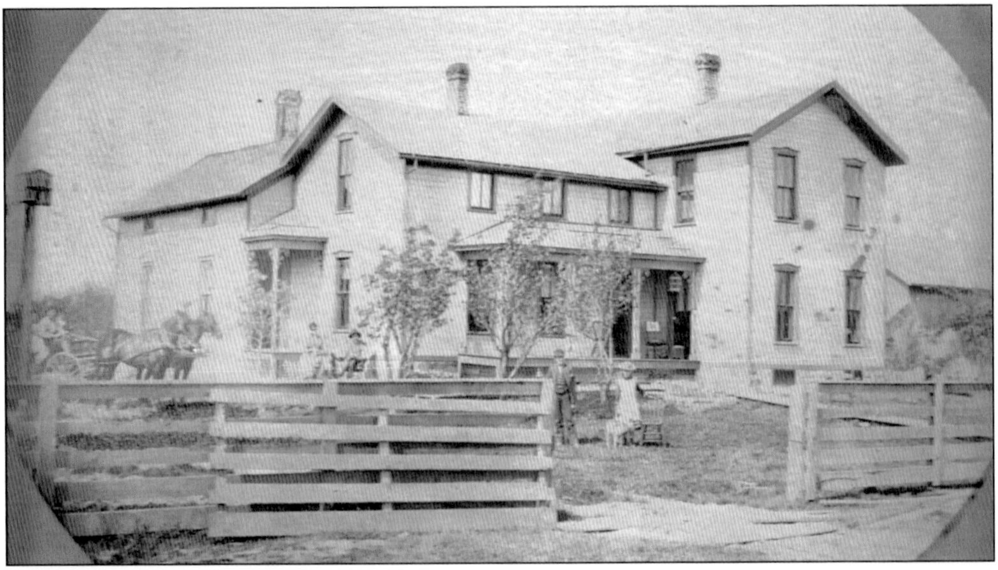

Renovations to the Bush Home. This photograph is believed to show the Bush home late in the 19th century or early in the 20th century. The wing of the house (front left) as compared to the previous photograph now has an upper floor, the wrap-around porch has been reduced, and a side door and small porch (far left) have been added. Bush is believed to be the person sitting in the yard (far left). (Courtesy of Patricia Frazer.)

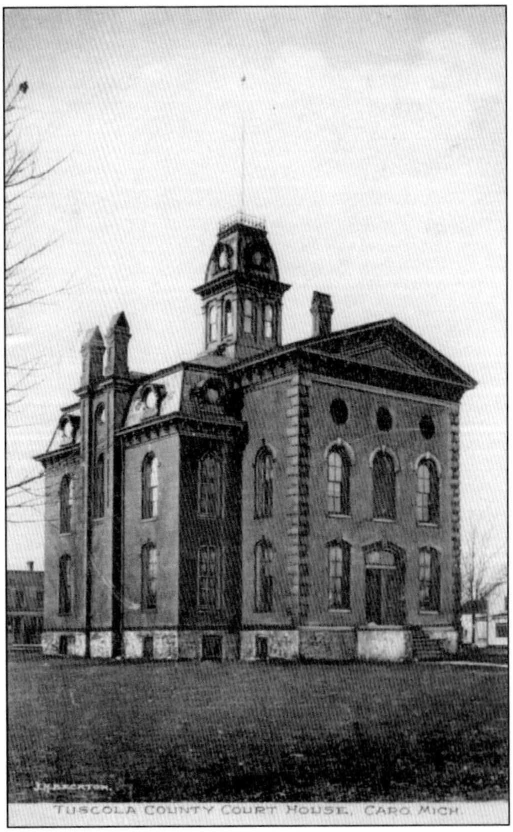

Old Tuscola County Courthouse. In 1866, Peter DeWitt Bush, the second permanent settler of Caro, donated land for the courthouse square. In a combined effort, the old Universalist church building was moved onto the site to become a temporary courthouse. In 1873, this brick building was erected and served until 1931, when it was razed and replaced by the current courthouse. (Courtesy of Gloria Hall.)

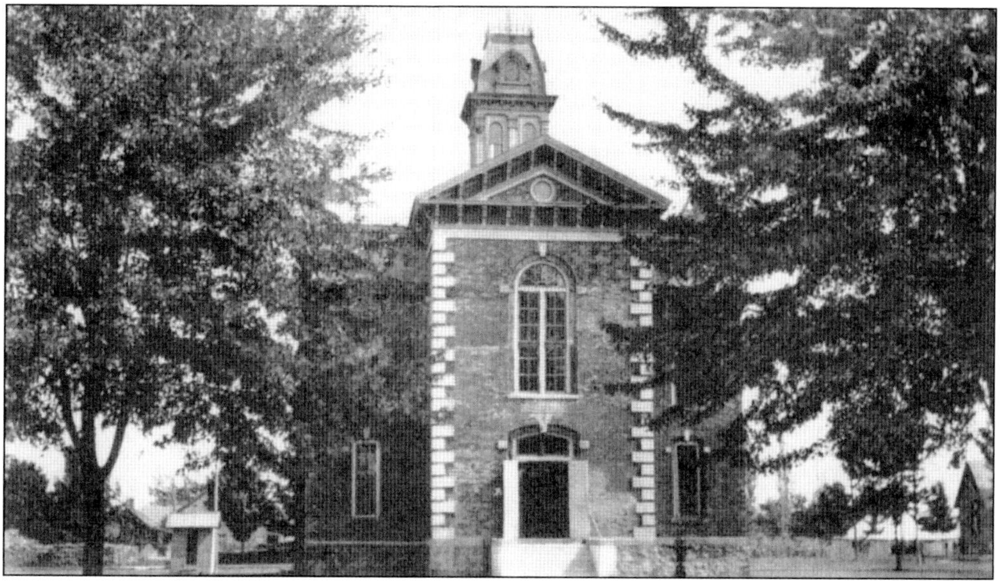

Rear Entrance, Courthouse. This is a view of the rear entrance to the 1873 brick courthouse. This side of the courthouse faced Court Street and was conveniently across the street from the county jail building, much as it is today. (Courtesy of Gloria Hall.)

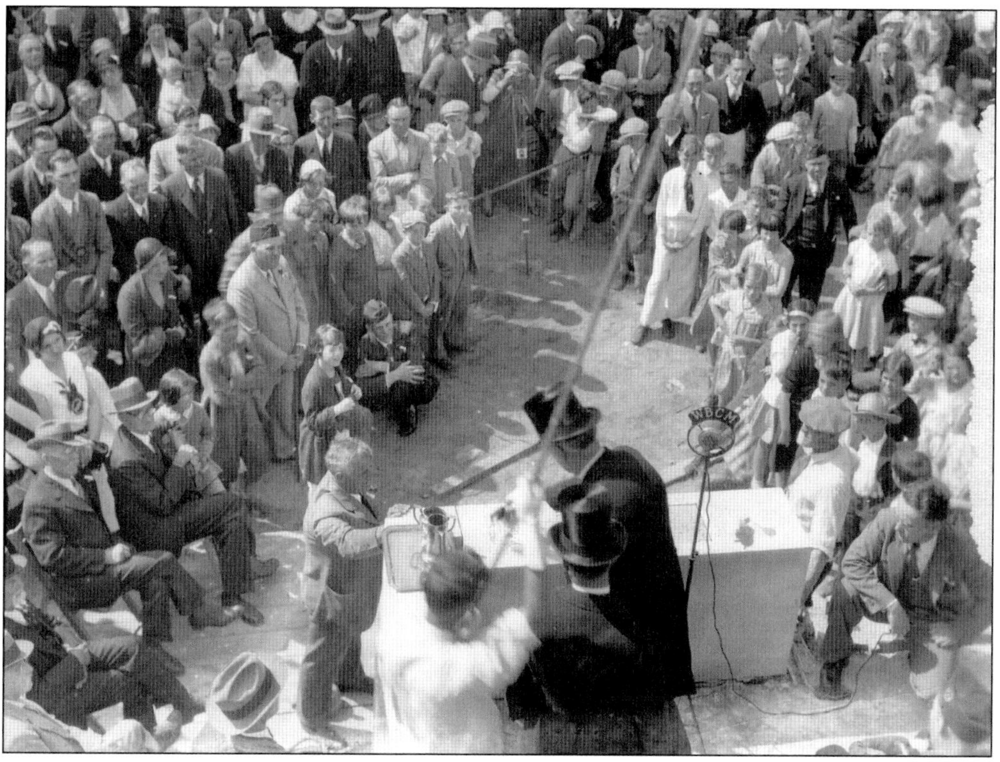

Laying the Cornerstone. On May 27, 1932, the courthouse square was the site of much celebration, as the cornerstone of the beautiful new courthouse was laid. A service was conducted by the grand master of the Michigan Masons during the cornerstone ceremony. (Courtesy of Watrousville-Caro Historical Society.)

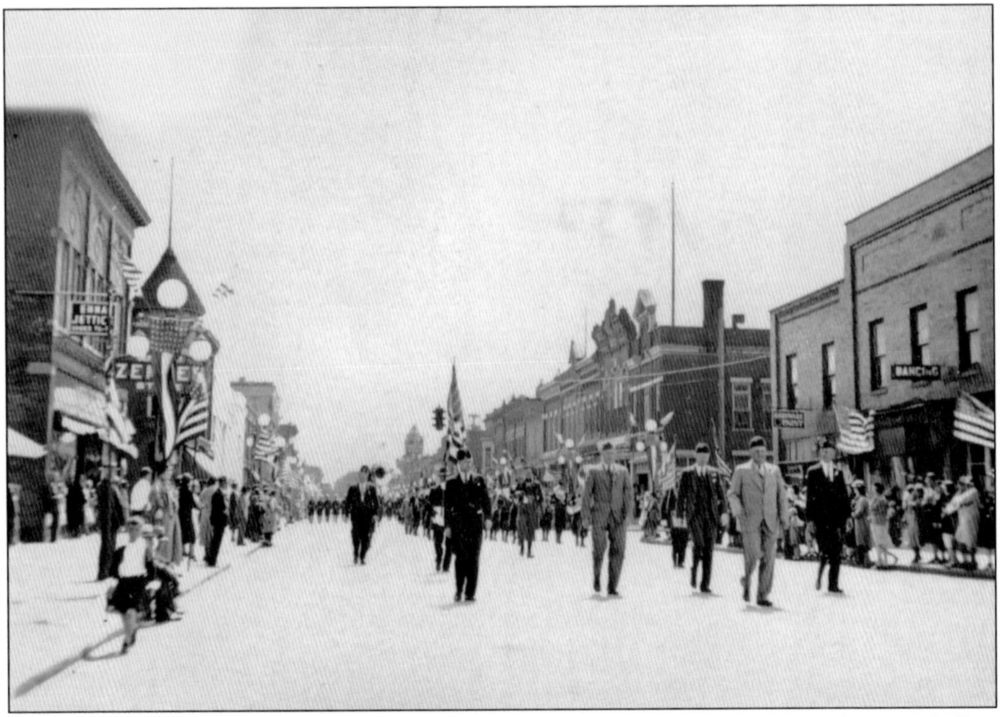

Courthouse Cornerstone Parade. On May 27, 1932, this parade led spectators from city hall to the cornerstone-laying festivities at the courthouse square. Pictured is the procession of mounted units, flag bearers, and dignitaries as it passes the intersection of Burnside and State Streets in front of the Zemke store. (Courtesy of Watrousville-Caro Historical Society.)

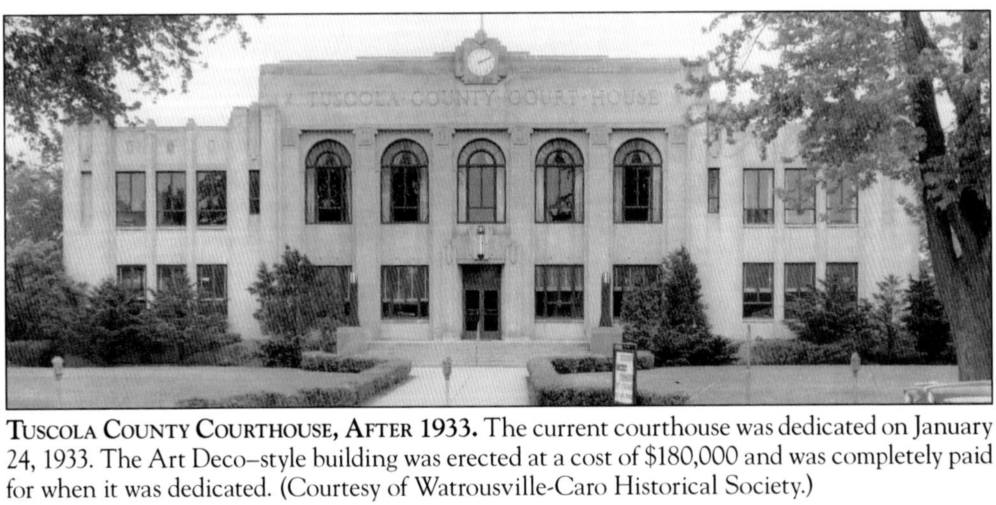

Tuscola County Courthouse, After 1933. The current courthouse was dedicated on January 24, 1933. The Art Deco–style building was erected at a cost of $180,000 and was completely paid for when it was dedicated. (Courtesy of Watrousville-Caro Historical Society.)

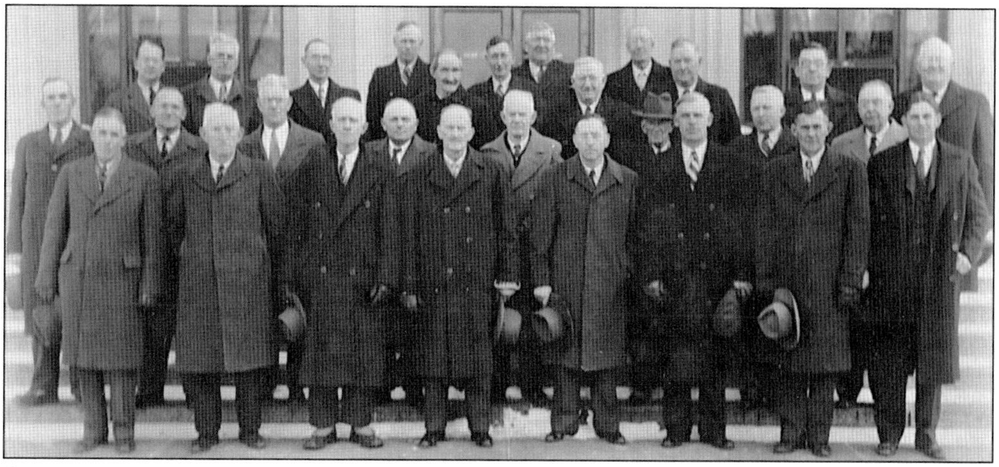

COURTHOUSE STAFF, C. 1933. In 1933, after the new Tuscola County Courthouse opened its doors to the public, these men were responsible for making things happen. The man in the back row, far left, is the only person identified in this photograph. He is Tim Quinn, who was the prosecuting attorney at the time and who later became a Michigan Supreme Court justice. (Courtesy of Norman Dorr Wiltse.)

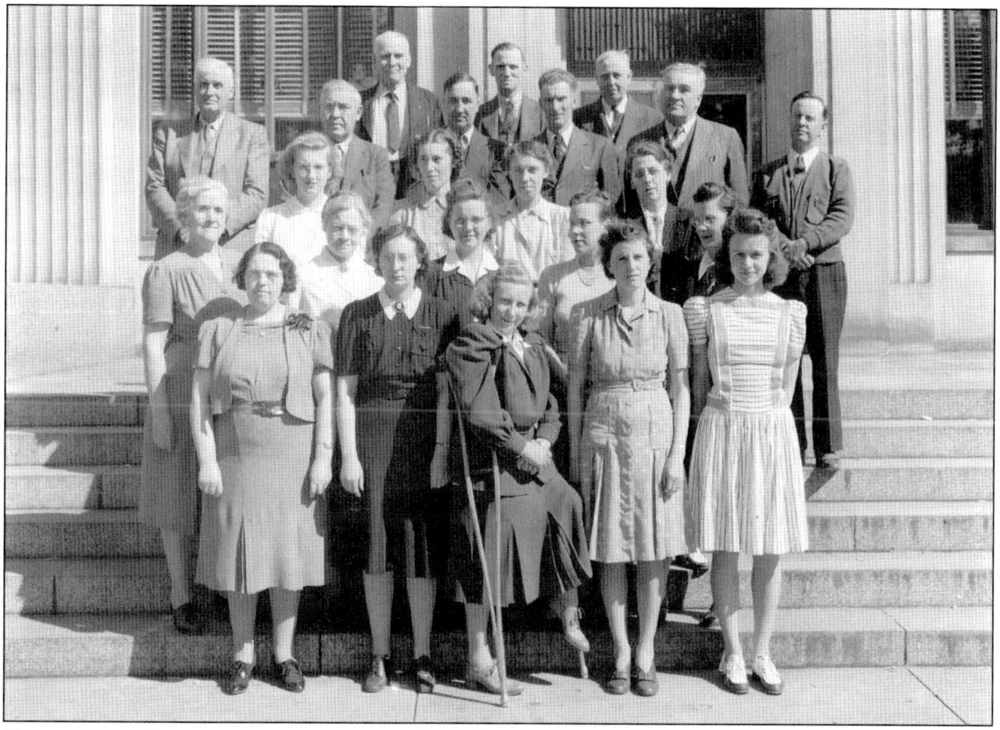

COURTHOUSE EMPLOYEES, 1942. Pictured are, from left to right, (first row) Ruth Tomlinson Dietz, Lucile Craig Miller, Jenney Mantey, Beryle Woodard Rocheleau, and Phyllis Greenfield; (second row) Carrie Hograver, Maud Ormes, Carolyn Ayre, Mildred Keilitz, and Rose Nagy Wilkinson; (third row) Maxine Barriger Kelley, Alice Foster, Marguerite Carpenter, and Lola Reichert; (fourth row) Ben H. McComb, O.E. McPherson, Arthur Willits, Truman Ackerman, Carl Keinath, and Wellington Reid; (fifth row) George Childs, Almon C. Pierce, and D.M. Graham. (Courtesy of Watrousville-Caro Historical Society.)

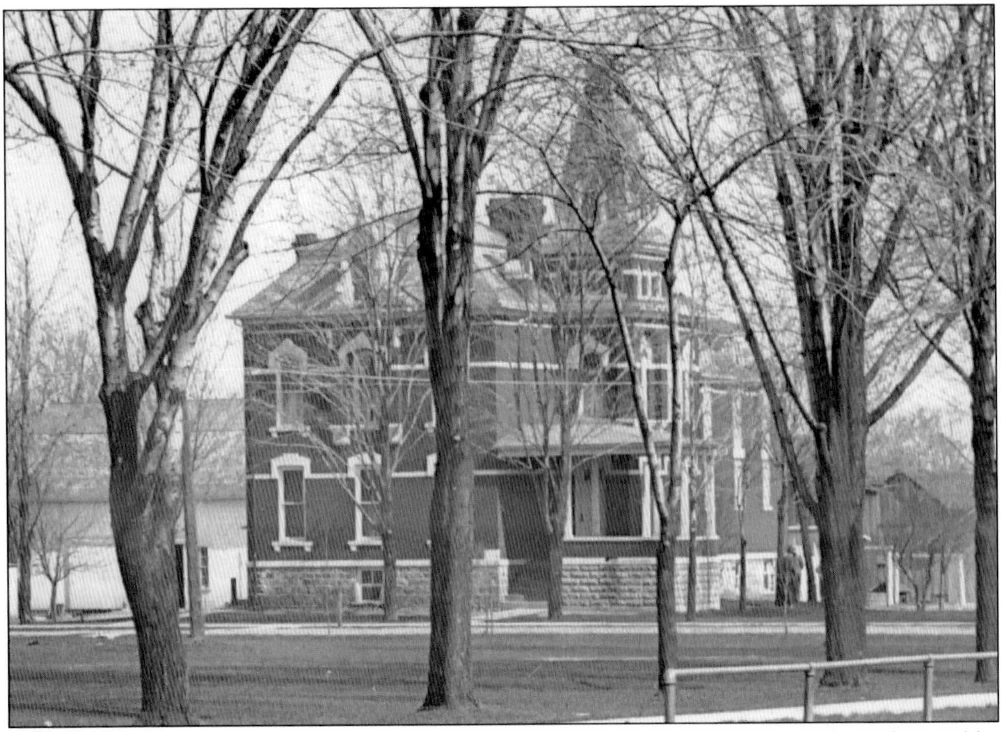

OLD TUSCOLA COUNTY JAIL. The old Tuscola County jail was built in 1878 on land donated by the earliest settler, Samuel P. Sherman. It was built at a cost of $8,800 and was the residence of the Tuscola County sheriff and the jail. It served until it was razed and replaced in 1966. (Courtesy of Watrousville-Caro Historical Society.)

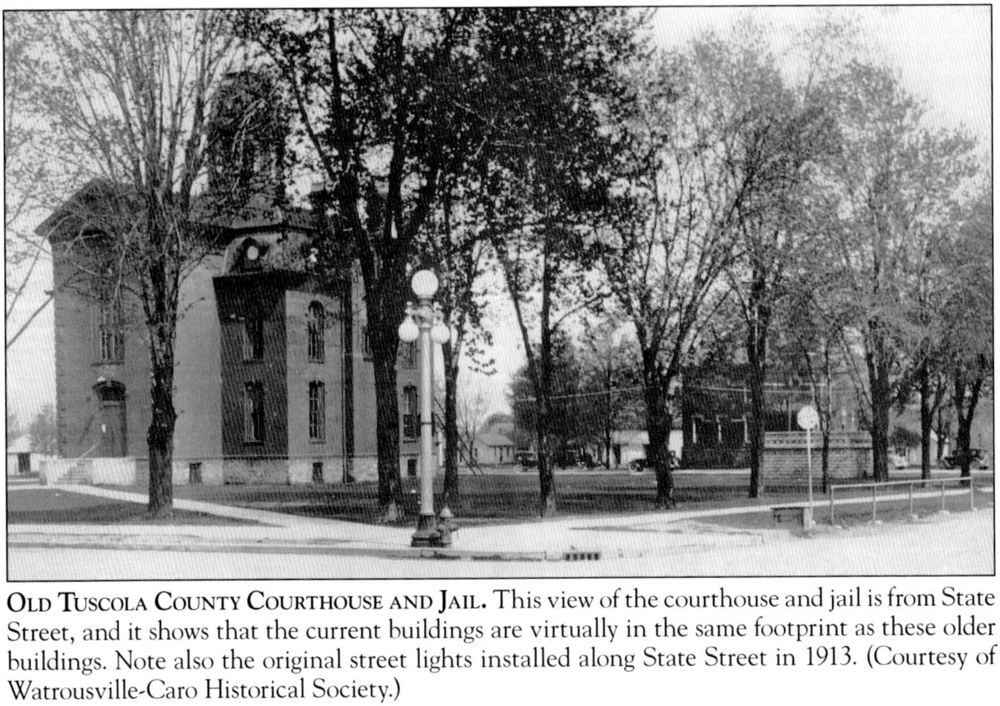

OLD TUSCOLA COUNTY COURTHOUSE AND JAIL. This view of the courthouse and jail is from State Street, and it shows that the current buildings are virtually in the same footprint as these older buildings. Note also the original street lights installed along State Street in 1913. (Courtesy of Watrousville-Caro Historical Society.)

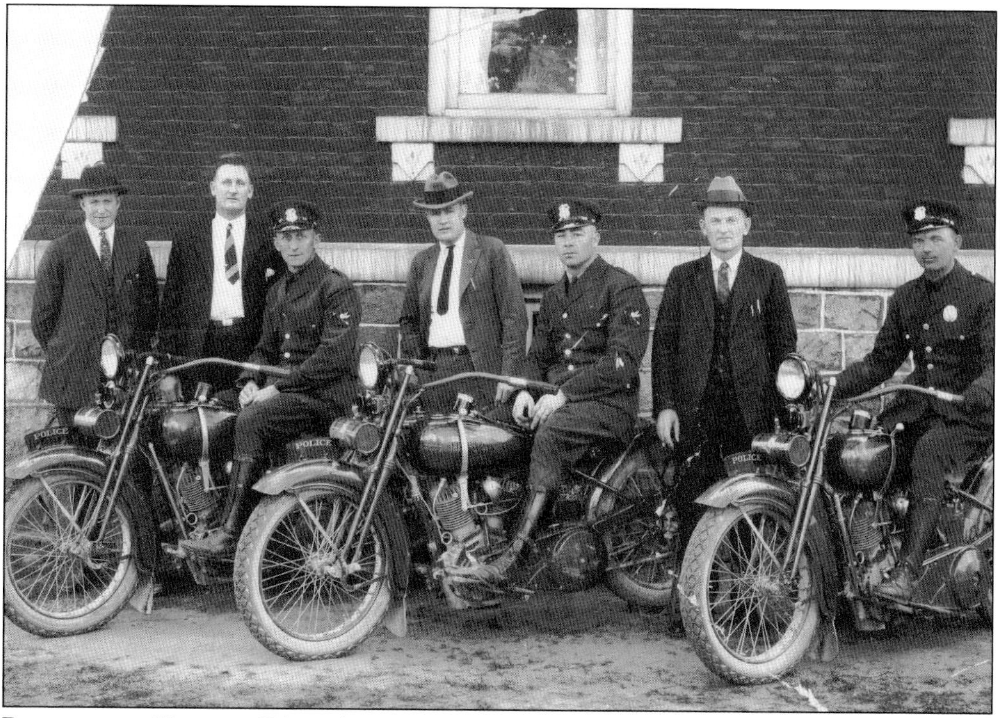

POLICEMEN ON HARLEYS. Taken about 1927, this photograph shows Tuscola County police officers. The motorcycles are limited model Harley-Davidsons made between 1926 and 1928. The officers are posed in front of the old Tuscola County jail and sheriff's residence. (Courtesy of Laureen Joslin.)

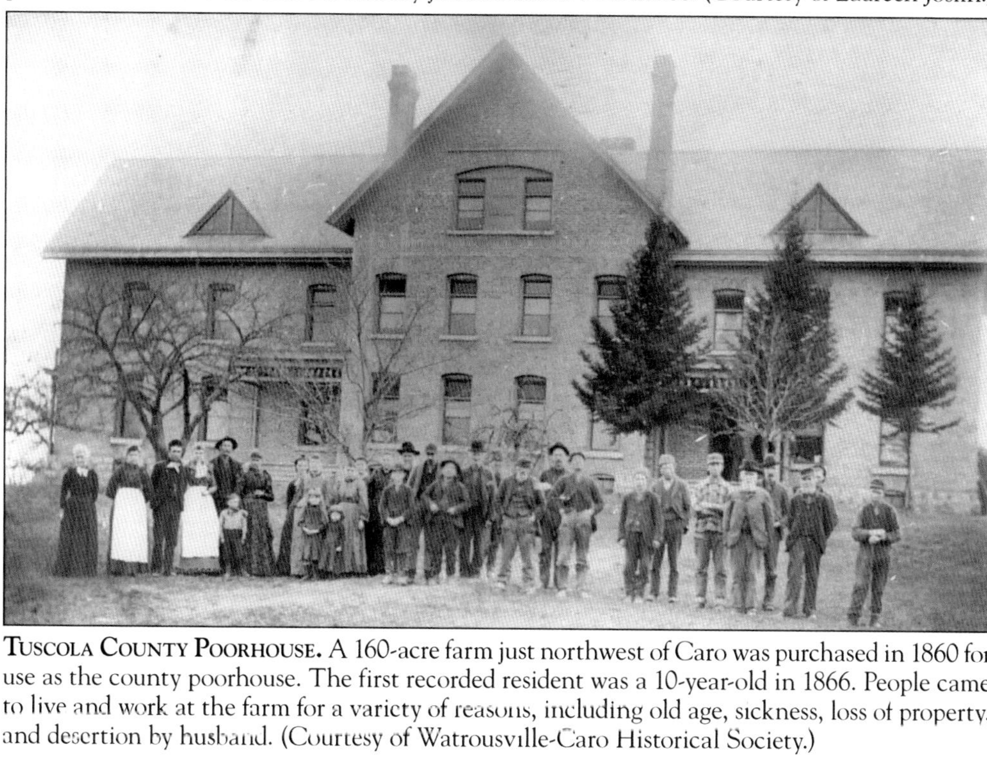

TUSCOLA COUNTY POORHOUSE. A 160-acre farm just northwest of Caro was purchased in 1860 for use as the county poorhouse. The first recorded resident was a 10-year-old in 1866. People came to live and work at the farm for a variety of reasons, including old age, sickness, loss of property, and desertion by husband. (Courtesy of Watrousville-Caro Historical Society.)

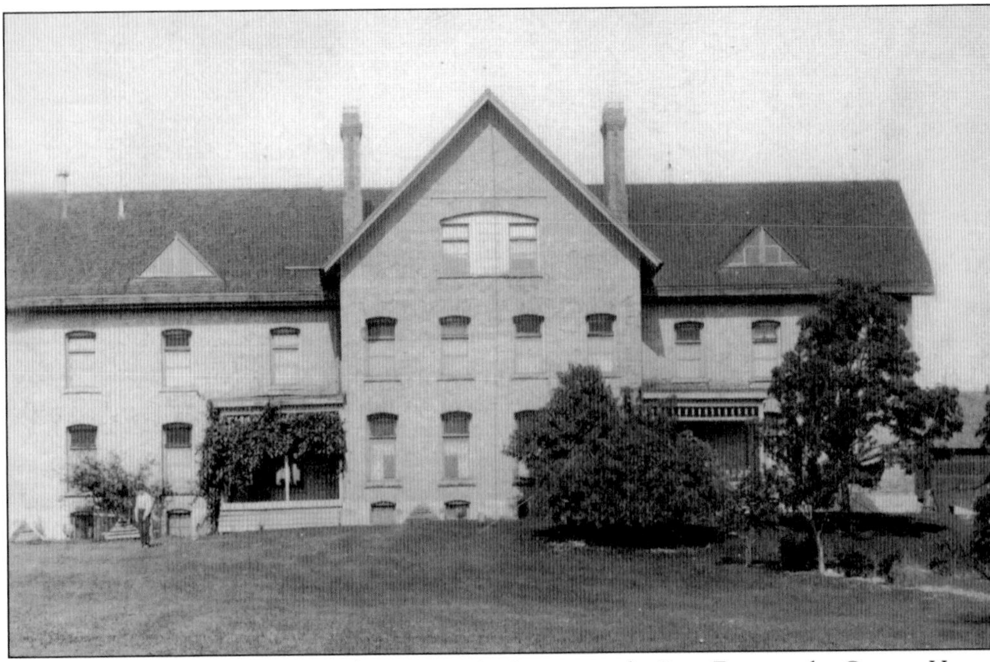

The Poor Farm, 1912. The poorhouse was also known as the Poor Farm or the County Home. In 1939, it became a hospital for the chronically ill and was then called the county infirmary. In November 1958, it became the Tuscola County Medical Care Facility with a new building. (Courtesy of Tim Romain/Cope collection.)

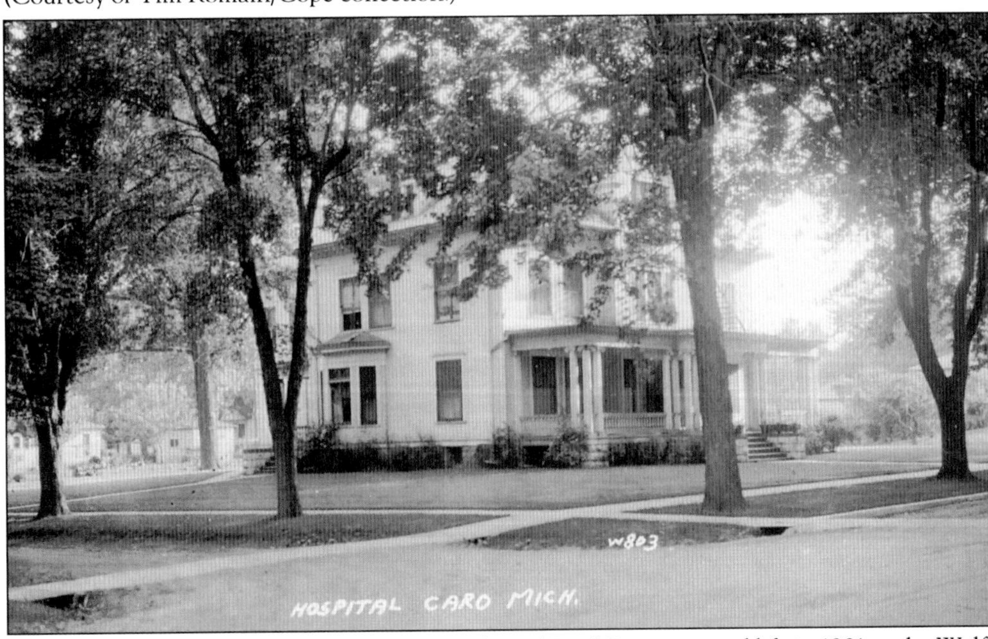

Caro Hospital. This building on West Burnside and Pearl Streets started life in 1901 as the Wolfe Himelhoch home and was sold to Theron Atwood in 1913. By 1920, it had become a combined hospital and residence of Dr. Charles Race. From 1922 to 1928, it was used by the Caro Schools as the Anna Black School, and it was later used as the Caro Hospital until 1963 when it was razed. (Courtesy of Gloria Hall.)

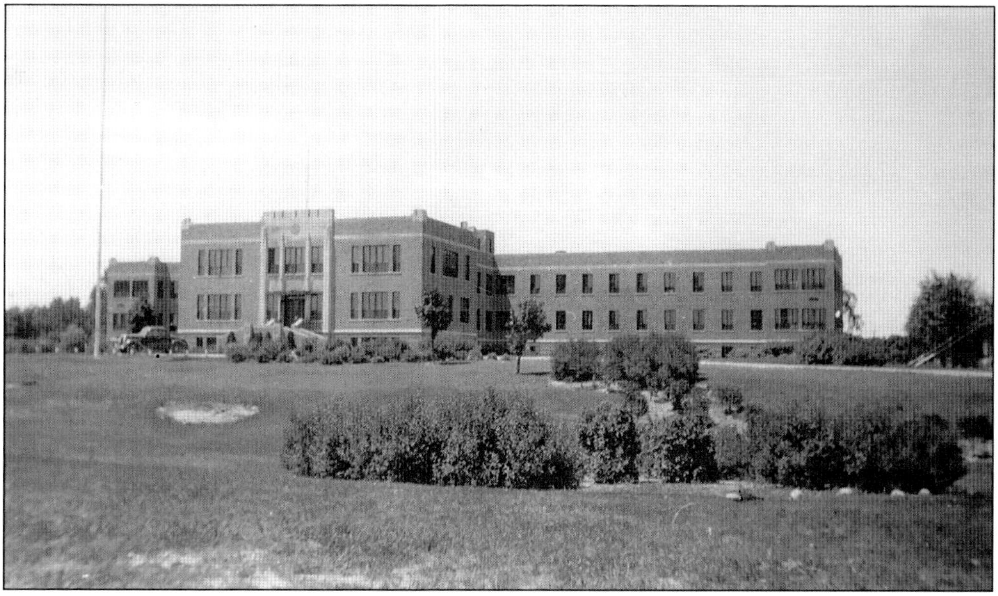

Caro State Hospital. Established in 1914 as the Farm Colony for Epileptics, this facility operated as a self-sufficient community. It became an institution for the developmentally disabled, then a home for the mentally impaired, and is now a forensic facility. This is a photograph of the administration building from around the 1940s. The hospital was a major employer in the Caro area for many years and is now known as the Caro Center. (Courtesy of Watrousville-Caro Historical Society.)

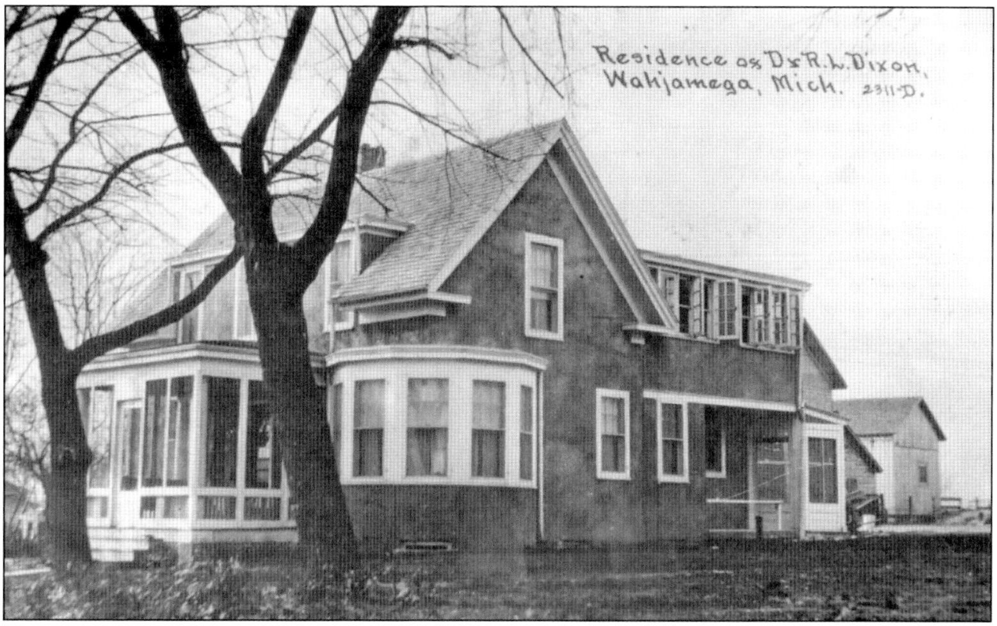

Superintendent's Home. Dr. Robert L. Dixon was superintendent at the Caro State Hospital from its beginnings as the Farm Colony in 1914 until 1949, with the exception of 1930–1937. This was the residence of the superintendent in 1916. The Farm Colony was built in Wahjamega, four miles south of Caro. The name *Wahjamega* was derived from the initials of six members of the William A. Heartt family. Heartt was the original settler of Wahjamega. (Courtesy of Gloria Hall.)

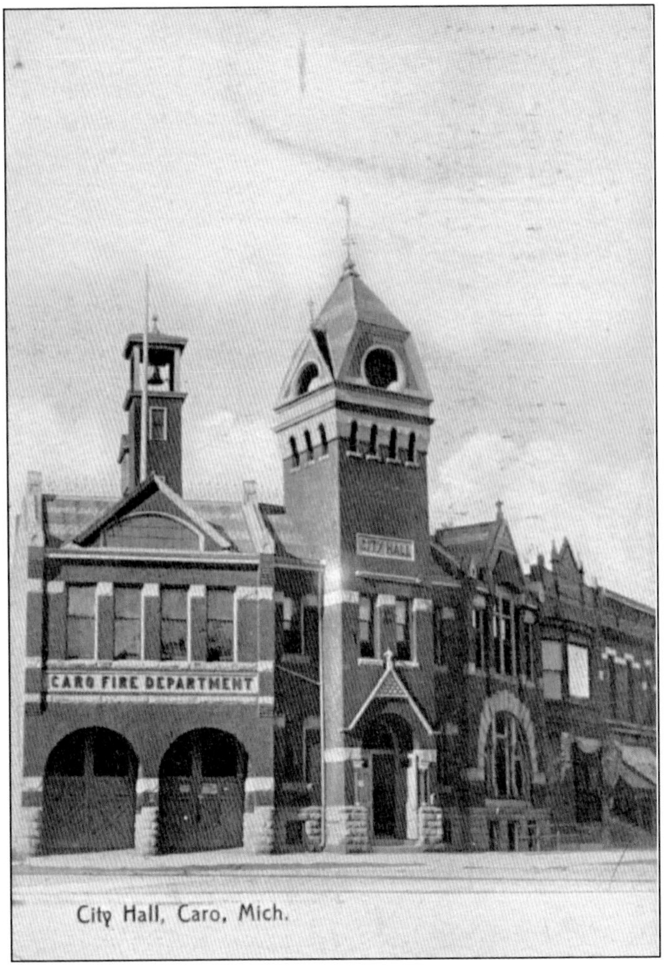

Caro City Hall. On December 9, 1887, Caro dedicated its new city hall, fire hall, and police station with all the pomp and circumstance due such a grand building. It was located at the corner of West Frank and State Streets, built at an angle that enabled it to face the village triangle. The city hall was the village centerpiece and a source of great civic pride. The building was razed in the 1950s. (Courtesy of Gloria Hall.)

"Caro's Great White Way." In 1913, State Street was paved, and electric street lights were installed. In honor of this great achievement, local poet Henry Dodge wrote the poem "Caro's Great White Way." His words speak to the changes that had occurred in 61 years and to the wonder that was felt for things we now take for granted. (Courtesy of Watrousville-Caro Historical Society.)

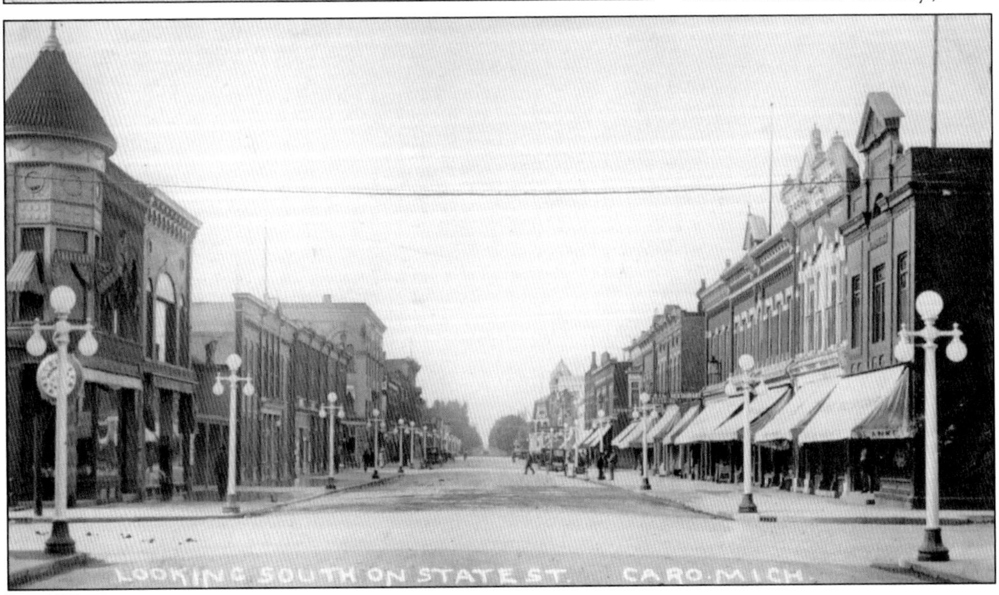

Caro's Great White Way

Our thoughts oft turn to years now past, some fifty-five or more,
'Twas then the virgin forest stretched, along our River's shore.
And where those giant pines then stood, and Red Men held their sway
We see at night the shining light, of Caro's Great White Way.

Of those who carved out early homes, and knew those days of toil,
Some passed away before their time, some died on Southern soil.
But few are left to know 'tis good, to be alive today,
To see the changes time has made, and Caro's Great White Way.

God gave to each a love of home, and may His will be done,
The men who chop'd and log'd the woods, were heroes every one.
And from their home beyond the flood, where it is always day,
May they look back on friends they loved, and Caro's Great White Way

Then let us cheer for lights and pave, 'tis best that we have known,
The gutter's filth and crossing mud, forever now have flown.
May street and light by day or night, seem bright as flow'rs in May,
To all who love the name of home, and Caro's Great White Way.

Caro, Mich., October 11, 1913. HENRY DODGE.

POEM BY HENRY DODGE. Here is the poem written by local poet Henry Dodge in honor of the great improvements on State Street in 1913. Dodge was an early settler, and his love of home brought forth many stories and poems celebrating life in the Caro area. (Courtesy of the *Tuscola County Advertiser.*)

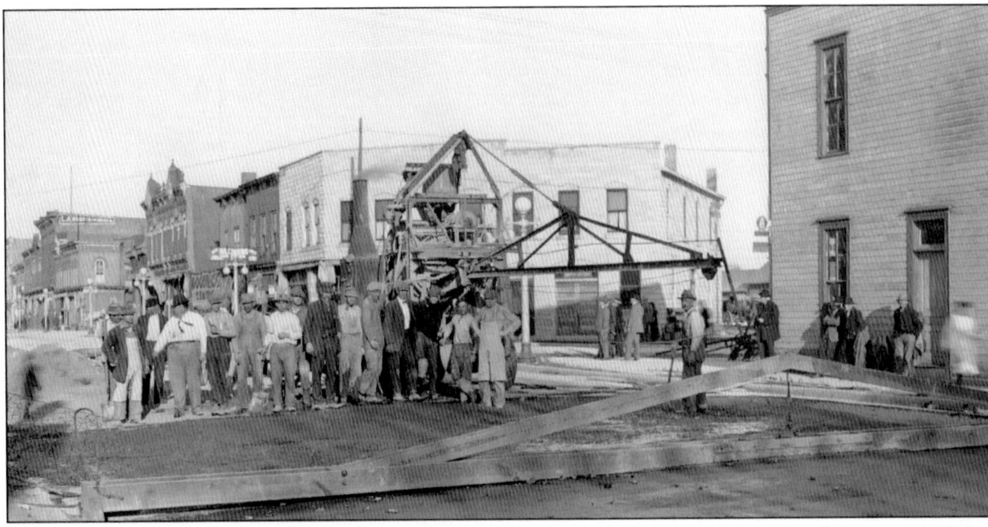

Paving Crew. This photograph shows the work crew and machinery involved in paving State Street at the corner of South Almer Street. The Morley Implement building is visible on the right. The street lights were already in place. There were also a number of observers along the street checking out the work. (Courtesy of Watrousville-Caro Historical Society.)

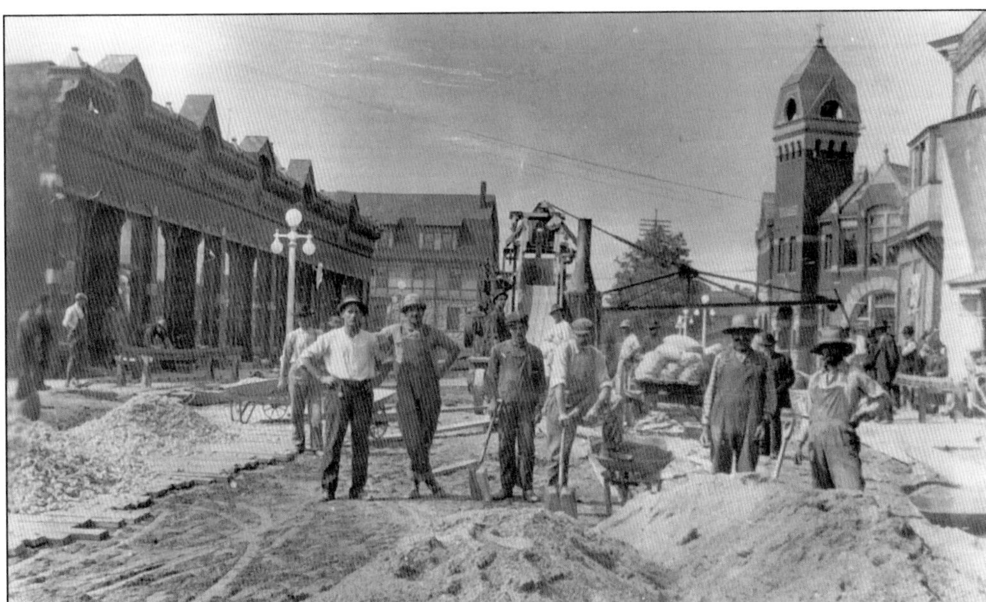

Paving East Frank Street. In September 1913, the paving crew was busy on East Frank Street. The city hall (right) and the Hotel Montague (middle left) are visible landmarks in this photograph. (Courtesy of Laureen Joslin.)

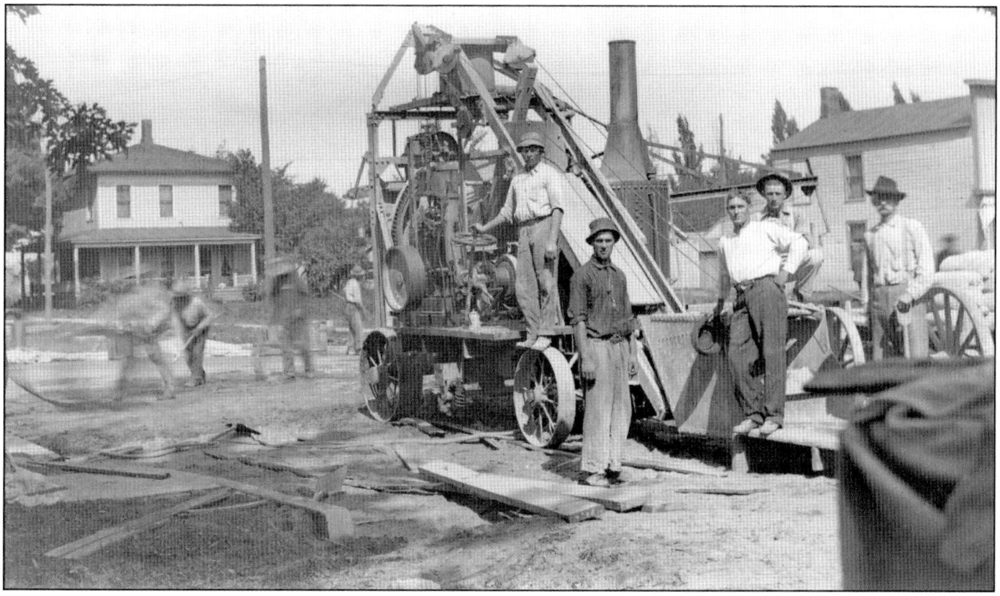

Paving at State and Grant Streets. Here is another paving crew at work in September 1913. This was obviously hard labor as shown by the blurs (left) of men at work with shovels. (Courtesy of Watrousville-Caro Historical Society.)

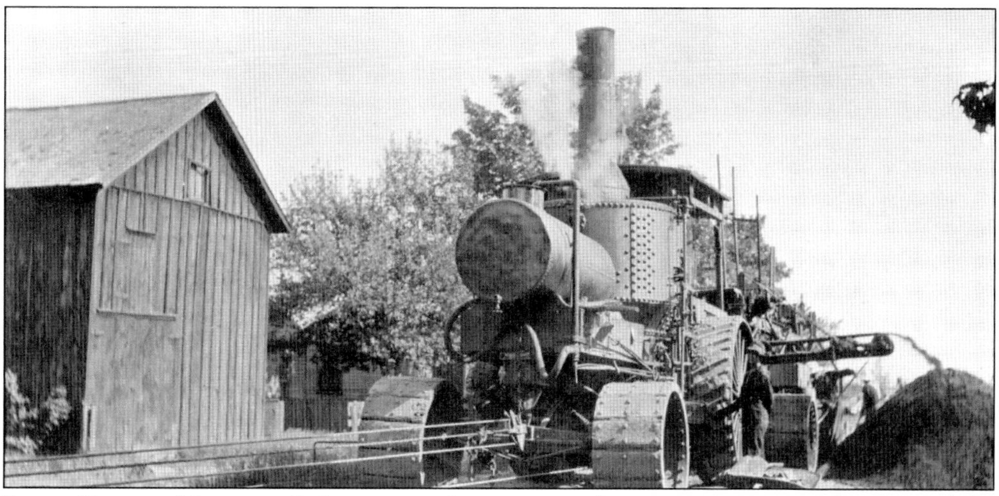

Sewer-Digging Machine. Before paving the streets, work crews put sewers in place around the village. This is a photograph of the digging from about 1910. The machines are steam driven. (Courtesy of Watrousville-Caro Historical Society.)

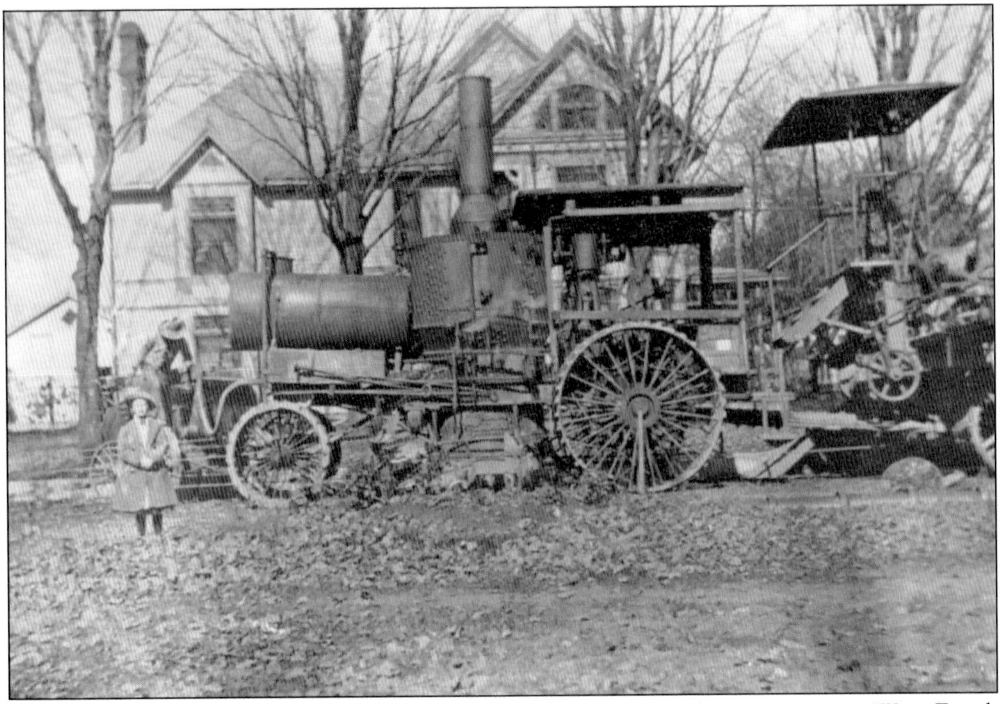

WEST FRANK STREET, 1912. In this photograph, the sewer was being put in on West Frank Street in front of John F. Seeley's home. Alice Seeley Zemke is the child in front of the machine. (Courtesy of Jack Gee/Watrousville-Caro Historical Society.)

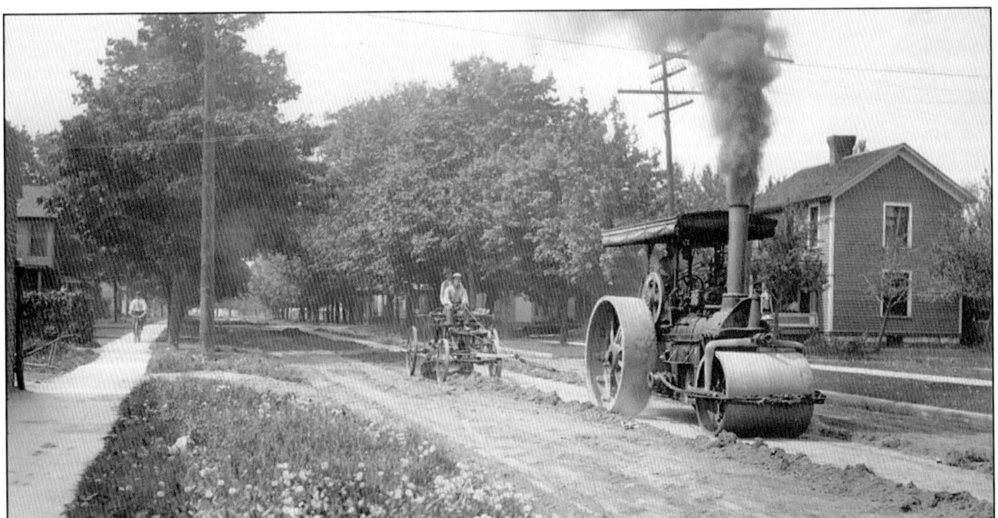

SHERMAN STREET, 1914. In this 1914 photograph, Sherman Street was being graded by a steam roller, which pulled the machinery behind it. A bicyclist follows (left) on the sidewalk. (Courtesy of Watrousville-Caro Historical Society.)

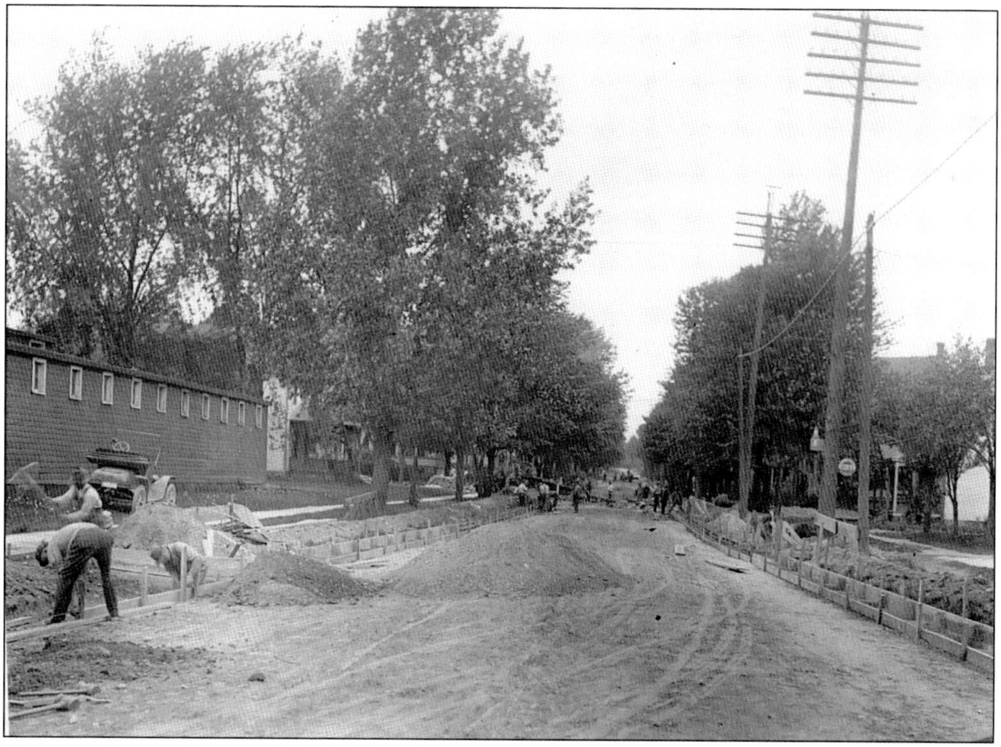

Curbing Almer Street. On July 17, 1921, a crew was busy laying the groundwork for the curbing of Almer Street. Just behind the crew (left) is a portion of Walter T. York's 10-cent horse barn, located at the corner of West Frank and North Almer Streets. (Courtesy of Watrousville-Caro Historical Society.)

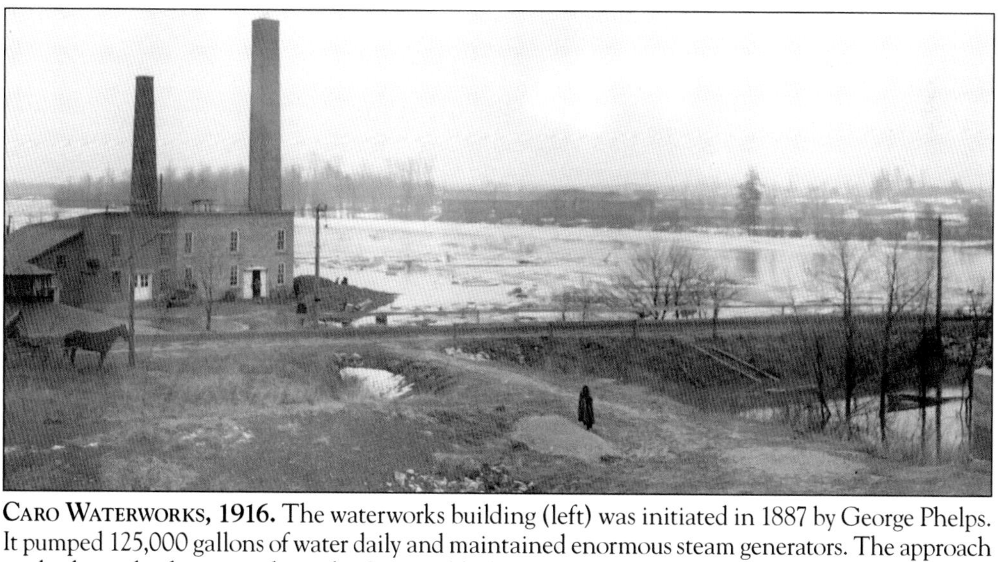

Caro Waterworks, 1916. The waterworks building (left) was initiated in 1887 by George Phelps. It pumped 125,000 gallons of water daily and maintained enormous steam generators. The approach to the lower bridge is on the right. Just visible (middle center) across the river is the large, dark silhouette of Lou Deming's icehouse, located approximately where the M-24 bridge stands today. (Courtesy of Watrousville-Caro Historical Society.)

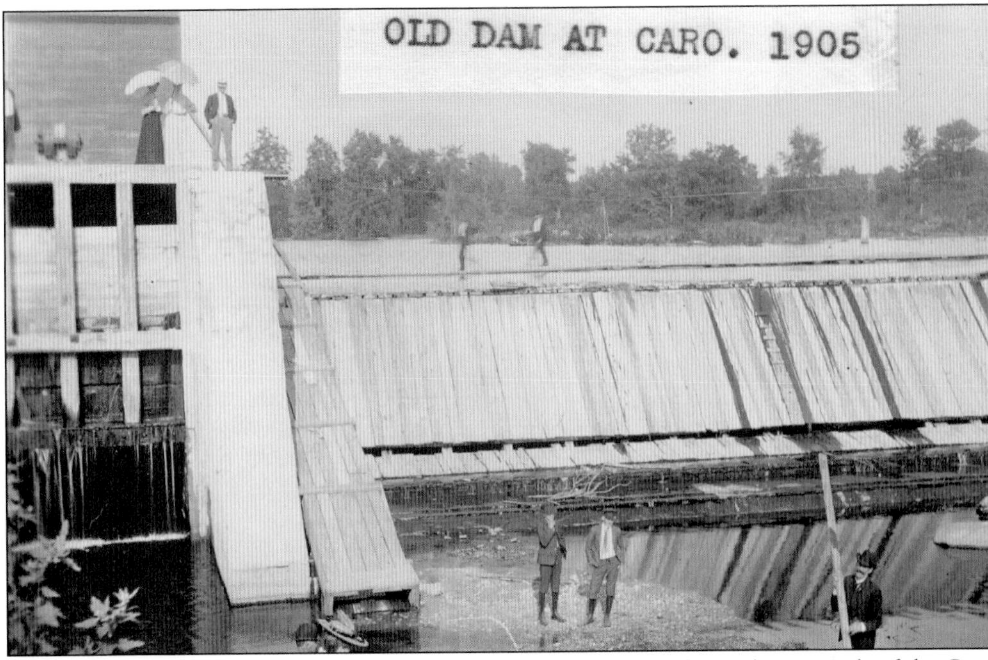

OLD DAM, 1905. This photograph, taken by William J. England, shows the west side of the Caro Dam on the Cass River. Situated two miles south of Caro, the dam was the dream and near-obsession of local entrepreneur Charles Montague. The dam head was 16 feet and flooded 20 acres at the time of construction. (Courtesy of Watrousville-Caro Historical Society.)

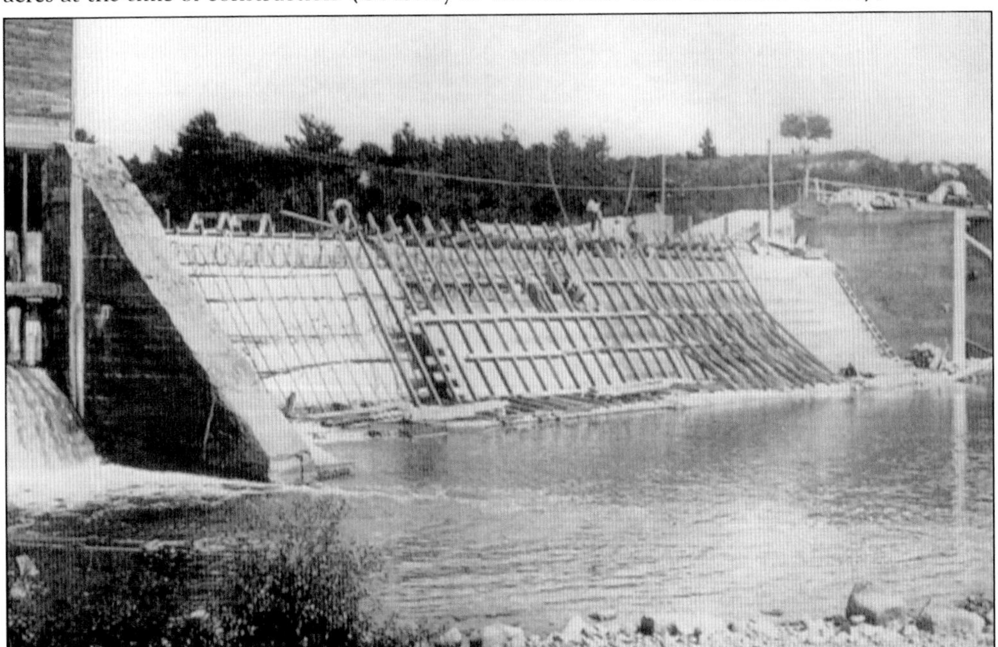

REBUILDING THE DAM, 1914. August 1914 saw crews of workers on the face and footings of the dam. The hope was to stabilize the honeycombed and undermined construction while also restoring the power generating capability to its former levels. In its glory days, the dam provided all the power for the village of Caro. (Courtesy of Laureen Joslin.)

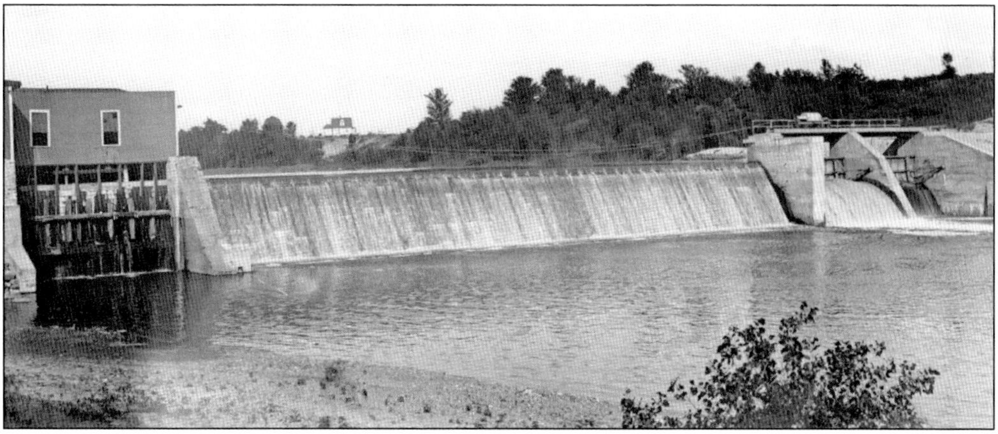

Dam, 1915. In 1915, the dam's future was in question. The original proponent and owner of the dam, Charles Montague, had devoted years and enormous financial support to the dam's construction. He suffered hardship with each failure. By the time of this photograph, Montague had gone broke and had sold his interests to Theron Atwood. (Courtesy of Watrousville-Caro Historical Society.)

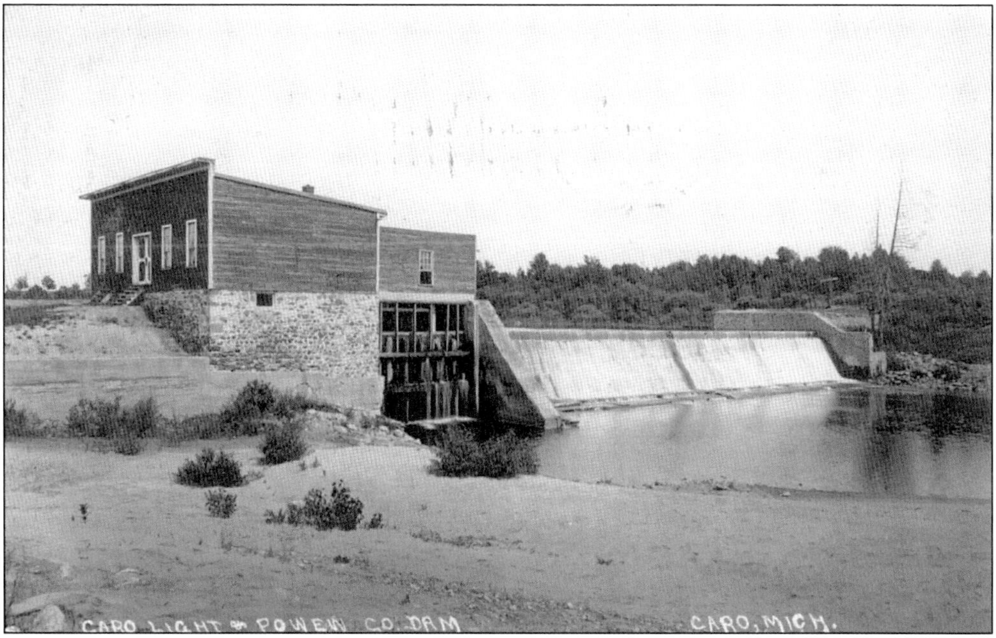

Dam Power House. This photograph from about 1912 is labeled Caro Light and Power Company. It provides a good view of the dam and its power house. The company was incorporated in 1898 under this name, with Charles Montague as president. After various ownership and name changes, Detroit Edison became the owner in 1935. (Courtesy of Gloria Hall.)

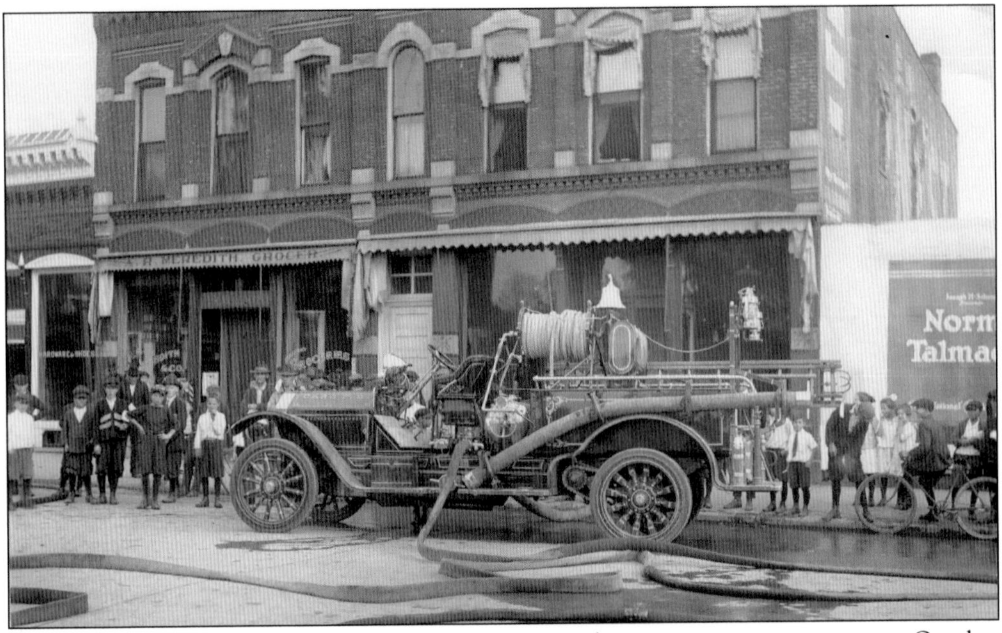

CARO FIRE DEPARTMENT, 1920. The fire department is shown testing its equipment in October 1920, to the delight of many villagers. This was the department's new 1919 American LaFrance pumper truck in a State Street demonstration. The department was organized in 1872 and by 1880 had 17 volunteers and an ever increasing complement of equipment. In December 1887, they took up residence in the new city hall. (Courtesy of Watrousville-Caro Historical Society.)

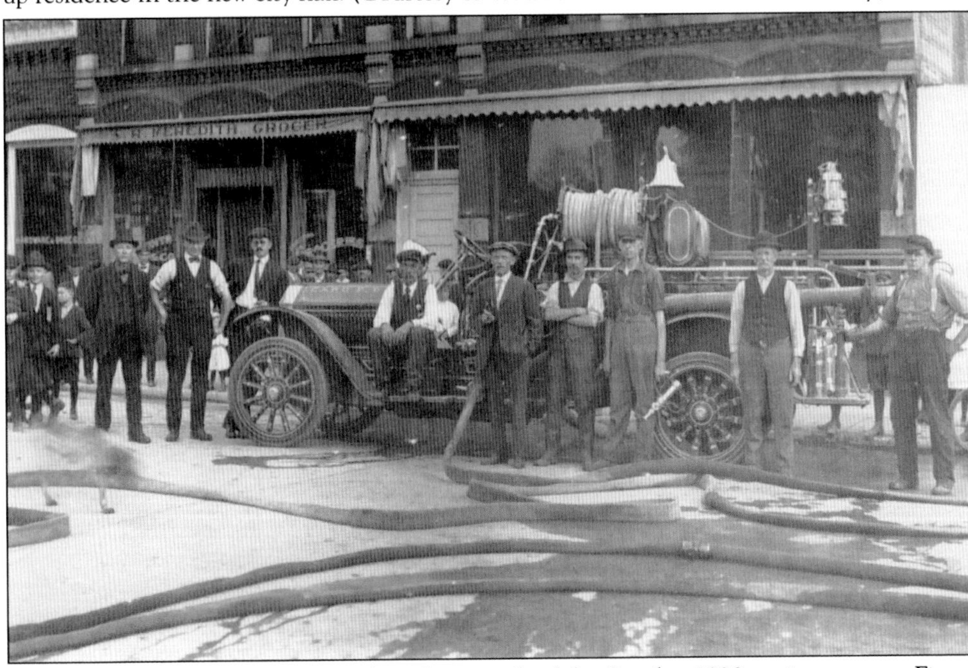

ANOTHER VIEW, 1920. This is another photograph of the October 1920 equipment test. Fire was always a significant danger in the village, and the Caro Fire Department was dedicated to its mission of keeping the village safe. Standing to the right of the rear wheel is first chief, Frank D. Riddle. To his left is Charles E. Middaugh, who followed Riddle as chief. (Courtesy of Gloria Hall.)

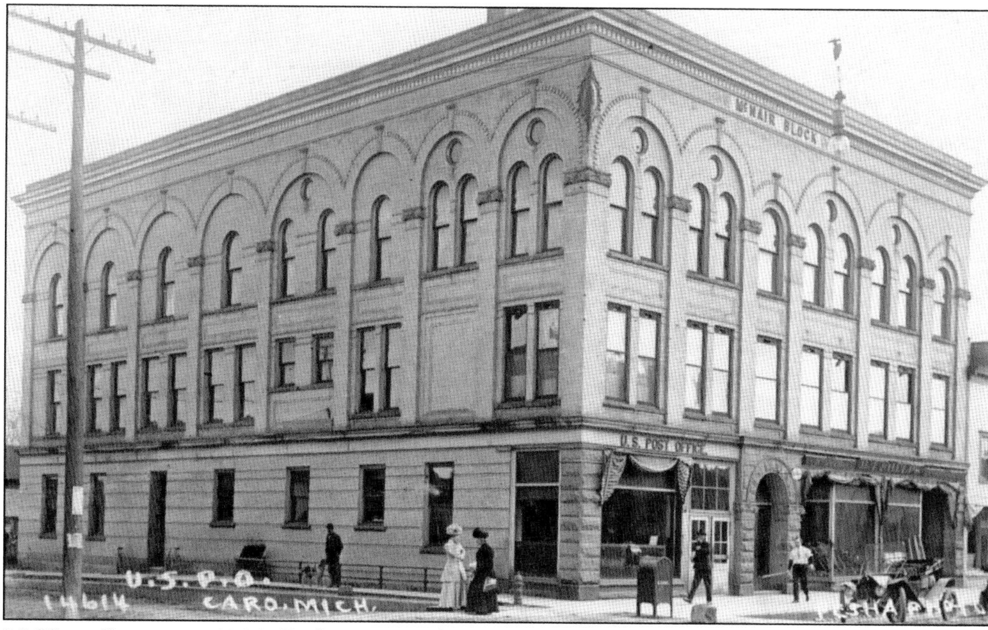

McNair Block, c. 1900. Built in 1899, the McNair Block, on the corner of State and Lincoln Streets, housed the US Post Office. The other original tenants were Turner's Hardware, the national headquarters of the Ancient Order of Gleaners, and the Independent Order of Odd Fellows. This location was a major upgrade for the post office, which saw increasing business as the village grew and prospered. (Courtesy of Watrousville-Caro Historical Society.)

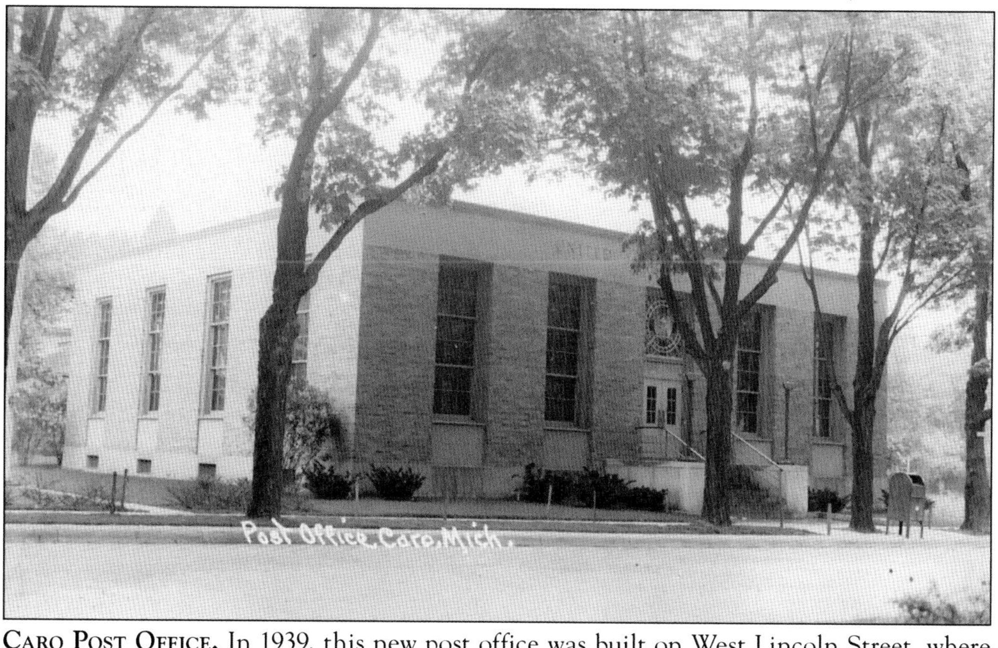

Caro Post Office. In 1939, this new post office was built on West Lincoln Street, where schoolteacher Cora Gibbs had lived in her brick home and tended her gardens. Costing $80,000, the modern brick and limestone building boasted dark wood counters and trim, brass and bronze Art Deco features, torchieres, and a wall mural entitled *Mail on the Farm*, painted by David Fredenthal. (Courtesy of Gloria Hall.)

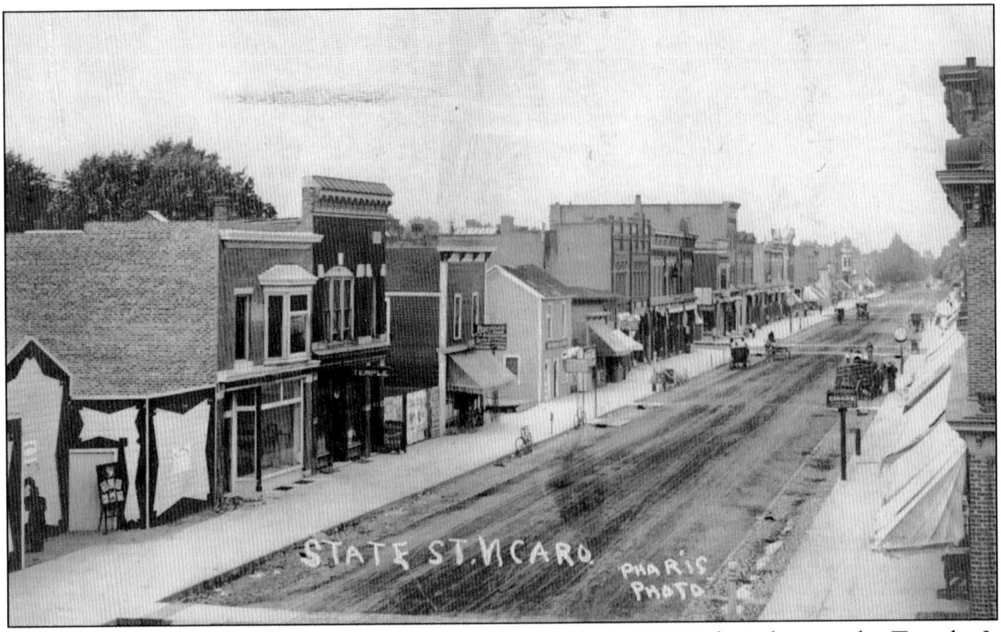

THE TEMPLE, STATE STREET, 1909. This photograph shows Caro's first theater, the Temple. It is the second building on the left, a two story structure built in 1882 by Jane Ryan, who was a successful milliner. She sold the building in the early 1890s. It became a harness shop, then the Temple Theater. The early movie matinee idols came to life in Caro at the 5¢ Saturday matinees. (Courtesy of Gloria Hall.)

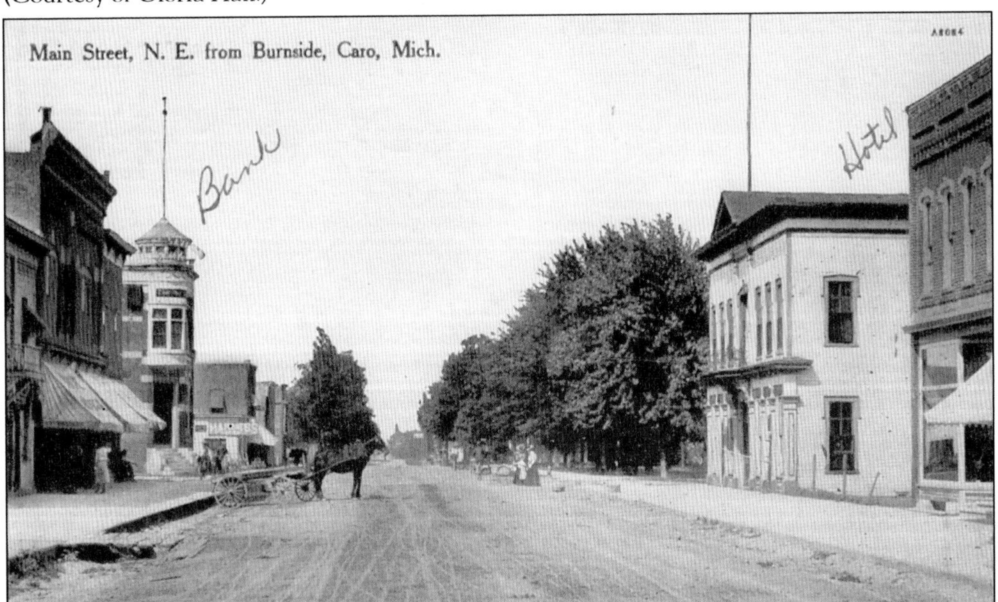

LOOKING NORTHEAST DOWN STATE STREET. This view from Burnside Street looks northeast down State (Main) Street, sometime before 1913. On the far left is a small corner of the Exchange Hotel, and the round, towered building is the Carson-Ealy Bank. On the right, next to the trees, is the Truesdell Hotel. It started as the Medler Hotel and was last known as the Edmunds. (Courtesy of Watrousville-Caro Historical Society.)

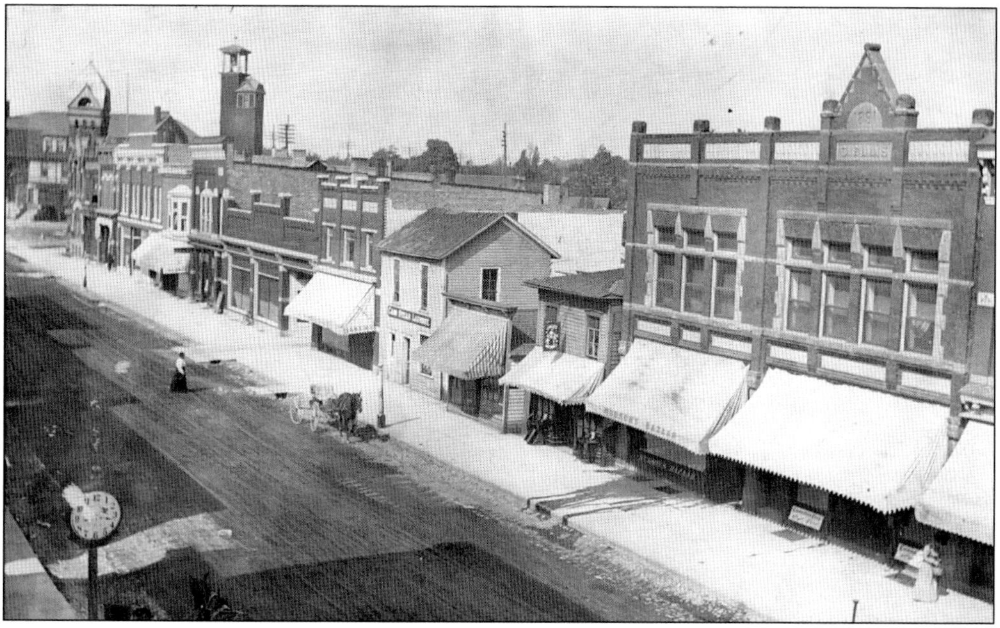

State Street, 1911. Looking west toward the city hall (upper far left), the Hotel Montague is just visible. The two-story frame building shown mid-block is Frank B. Ransford's Caro Steam Laundry. The sidewalk clock in the lower left belongs to Dyer Jewelers. (Courtesy of Gloria Hall.)

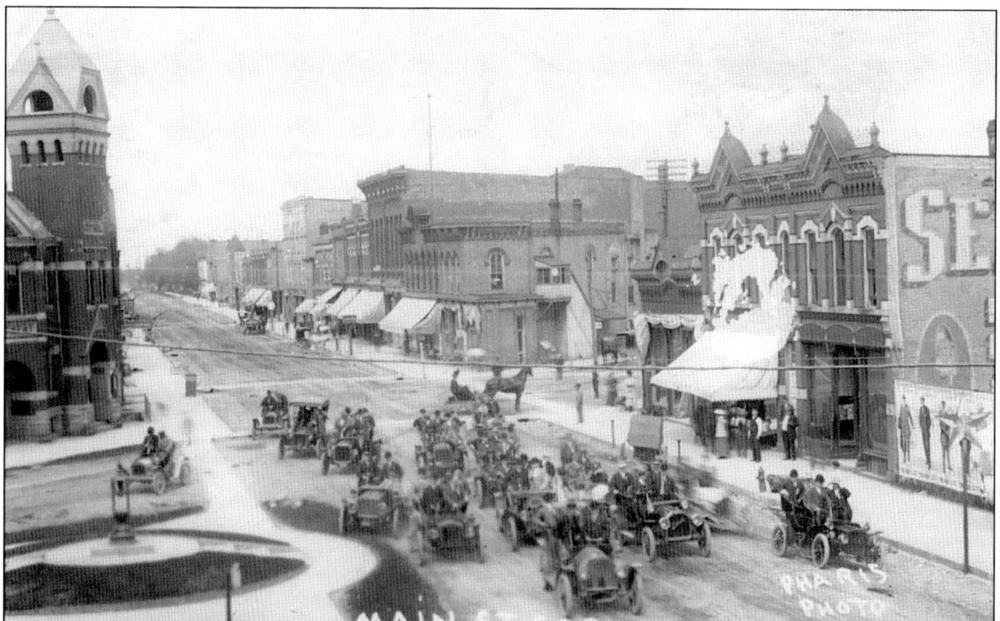

Road Rally, 1909. Taken on May 25, 1909, this photograph of local residents exudes the excitement of early motor cars. They are gathered before the Phelps Fountain on the triangle in front of the Hotel Montague. Among the residents pictured are Tiny Van Tyne (first row left, second car), Roy Riddel (first row left, first car), and William J. Moore (front, far right). (Courtesy of Watrousville-Caro Historical Society.)

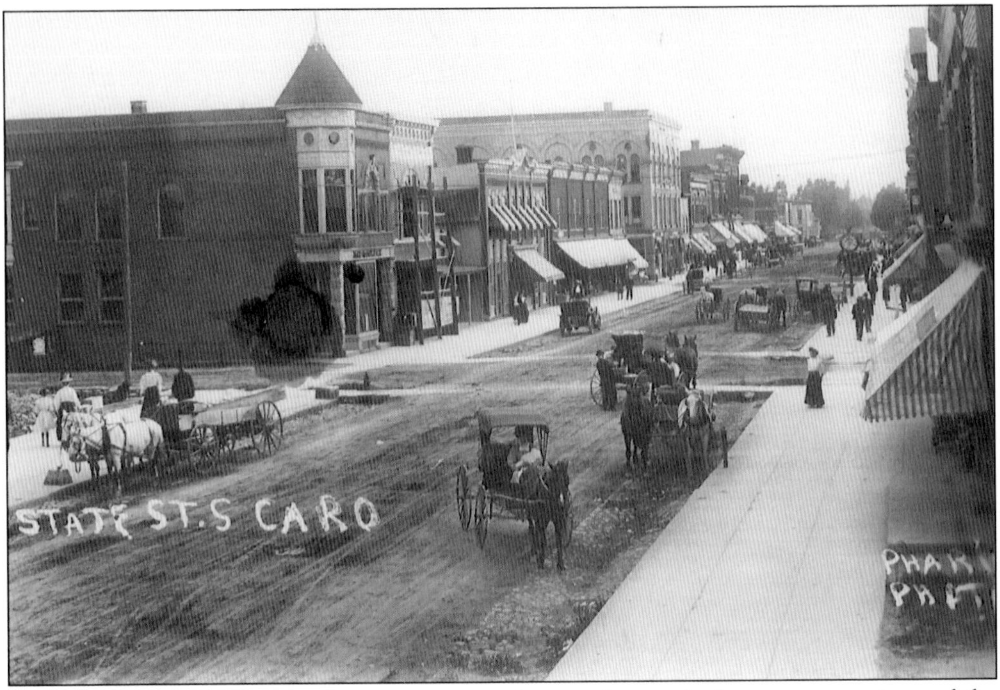

Busy Street Scene. This interesting viewpoint shows a close-up look at transportation and the state of the streets and sidewalks in about 1909. It also gives us a glimpse of a productive, busy center of business. The building with the turret (near left, top) was the home of the *Tuscola County Courier*, a newspaper with a Democratic political view. (Courtesy of Laureen Joslin.)

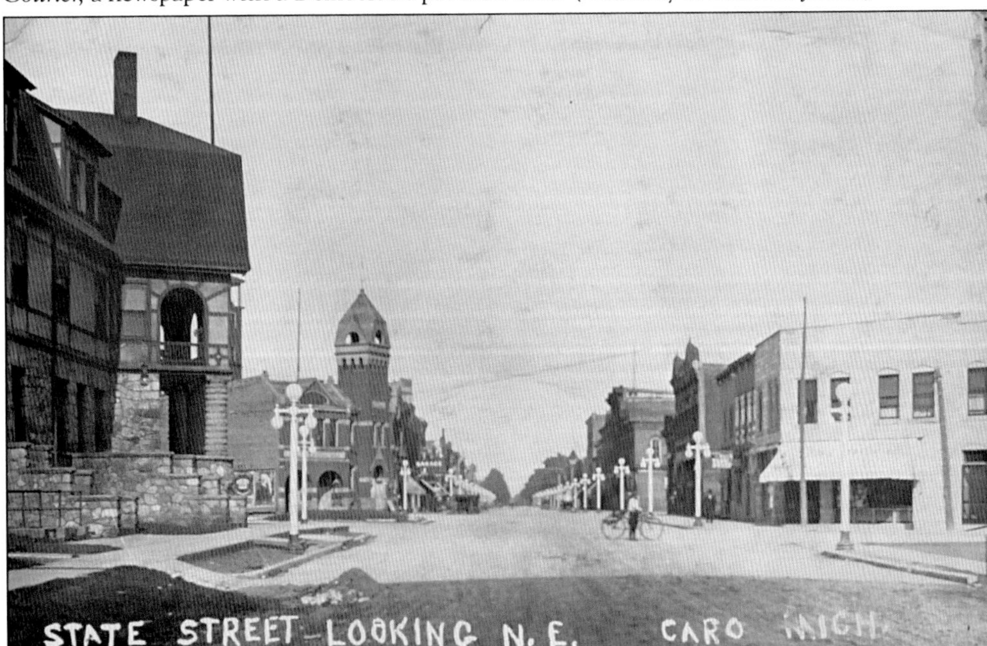

A Street with a View. This is a 1913 long view down State Street at a time between the installation of the street lights and the paving of the street. It is a perspective on the long stretch of State Street not often seen in other period photographs. (Courtesy of Gloria Hall.)

Two

AN ENTERPRISING CARO

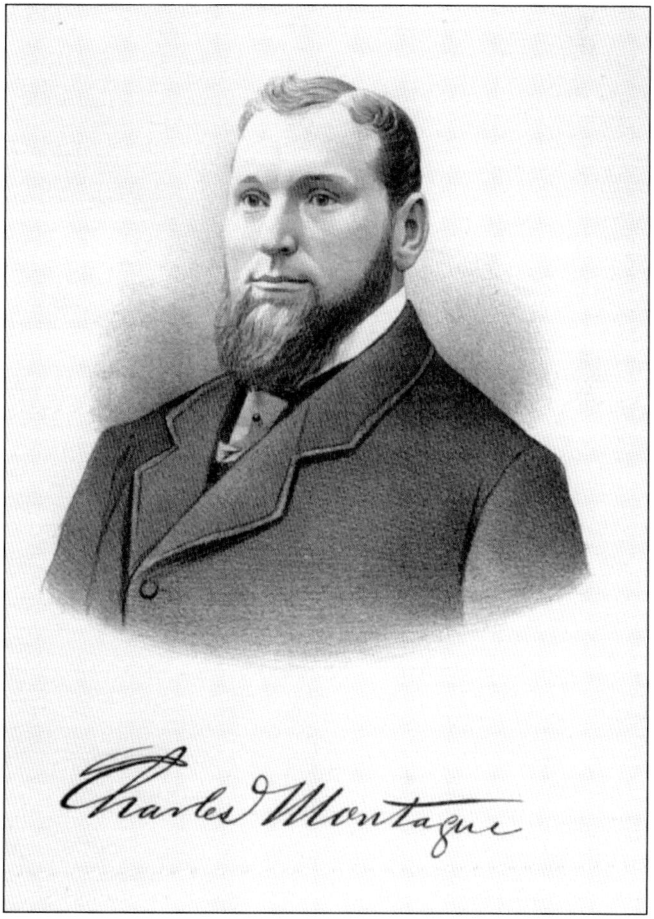

CHARLES MONTAGUE. Montague came to Centerville in 1863 at age 18. He spent two years in the Union army, returning in 1865 and commencing his life as an entrepreneur. He was a lumberman, a merchant, a banker, and a builder—often acting as all of these at the same time. He was instrumental in bringing the railroad to Caro and in establishing the waterworks. He was devoted to the development and prosperity of Caro. (*History of Tuscola and Bay Counties.*)

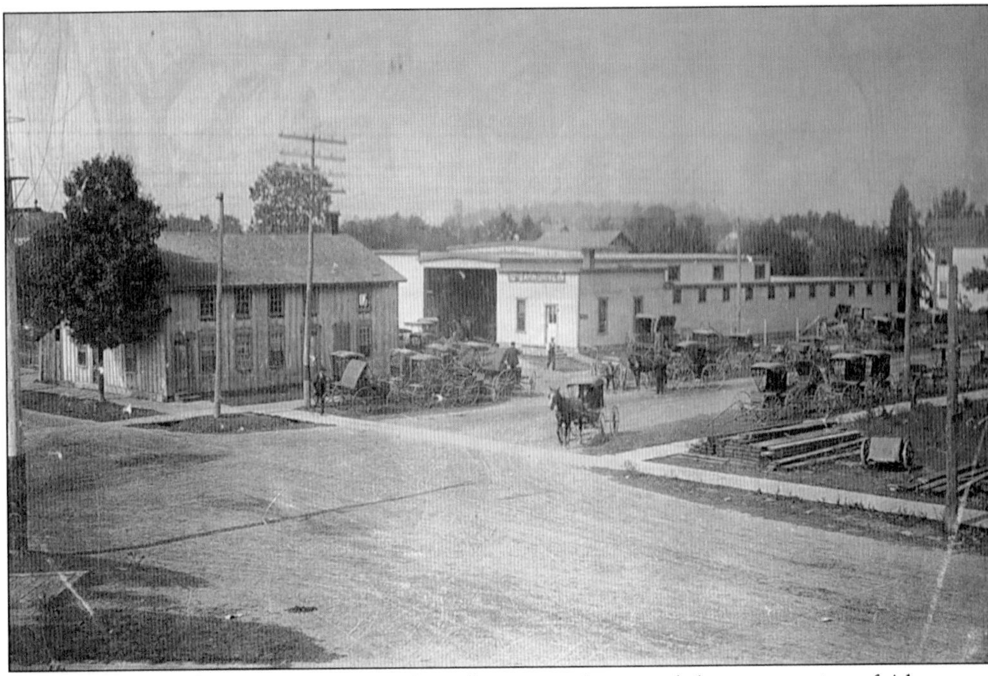

Gibbs House, c. 1897. Looking from the village triangle toward the intersection of Almer and Frank Streets is the Gibbs House (left). Built in 1858 by early settler Melvin Gibbs, the Gibbs House was the first hotel in Caro. The long building (right) behind the Gibbs House is Walter T. York's 10-cent horse barn. Used as a parking lot for horses and buggies, the barn had enough room for 200 horses. (Courtesy of Gloria Hall.)

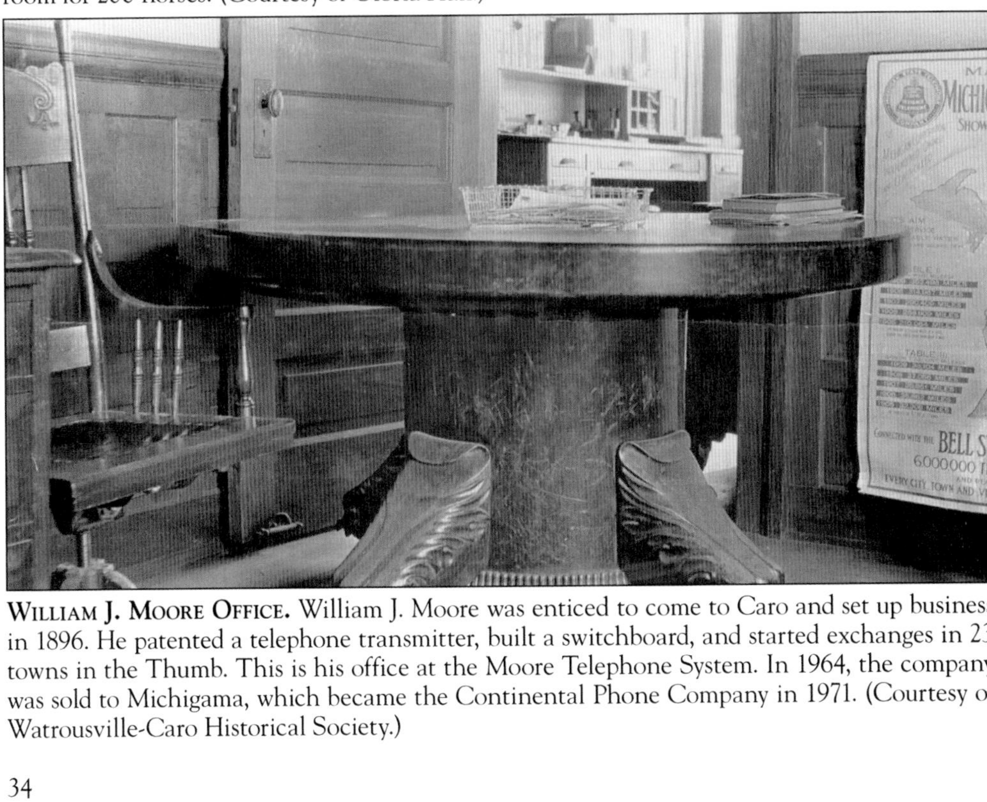

William J. Moore Office. William J. Moore was enticed to come to Caro and set up business in 1896. He patented a telephone transmitter, built a switchboard, and started exchanges in 23 towns in the Thumb. This is his office at the Moore Telephone System. In 1964, the company was sold to Michigama, which became the Continental Phone Company in 1971. (Courtesy of Watrousville-Caro Historical Society.)

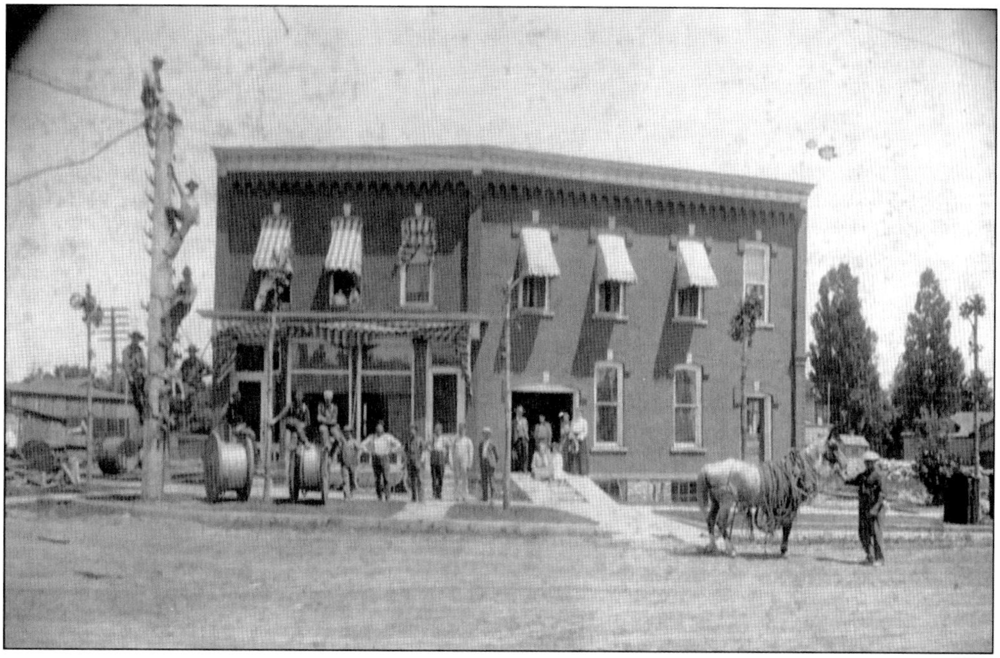

Moore Telephone System. This is the home office and factory of the Moore Telephone System. The building was at the corner of Joy and Montague Streets. It was torn down in 1973, completing the story of a unique businessman and inventor, William J. Moore. (Courtesy of Almona Pierce Bradley.)

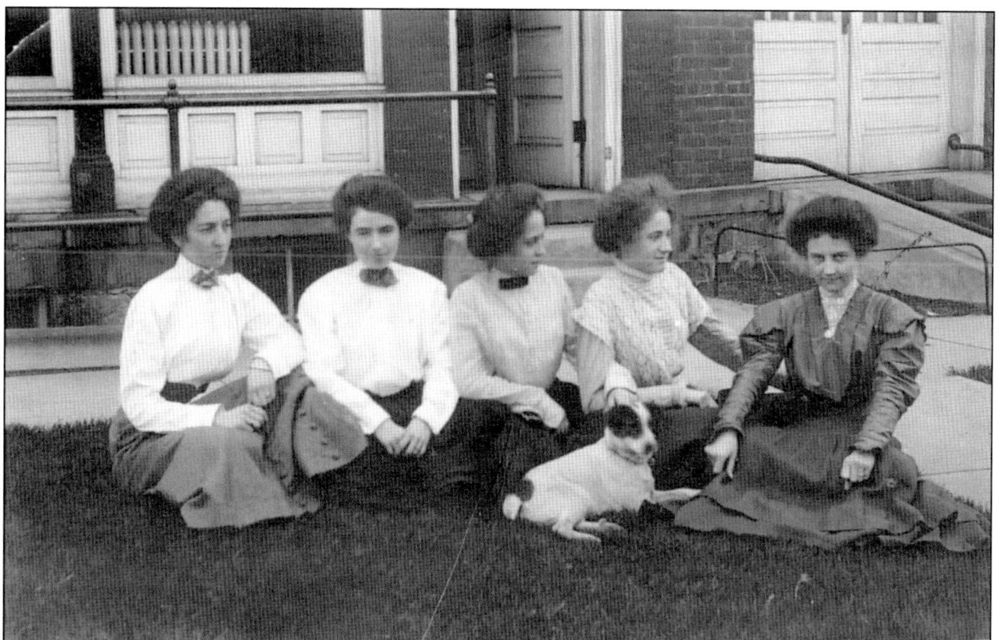

Moore Telephone Operators. Pictured about 1909 are the Moore Telephone System switchboard operators. From left to right are Alta Honsinger, Viola Geron Orr, Harriet Rounds Ayre, Etta McLane Watrous, and Alta Case. Operators continued to run the local switchboard until 1980. (Courtesy of Watrousville-Caro Historical Society.)

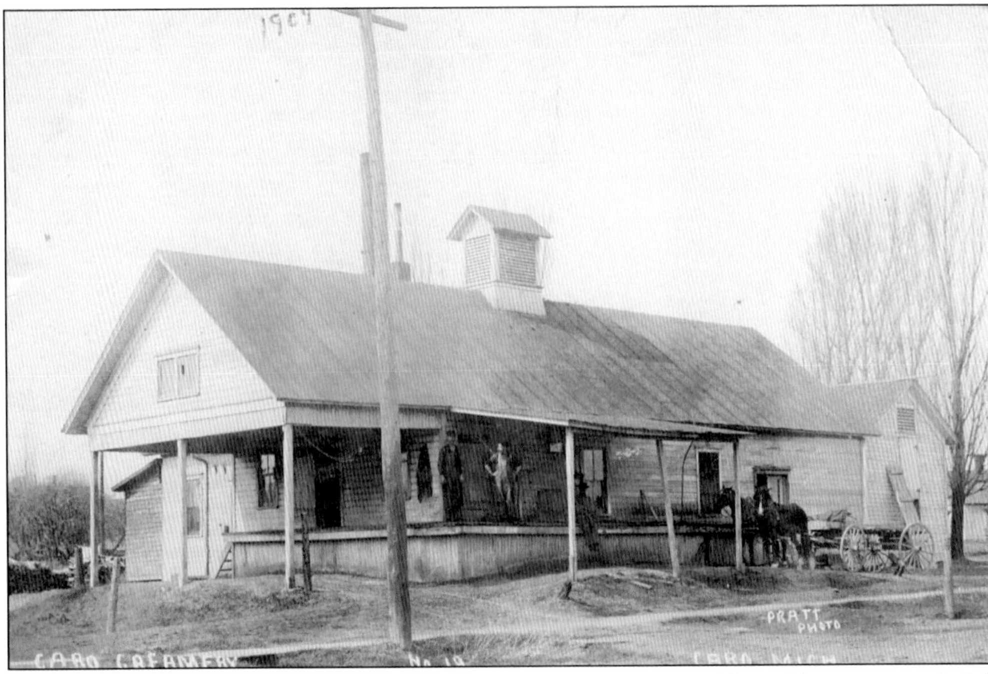

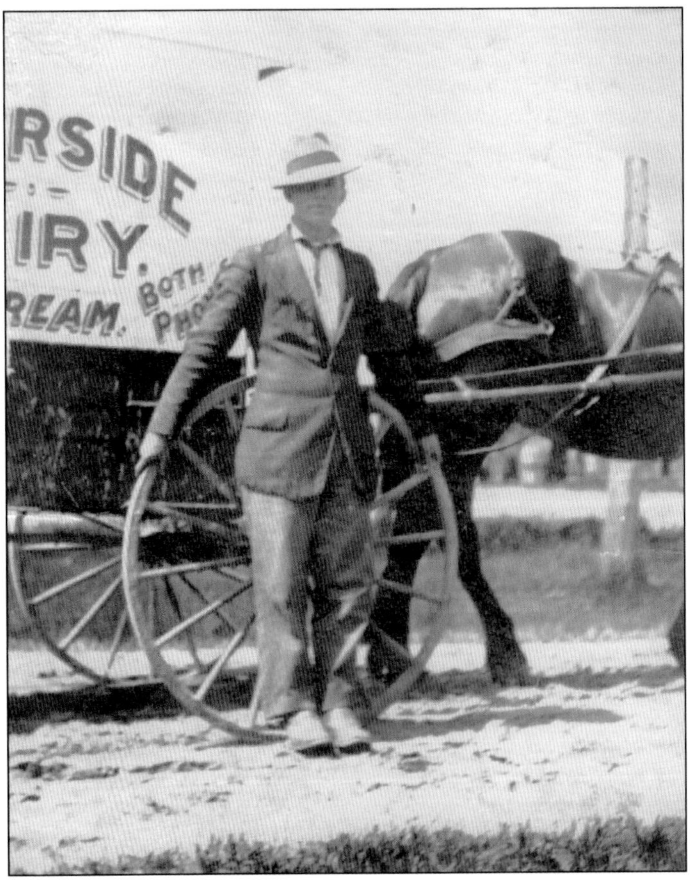

CARO CREAMERY, C. 1909. The Caro Creamery grew out of the failed Caro Elgin Butter Company. W.H. Bechtel was the general superintendent and later became the owner. Farmers delivered milk by horse and wagon to this location on Montague Street where it was processed, distributed to retailers, or sent out on a delivery route. (Courtesy of Gloria Hall.)

DAIRY DELIVERY. This milkman has been photographed next to his company horse and buggy. He would have had a delivery route to follow. The year of this photograph is unknown and could be from the early 1900s to the 1930s. (Courtesy of Watrousville-Caro Historical Society.)

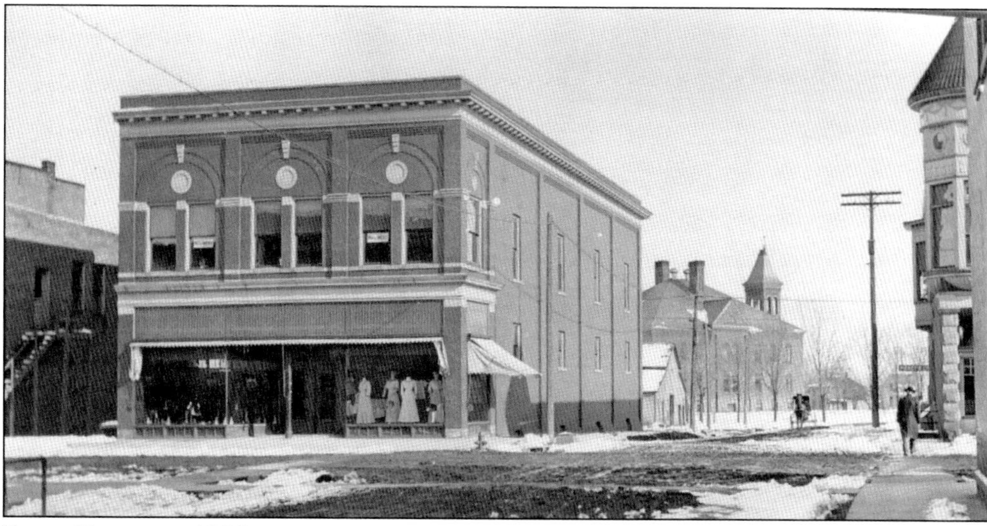

Zemke Building, 1909. Brothers Otto and Max Zemke arrived in Caro in the first decade of the 20th century. They established a clothing and department store on the Himelhoch Brothers and Company site, at the corner of State and Burnside Streets. The old Caro High School is visible behind the Zemke Building, and a corner of the Courier Building (right) is across from the Zemke Building. (Courtesy of Watrousville-Caro Historical Society.)

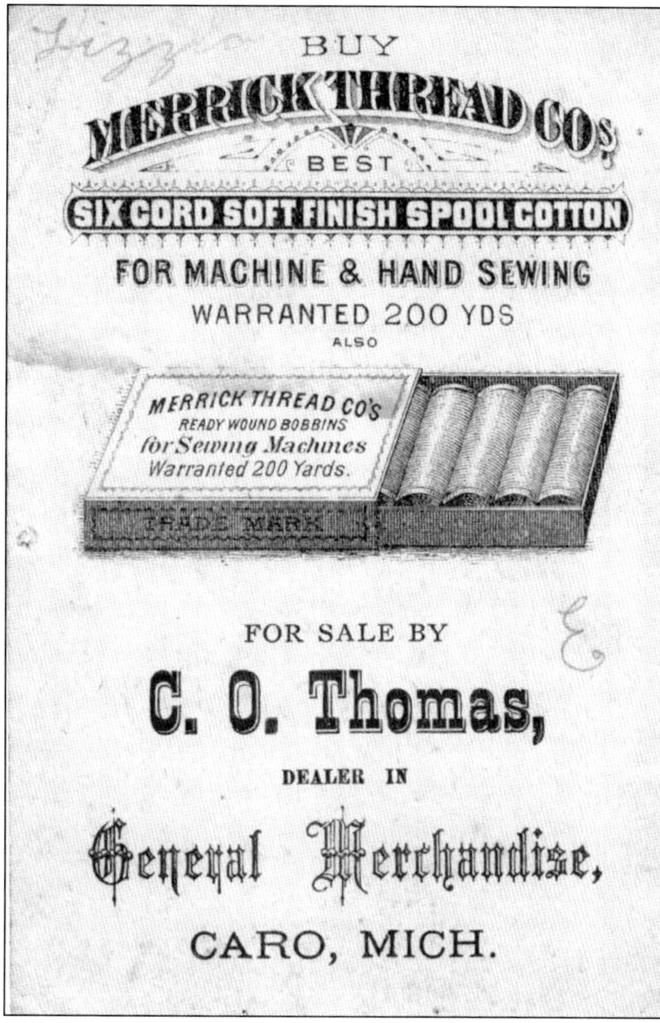

Advertising Card. This was a popular and effective method of advertising after the Civil War, with the development of consumer markets and the rapid growth of manufactured goods available to the public. Advertising cards had their zenith from the 1870s through the early 1900s. The card pictured advertises sewing thread for local merchant C.O. Thomas. (Courtesy of Gloria Hall.)

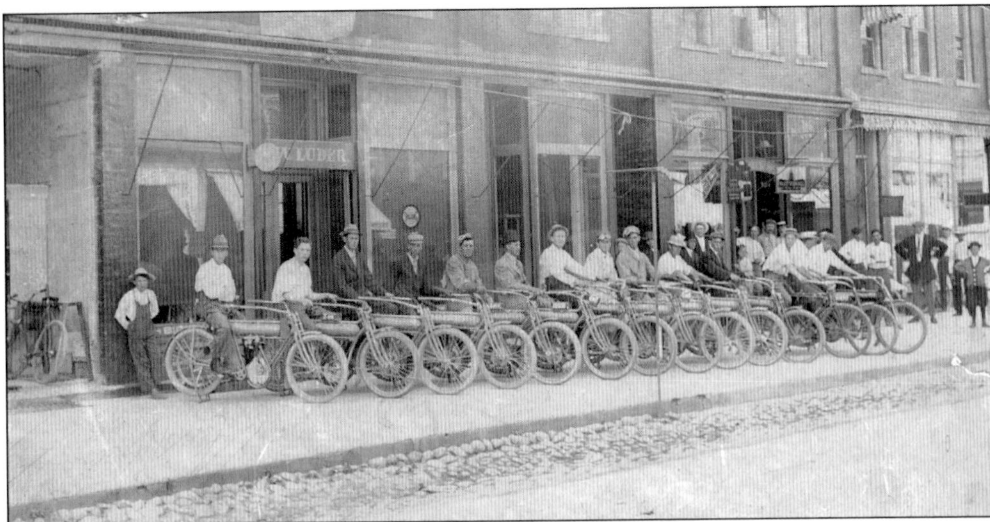

Luder Shop, c. 1910. At this time, the Luder Shop occupied a section of storefront adjacent to the McNair Block. The inventory in this photograph appears to be pedal-start, belt-drive motorcycles, possibly early Harley-Davidson bikes. Selling his sporting goods store behind the McNair Block in 1913, Louie Luder took his family on a 2,800-mile motorcycle (including sidecars) tour of the eastern United States. (Courtesy of Watrousville-Caro Historical Society.)

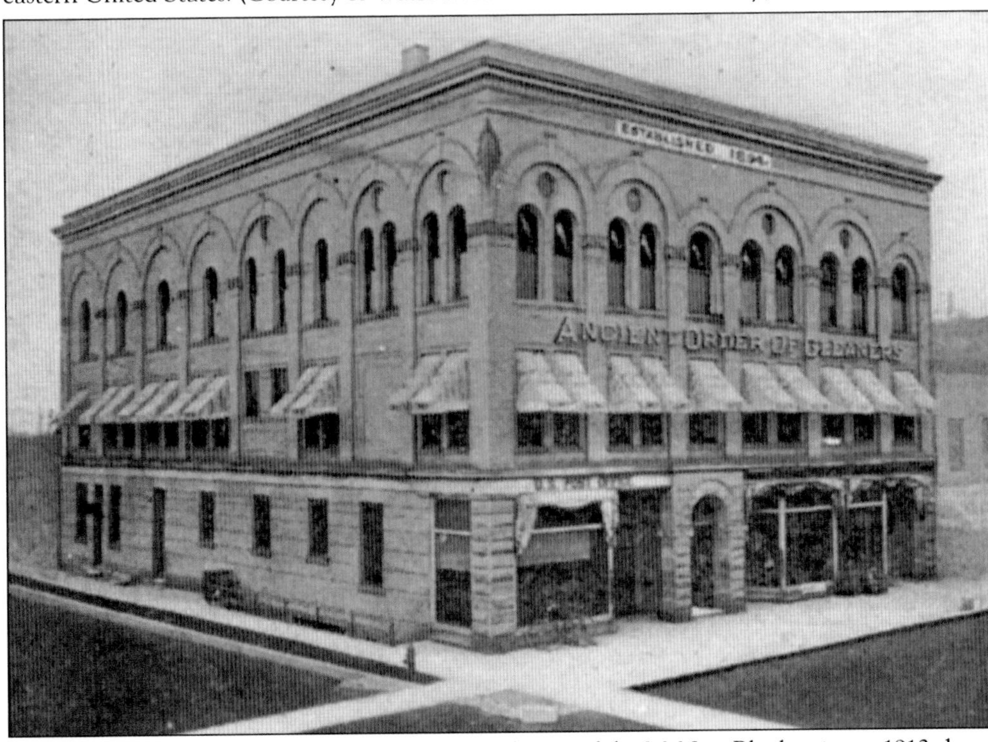

US Post Office, McNair Block. This postcard view of the McNair Block prior to 1913 shows one of Caro's most impressive buildings. Erected in the late 1890s, this block housed the US Post Office, various businesses, the Ancient Order of Gleaners, and later the Indianfields Township Library. The Ancient Order of Gleaners was a fraternal insurance organization started in Caro and still in existence. (Courtesy of Watrousville-Caro Historical Society.)

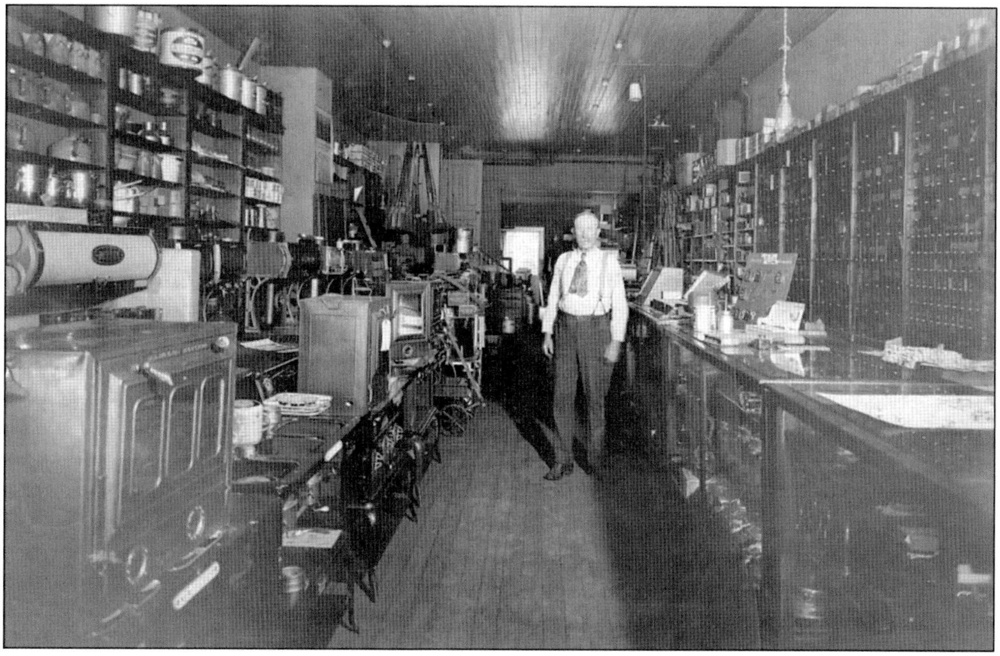

Phelps, Riley & Company. This is an interior view of the Phelps, Riley & Company hardware store. Located on the first floor of the McNair Block in 1880, the store remained there until 1912 when it relocated to the building that later became the J.C. Penney store. The store carried general hardware merchandise, harnesses, paints, and fencing. They also did plumbing, steam fitting, and sheet iron work. (Courtesy of Watrousville-Caro Historical Society.)

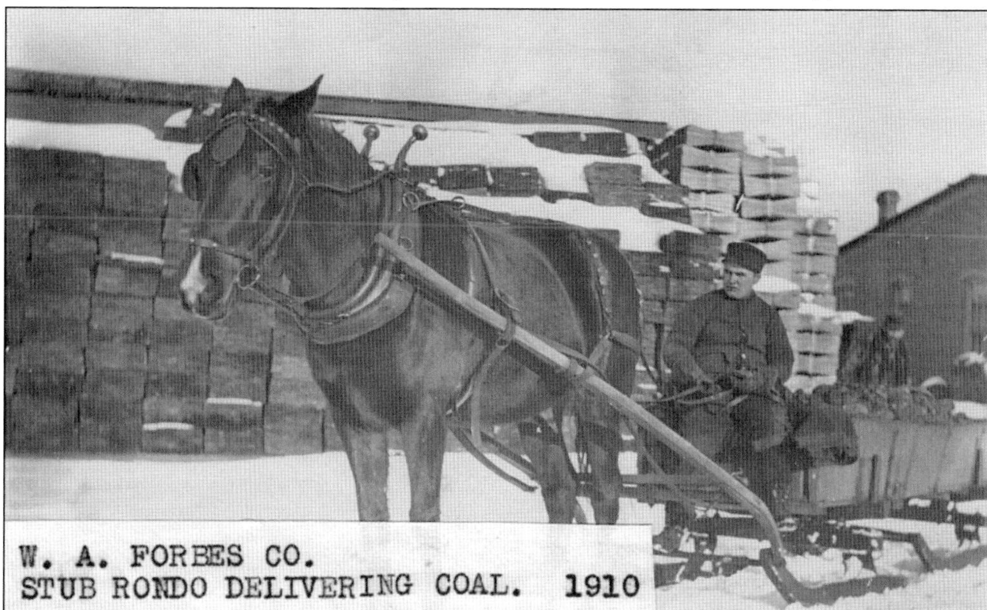

Winter Delivery, 1910. Stub Rondo delivers coal by sledge for the W.A. Forbes Company. The W.A. Forbes Lumber Company was in business from 1880 to 1969 and was located at 429 Montague Street. In the early years, most of the lumber was local pine and basswood, primarily harvested along the Cass River. (Courtesy of Watrousville-Caro Historical Society.)

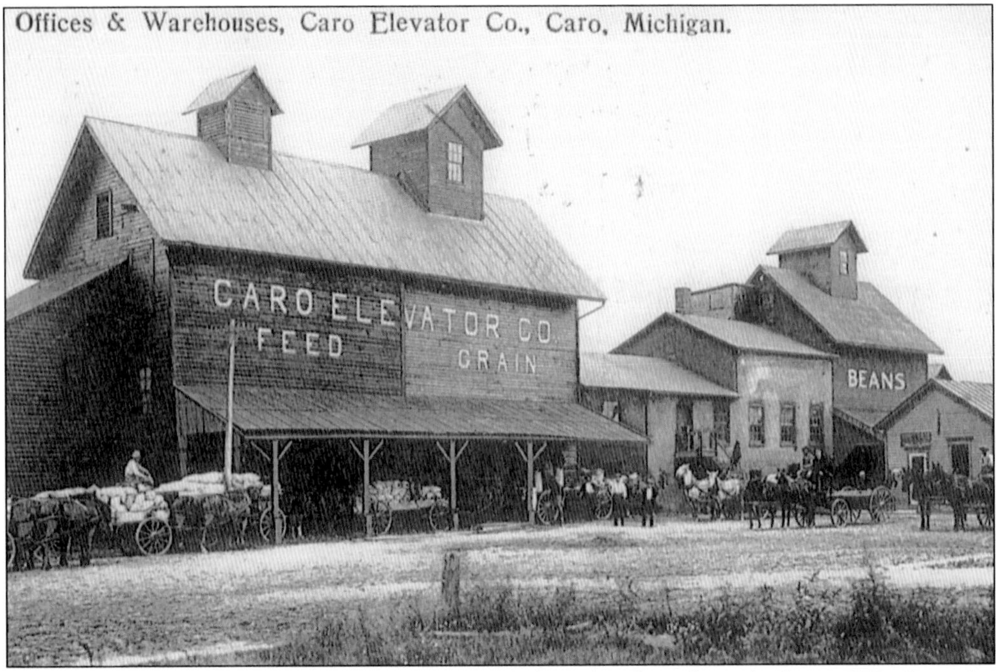

CARO ELEVATOR COMPANY. The first elevator is believed to have been built in 1875, along the siding of the Michigan Central Railroad for easy shipping. Originally, the elevator was operated by horsepower and later by steam power. It was converted to electrical power in the 1920s. This was a vital business for local farmers and the agricultural industry for many years. It was destroyed by fire in 1973. (Courtesy of Laureen Joslin.)

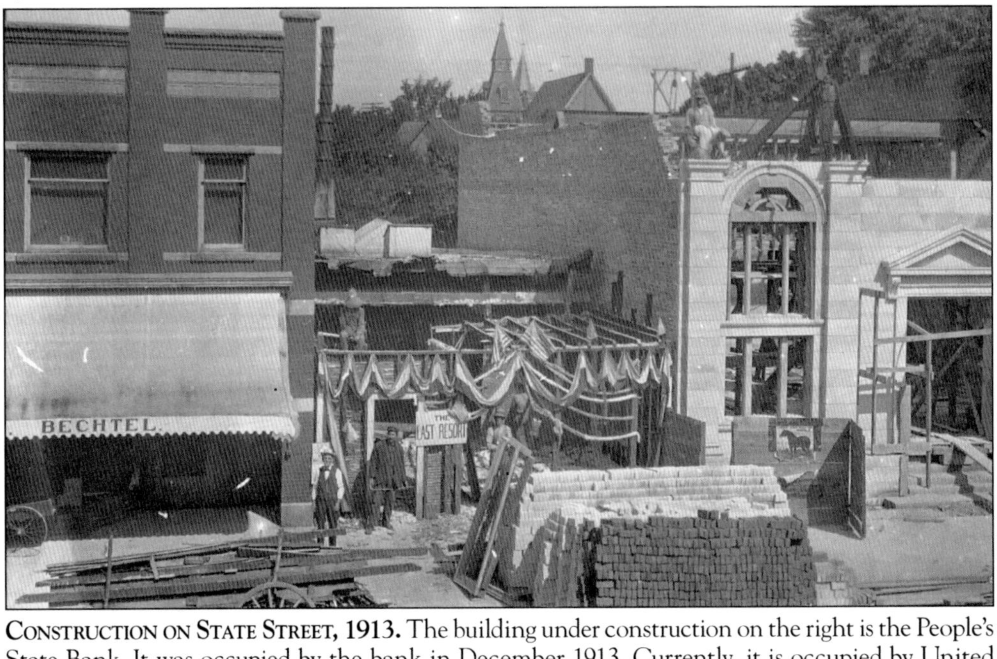

CONSTRUCTION ON STATE STREET, 1913. The building under construction on the right is the People's State Bank. It was occupied by the bank in December 1913. Currently, it is occupied by United Health Services. The construction in the middle is F.B. Ransford's Caro Steam Laundry. On the left is the Bechtel Bakery and Ice Cream shop. (Courtesy of Watrousville-Caro Historical Society.)

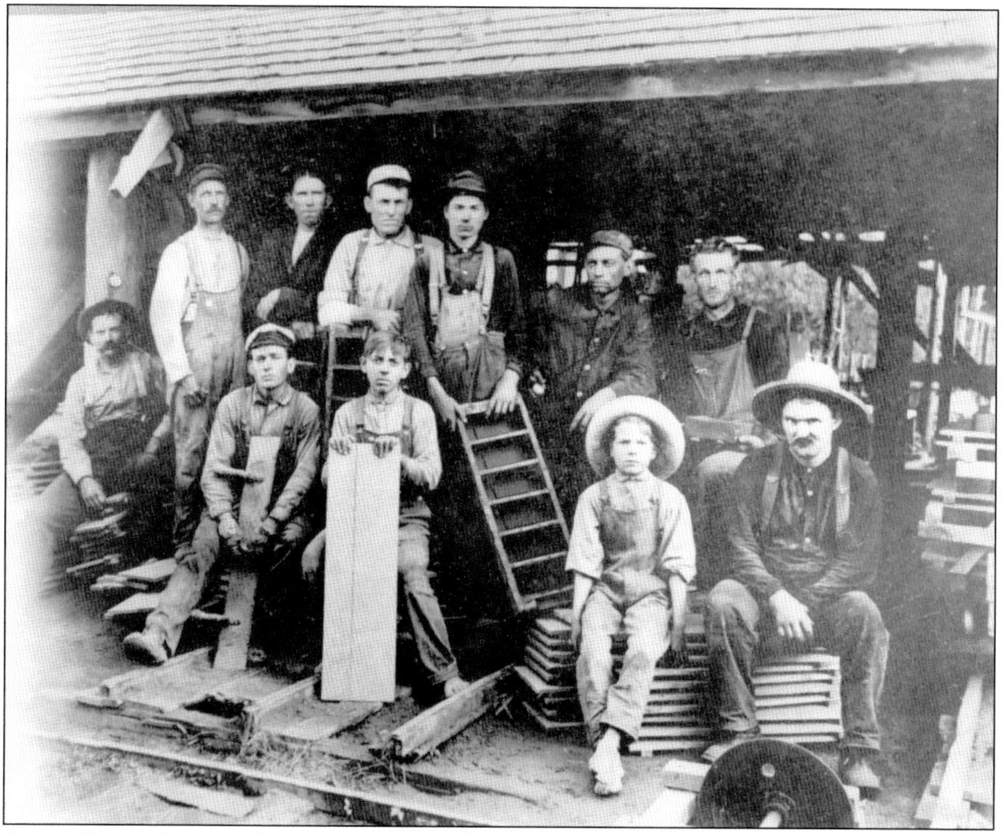

Almer Brick & Tile Company. Many of the bricks used in Caro area homes and businesses came from this firm. Pictured from left to right are work crew members (seated) operator P.J. Peterson, Clarence Drake, Clyde Peterson, Carl Peterson, and Lew Rowley; (standing) Perry Whitney, George Black, Del Mosshier, Tim Beyette, Orrin Garris, and Will Stoner. (Courtesy of Norman Dorr Wiltse.)

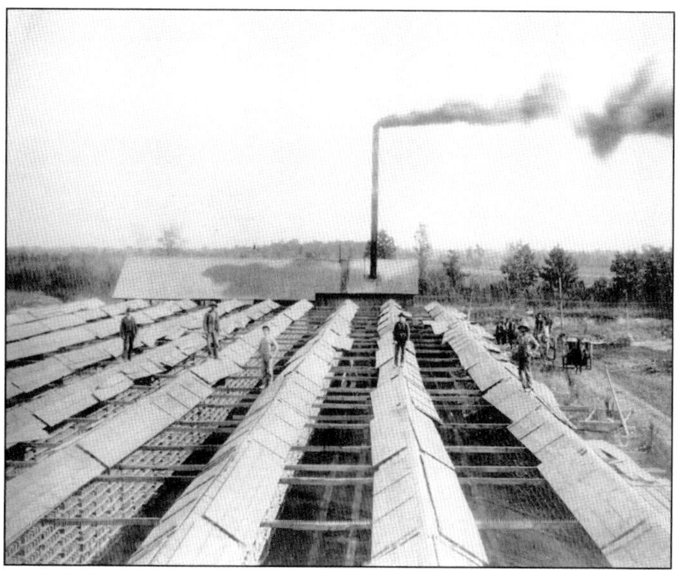

Drying Bricks. The drying area of the Romain Road brickyard was east of Caro, near the curve by the Cass River. It was one of several area brickyards that supplied the building needs of nearby communities. Primarily using local raw materials—and hard work—the bricks they made are evident in the brick buildings still standing today. (Courtesy of Norman Dorr Wiltse.)

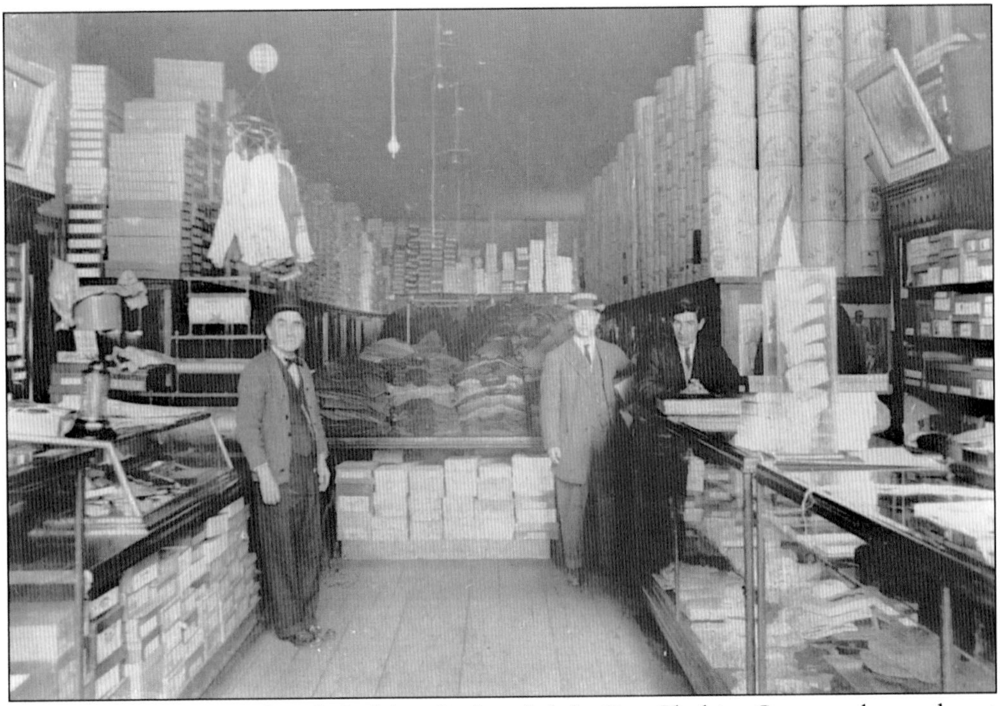

Star Clothing Store. Joseph St. Mary Sr. founded the Star Clothing Store on the northwest corner of State and Lincoln Streets. Under St Mary's watchful eye and those of his sons Joseph, Frank, and Edward, the store was a State Street constant for many years; it was also called St. Mary's Clothing House. Joseph Sr. poses, presumably, with two of his sons among the inventory. (Courtesy of Watrousville-Caro Historical Society.)

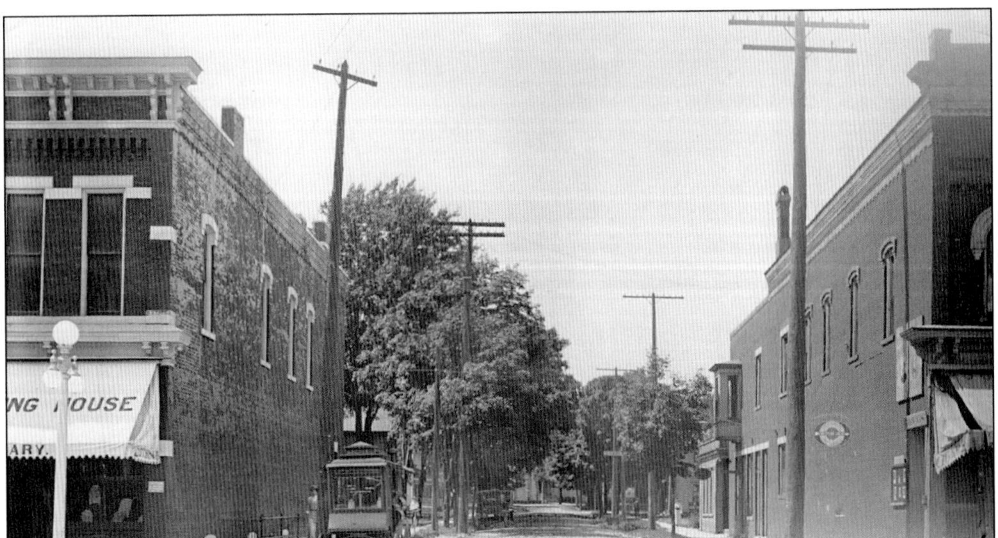

Snyder's Popcorn Wagon. Snyder's Popcorn wagon is shown at the corner of State and West Lincoln Streets on a July day in 1914. The St. Mary's Clothing House is on the left. Dell Patterson was the first one to operate a popcorn wagon. (Courtesy of Watrousville-Caro Historical Society.)

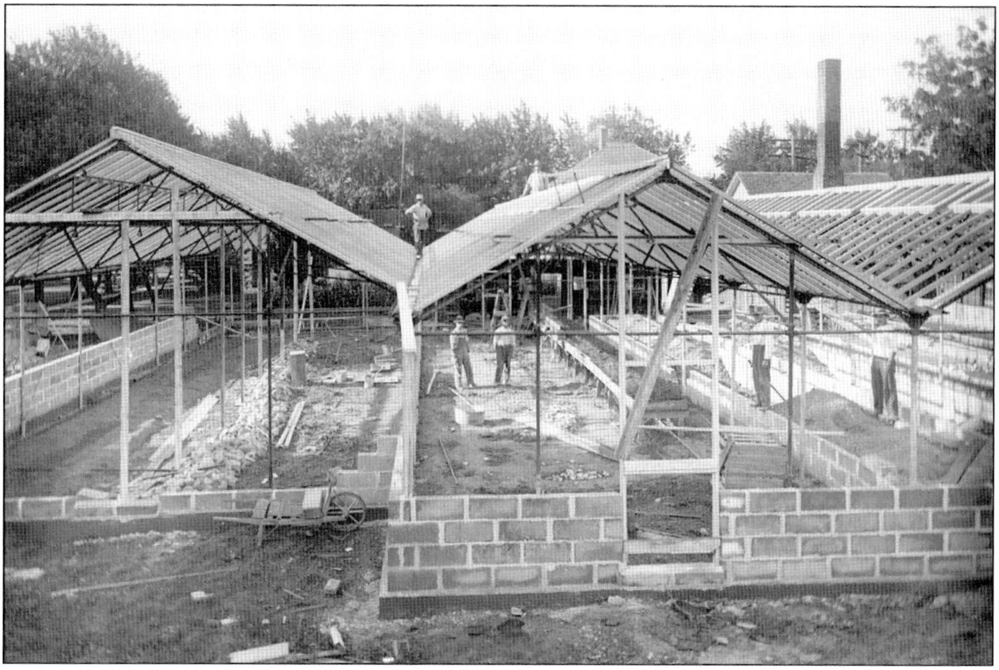

Building Greenhouses. Labeled August 14, 1914, this photograph shows the Caro Greenhouse being erected on Pearl Street for Arthur J. Packer. Packer sent village children door to door with baskets to sell his greenhouse vegetables. In 1921, Sumner Wesley Holden opened the Caro Floral Company at the location. The company was later owned by Burnell Holden and finally by Carson Dalton. (Courtesy of Watrousville-Caro Historical Society.)

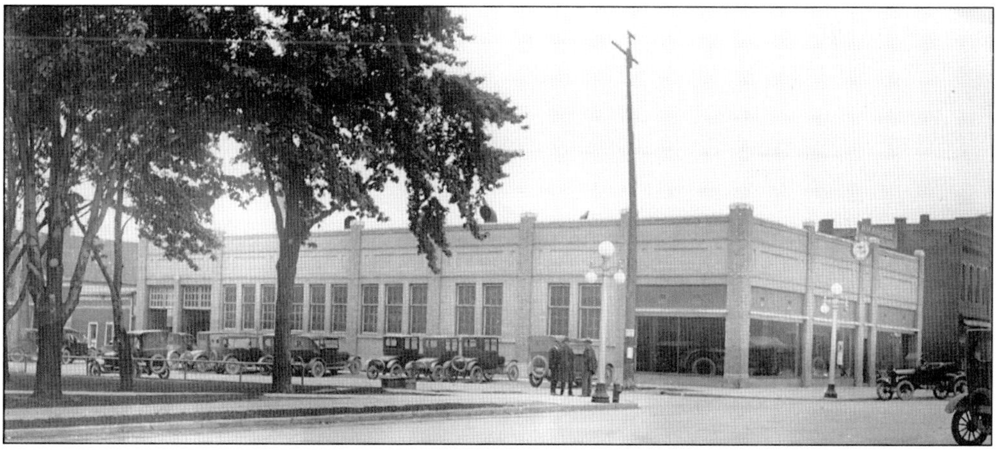

Cooper and Striffler Buick Garage, 1922. The Cooper and Striffler Buick Garage was on the corner of State and Sherman Streets. This was previously the location of the Edmunds Hotel and is now the location of Continental Rental. New Buick models are lined up next to the building. (Courtesy of Watrousville-Caro historical Society.)

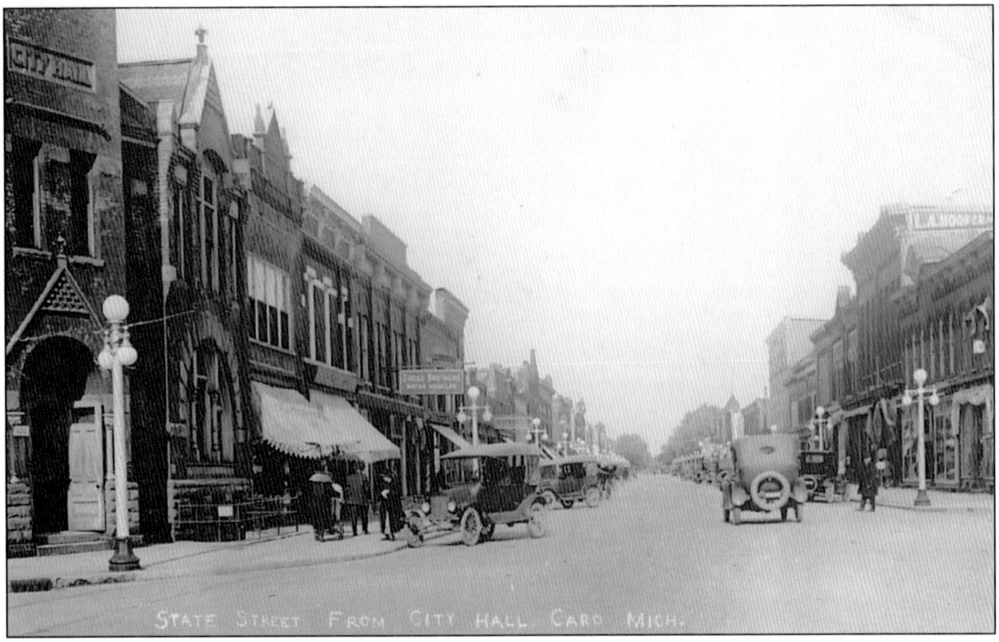

LOOKING NORTHEAST DOWN STATE STREET. In 1922, downtown Caro was a bustling, busy place. Looking northeast down State Street, we see the changeover from horses to automobiles has made great strides, with automobiles lining both sides of the street. With the wide, paved street, elegant streetlights, and well-kept storefronts, Caro was the picture of success in 1922. (Courtesy of Watrousville-Caro Historical Society.)

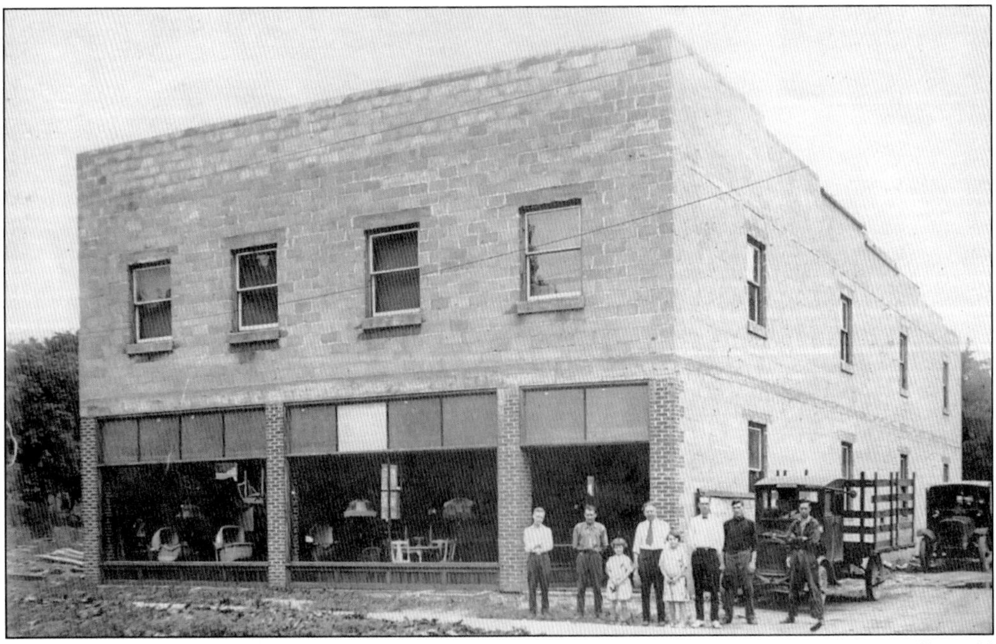

GUNSELL'S, 1924. Built in late 1923 and located at 130 West Burnside Street, Gunsell's sold furniture, rugs, coal and wood ranges, heating stoves, and hand-wringer washing machines. This building is now occupied by Dental Health Care PC. William Gunsell stands between his two young daughters in this photograph. (Courtesy of Watrousville-Caro Historical Society.)

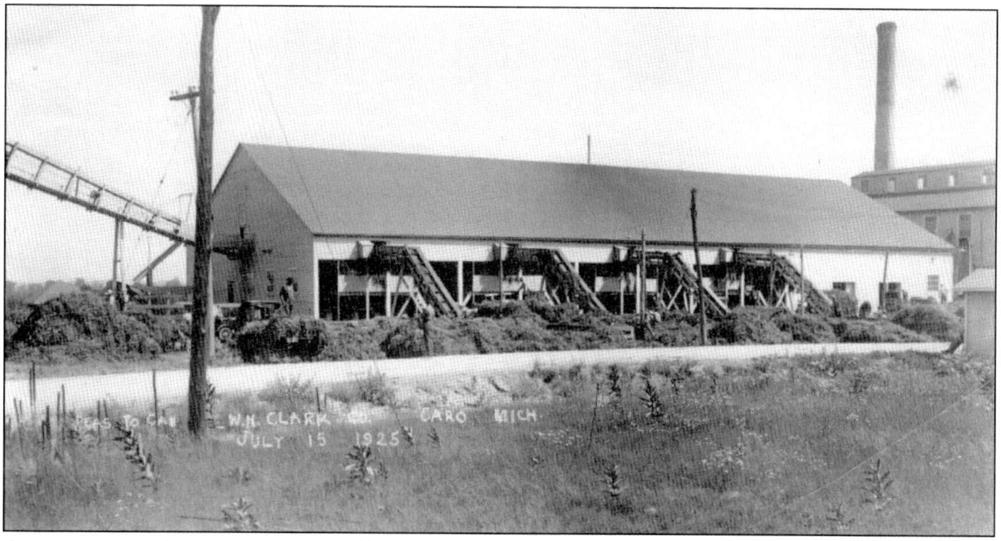

Cannery and Peas, 1925. This W.N. Clark Canning Company building was erected in 1923 along a railroad siding in Caro. The large piles of fresh peas shown were fed onto the conveyer belts and into the plant for processing. This building was later replaced with a cement structure. The company provided employment for hundreds of local residents. The plant was closed in 1970. (Courtesy of Watrousville-Caro Historical Society.)

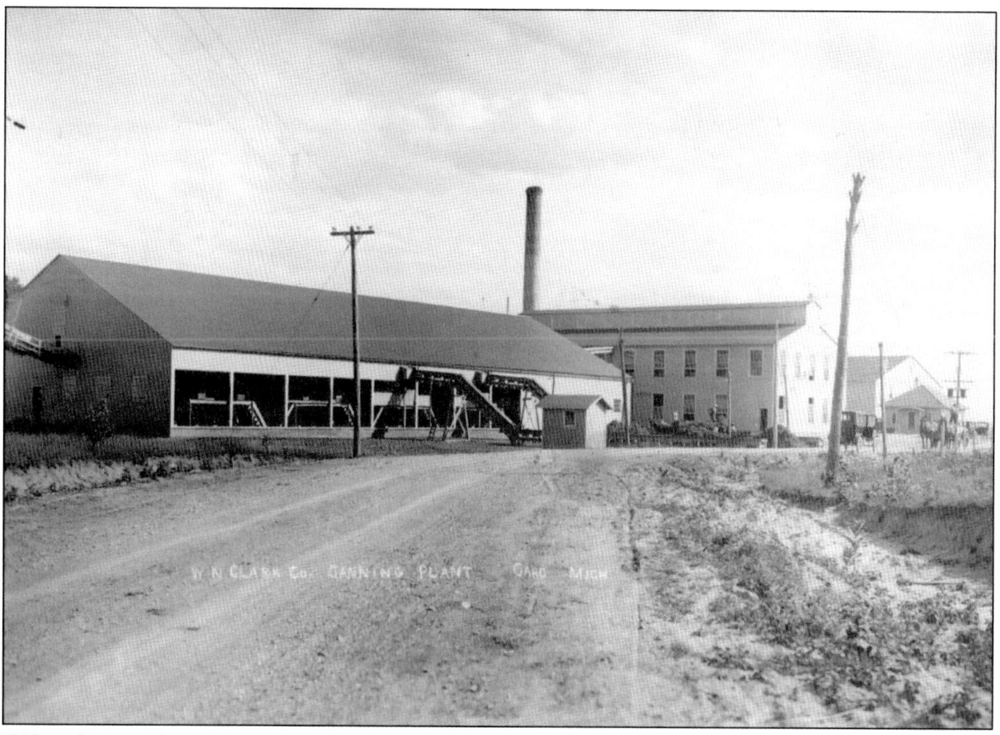

W.N. Clark Canning Company. This 1929 photograph gives a more extensive view of the company buildings on Columbia Street. In addition to peas, snap beans and lima beans were also processed at the cannery. This company was an important part of the area's economy through the first half of the 20th century. (Courtesy of Norman Dorr Wiltse.)

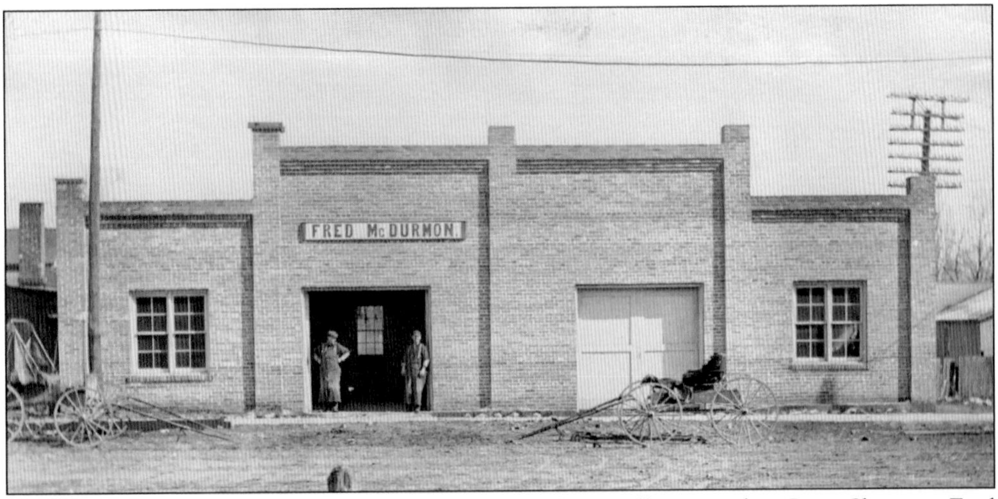

BLACKSMITH SHOP. In the 1920s, several blacksmith shops still operated in Caro. Shown is Fred McDurmon's shop on Montague Street in about 1930. Blacksmiths still shoed horses but they could also make almost any iron item a farmer might need. (Courtesy of Watrousville-Caro Historical Society.)

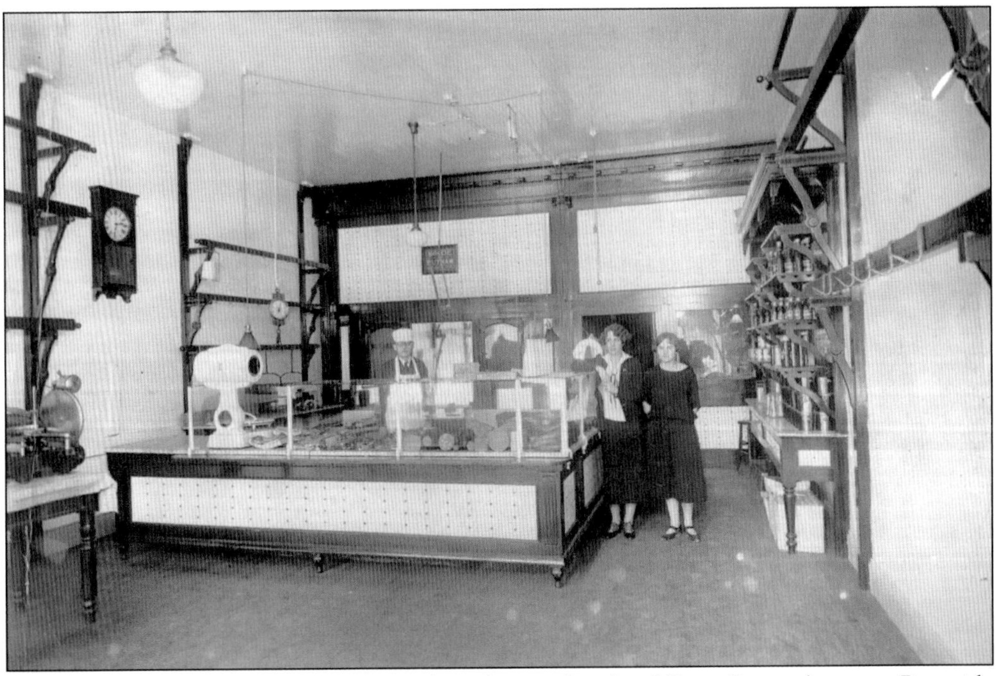

KINDE PUTNAM MEAT MARKET. Located on the south side of State Street, between Burnside and Sherman Streets, this meat market was the model of a clean, modern shop. Discriminating housewives and domestics had to maintain a close relationship with their butcher in the days before modern refrigeration. This shop was later torn down to make way for the Woolworth's store. (Courtesy of Watrousville-Caro Historical Society.)

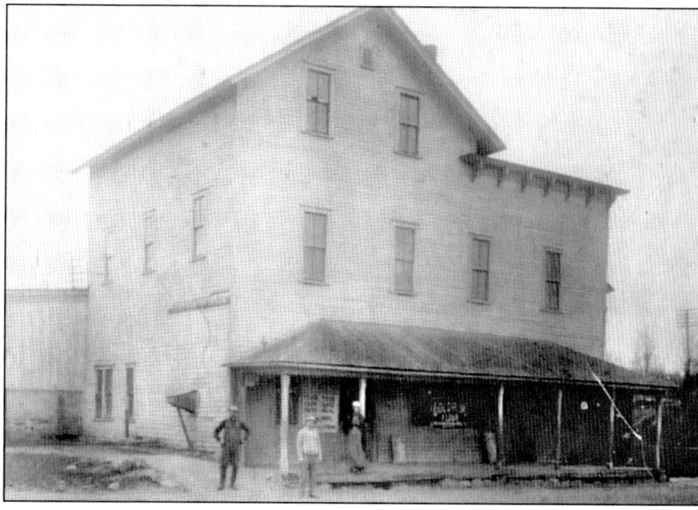

Gristmill. Started in the early days of Caro, by 1905 this was the Caro Milling Company, owned and operated by Albert J. Van Sickle. It was located at Monroe and State Streets, where the dry gully now runs under State Street. In those days, enough water gushed through the gully to power the behemoth mill as it ground corn and grain for feed and flour. (Courtesy of Norman Dorr Wiltse.)

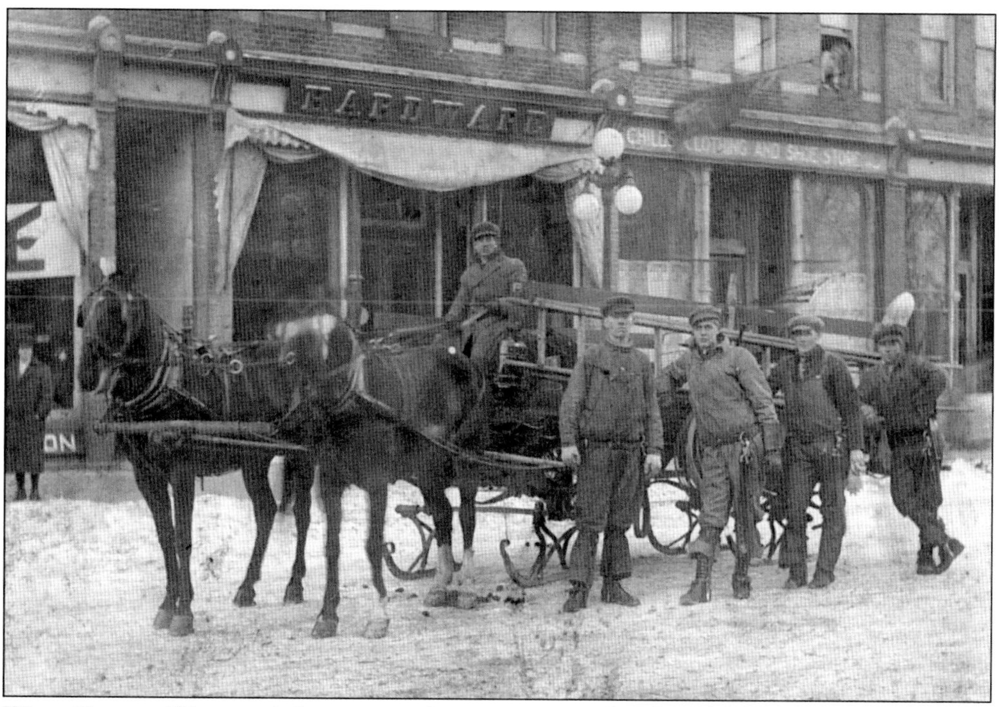

Work Crew in Winter. A five-man work crew is equipped with tool belts and a ladder, wearing what appear to be linemen's boots. They are posed around their horse-drawn sleigh on State Street. Possibly, they are part of an electrification crew, as a streetlight can be seen behind them. This identifies the date of the photograph to at least 1912–1913. (Courtesy of Norman Dorr Wiltse.)

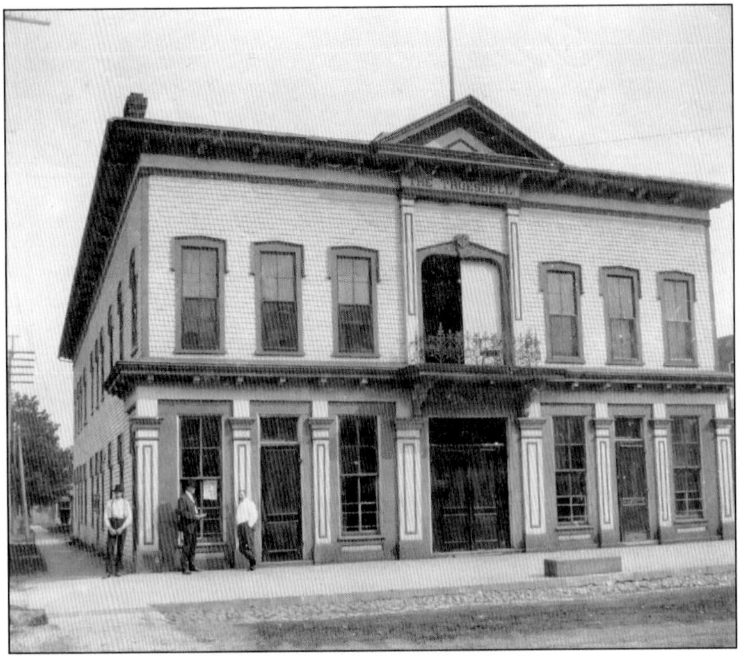

TRUESDELL HOUSE. Located on the corner of State and Sherman Streets, this hotel was built in 1880 as the Medler House. It was also known as the Truesdell House and the Hotel Edmunds. In the early 20th century, the Edmunds had an icehouse that was accessed by local children on hot summer days by climbing a series of cleats nailed to its exterior. (Courtesy of Watrousville-Caro Historical Society.)

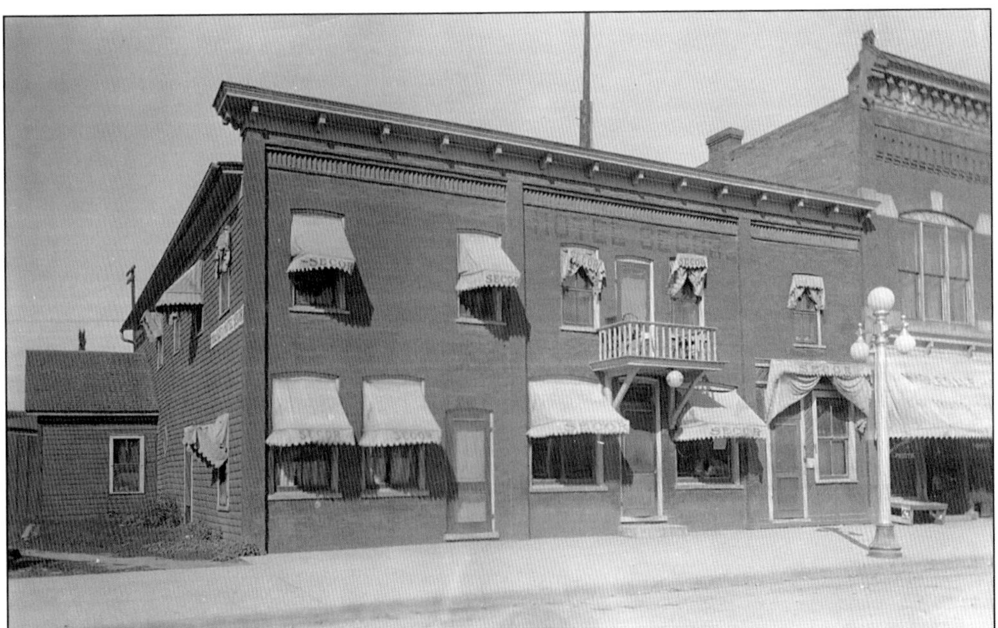

HOTEL SECOR. Located on State Street between Burnside and Sherman Streets, the Secor was built in 1867 as the Exchange Hotel. Above the front door, the Hotel Secor had a small balcony, used by residents to view circus parades. The hotel burned in the early 20th century. The site is now occupied by the Signature Bank. (Courtesy of Watrousville-Caro Historical Society.)

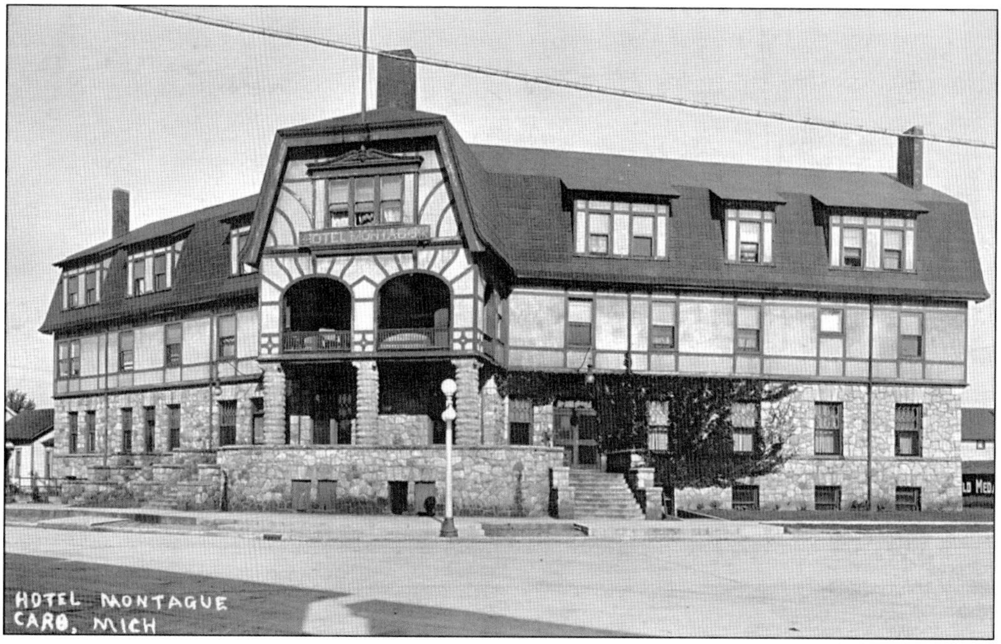

HOTEL MONTAGUE. The Hotel Montague was built in 1902 by prominent Caro businessman Charles Montague. It was considered one of the finest hotels in the region and was a source of great pride to the community. The Montague's dining room, complete with a mounted moose head over the fireplace, was the scene of many holiday celebrations. (Courtesy of Gloria Hall.)

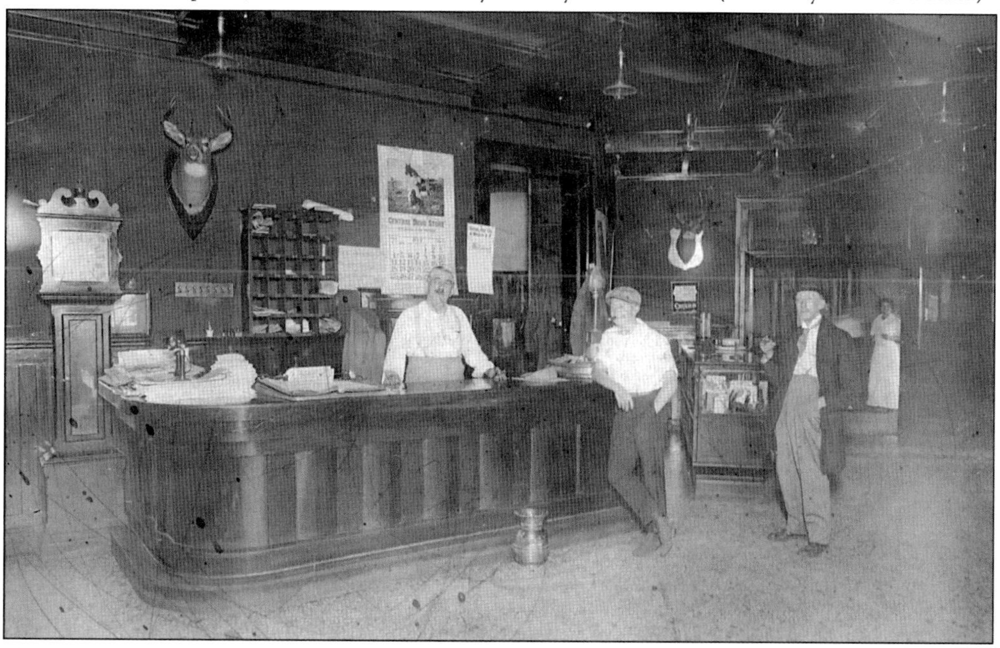

HOTEL MONTAGUE LOBBY. This is the original lobby of the Montague before the 1923 fire; it is 4:12 p.m. on a July day in 1913 or 1915. Notice the candlestick phone on the desk as well as the spittoon on the floor. Incandescent light bulbs hang from the vaulted ceiling and a panel of push-button switches is on the wall. The train schedule and a Central Drug calendar hang behind the desk. (Courtesy of Norman Dorr Wiltse.)

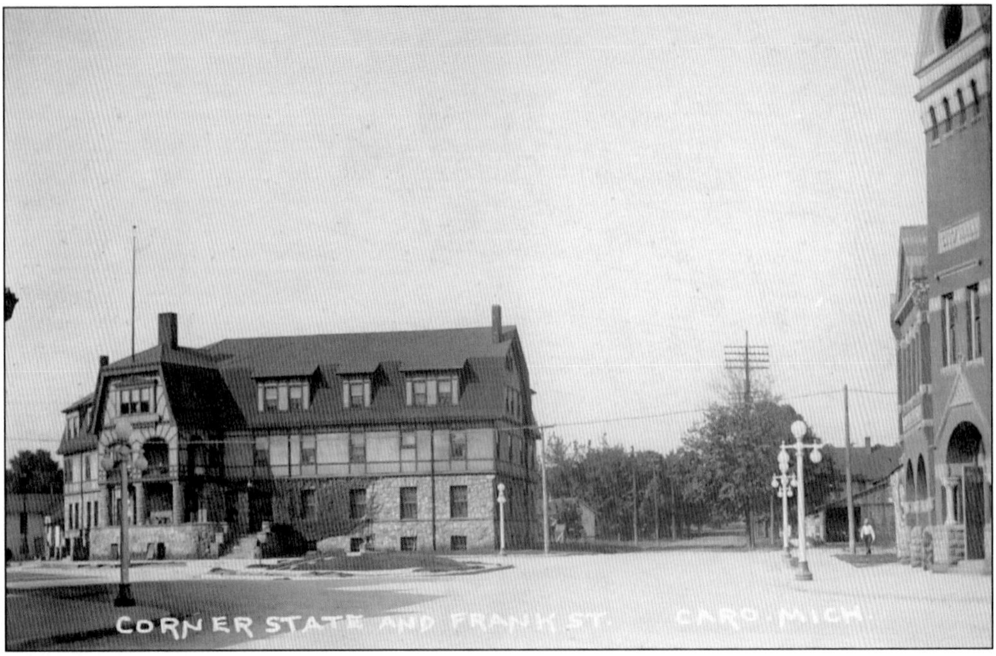

Frank and State Streets. This photograph presents another view of the Hotel Montague (left) as well as the city hall (right). The hotel had 60 rooms on three floors and a basement. The basement had bowling alleys, a billiard room, and a barbershop. The dining room and office were on the first floor. (Courtesy of Gloria Hall.)

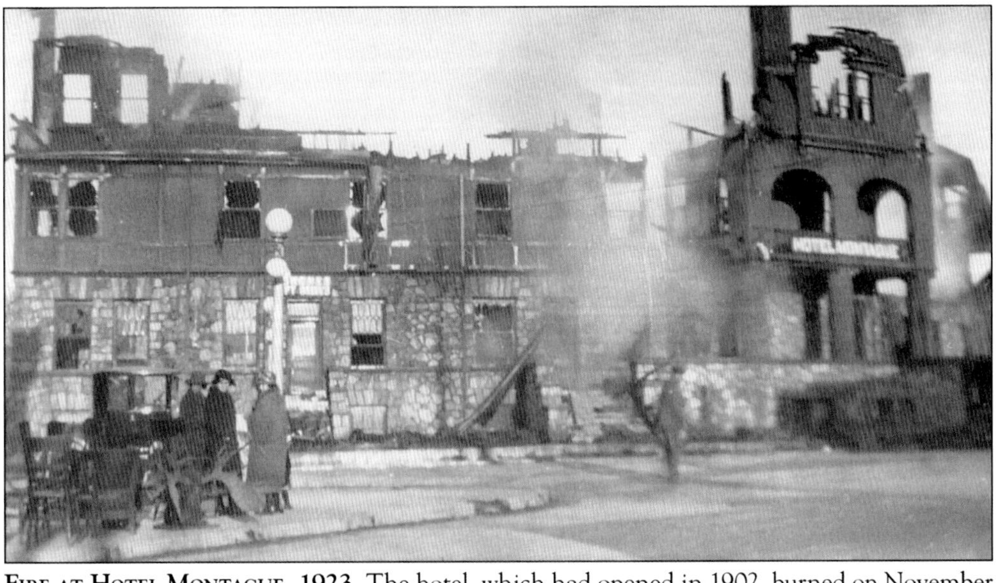

Fire at Hotel Montague, 1923. The hotel, which had opened in 1902, burned on November 21, 1923. The fire was visible in Saginaw 30 miles away. Both the Bay City and Saginaw Fire Departments were called for assistance. Saginaw fire chief John Krenzberger and Engine Company No. 2 responded, making the run to Caro in 47 minutes. (Courtesy of Watrousville-Caro Historical Society.)

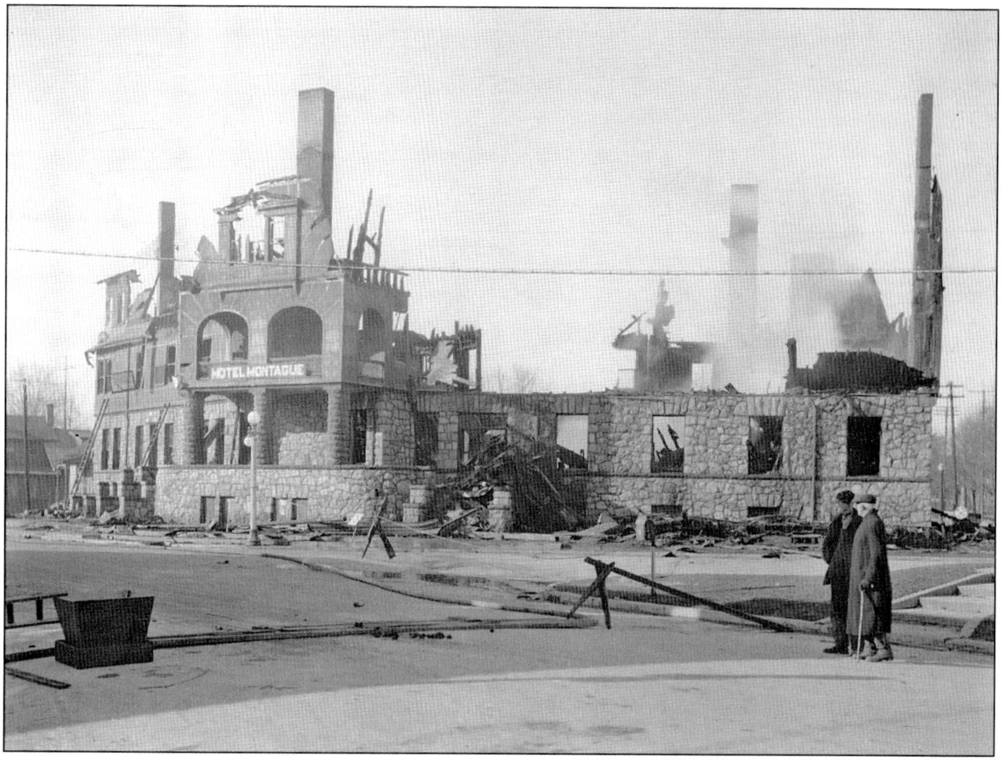

The Day After. This photograph, which appeared in the *Tuscola County Advertiser*, was labeled as having been taken the day after the fire, while smoke still rose from the ragged rubble of the once-grand hotel. Ladders still lean against the building, and the total destruction of the hotel is obvious. (Courtesy of Norman Dorr Wiltse.)

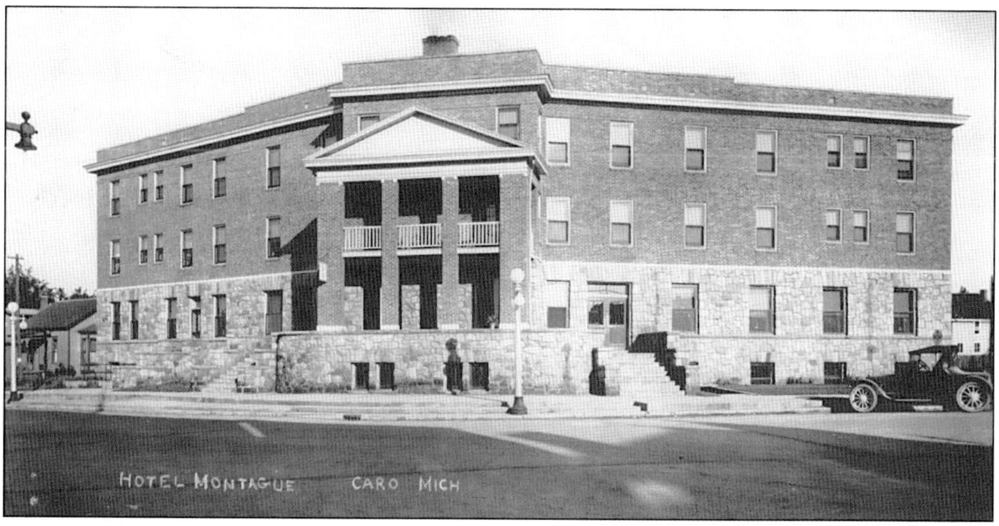

Rebuilt Hotel Montague, 1925. In 1924, the Caro community came together through the Hotel Montague Company and the Caro Board of Commerce to rebuild the Hotel Montague after it had been destroyed by fire in 1923. The upper two stories were now brick, and there were 50 sleeping rooms, all with running water, and 10 with baths. (Courtesy of Watrousville-Caro Historical Society.)

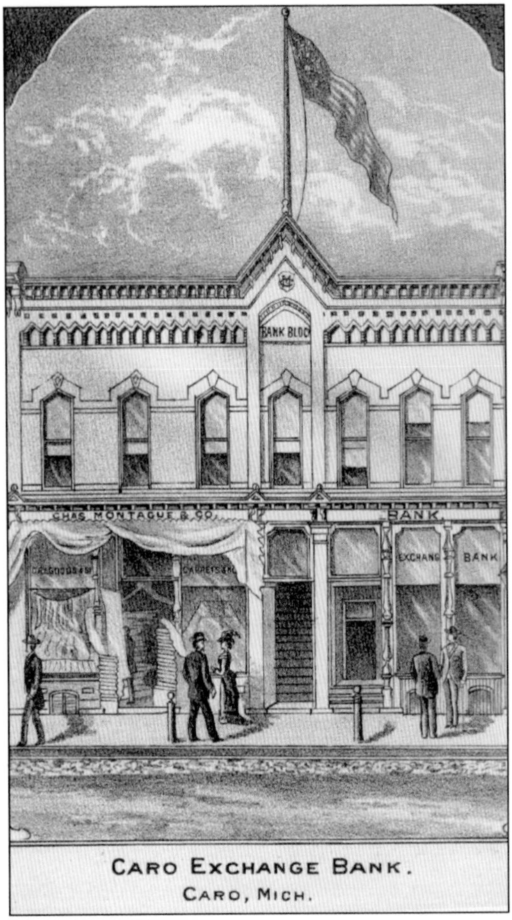

CARO EXCHANGE BANK. Established in 1875 by Charles Montague, this was the first bank in Caro. In 1879, the Bank Block pictured was built by Montague and a portion of the ground floor was devoted to the Exchange Bank. The second floor was the Masonic Lodge, and still is today. By 1903, Montague's heavy business losses and declining health resulted in the bank's closing. (*History of Tuscola and Bay Counties.*)

PEOPLES STATE BANK, 1915. The Peoples State Bank was organized in December 1912. This building was designed by architect Peter Miller and was completed in December 1913. United Health Services currently occupies the building. On the left is Frank Ransford's Caro Steam Laundry, and on the right is Hudson's Bazaar. (Courtesy of Watrousville-Caro Historical Society.)

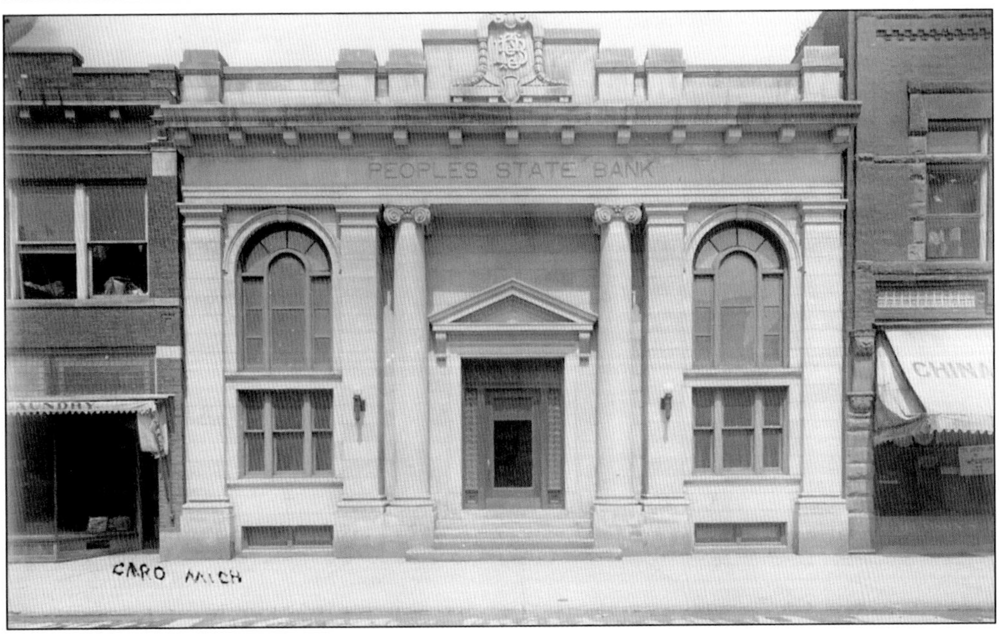

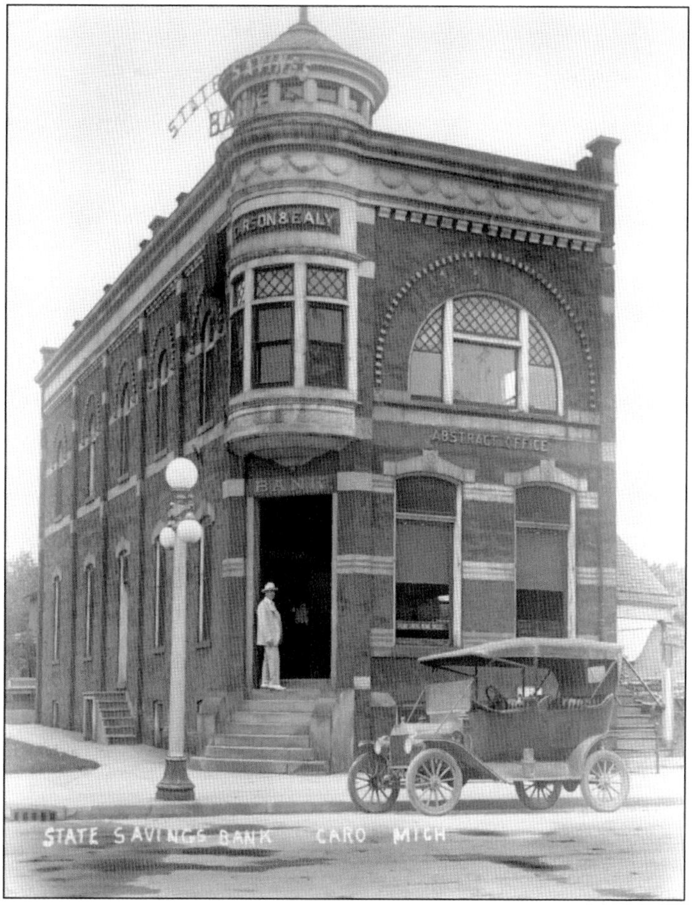

State Savings Bank, 1916. The State Savings Bank was organized in May 1904 and was the successor to the Carson & Ealy Bank. This building was on the corner of State and Sherman Streets. In 1921, the State Savings Bank moved to 240 North State Street. The State Savings Bank is now the Chemical Bank. (Courtesy of Watrousville-Caro Historical Society.)

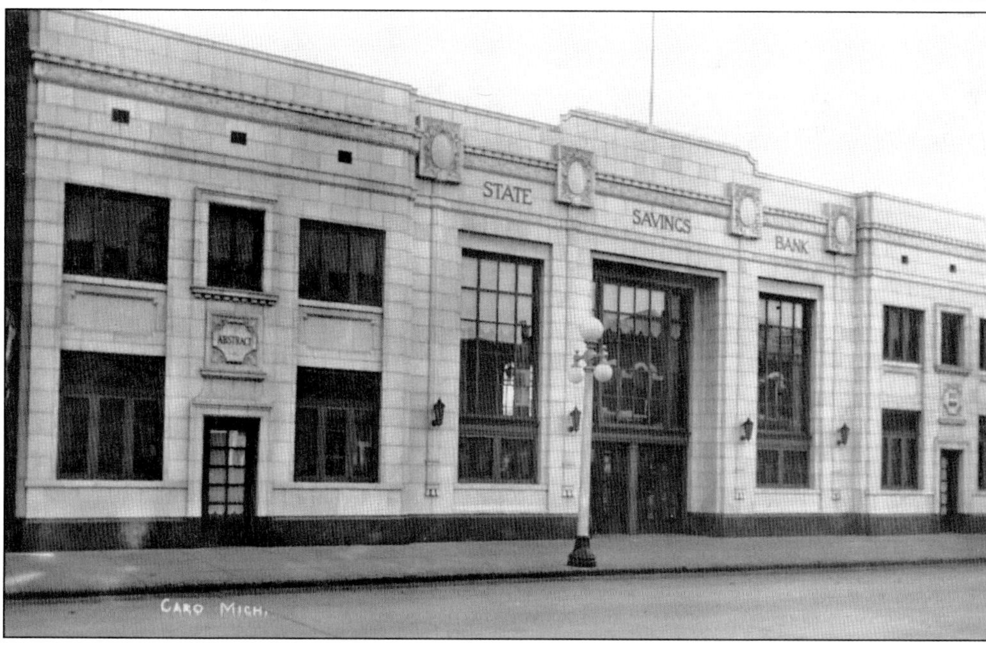

New State Savings Bank, 1922. This was the new building, completed in 1921. It was erected on the former site of the Caro House, one of the oldest hotels in the village. The white front of the bank in this photograph has been redone in red brick. (Courtesy of Gloria Hall.)

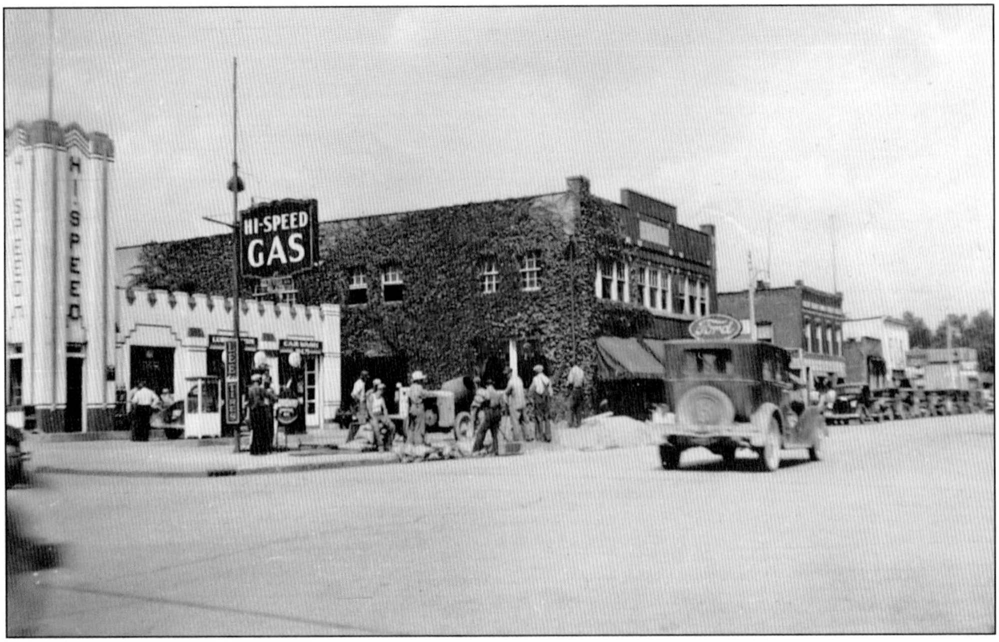

Hi-Speed Gas Station. This gas station replaced the Carson & Ealy Bank and State Savings Bank building on the corner of State and Sherman Streets. The Ford Garage next to the gas station was built in 1911. In recent years, the Botsford gas station has been on the Hi-Speed site. (Courtesy of Douglas C. Gallery/Watrousville-Caro Historical Society.)

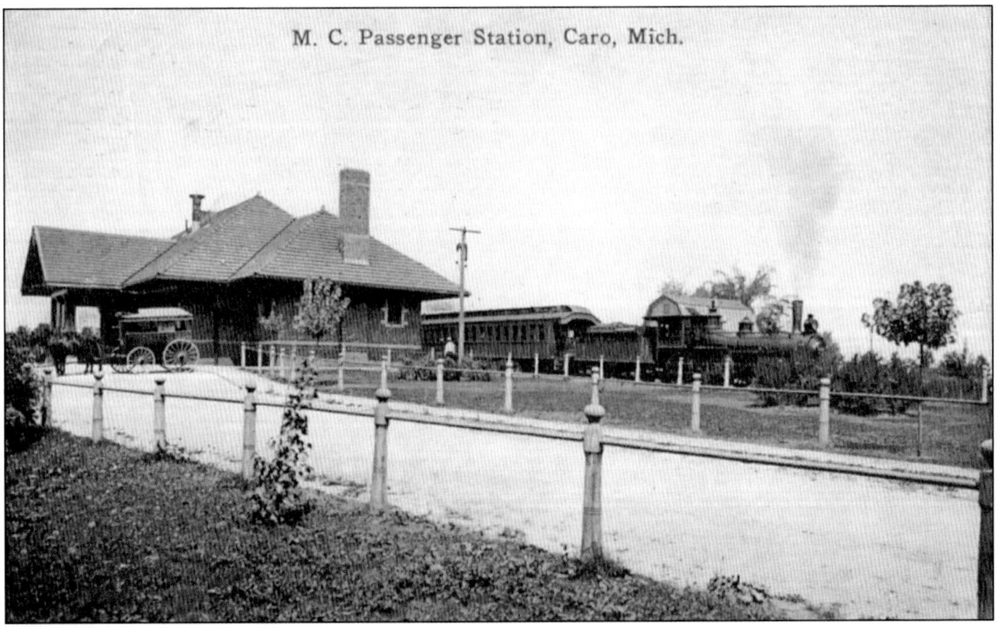

Michigan Central Depot. Railroad transportation was vital to Caro's prosperity in moving lumber products and agricultural goods. The Michigan Central Railroad Company arrived in Caro in 1879 through the sponsorship of Charles Montague and William A. Heartt, in particular. This photograph was taken in about 1905. The carriage is from the Hotel Caro and awaits passengers. (Courtesy of Watrousville-Caro Historical Society.)

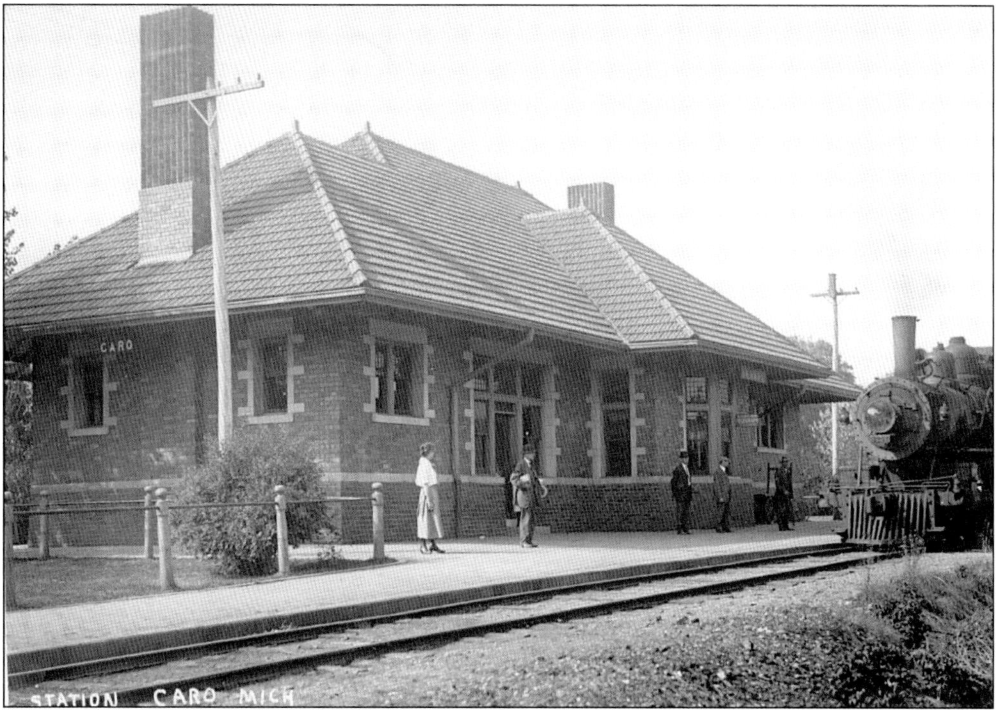

Michigan Central Depot, 1916. Located on North State Street near today's Rite Aid Store, this beautiful brick depot was the pet project of Theron W. "Tip" Atwood, who was the Michigan Commissioner of Railroads at the time. The epicenter of travel in its heyday, this picturesque building was demolished in 1971. Here, engine No. 8296 pulls into position at the platform. (Courtesy of Watrousville-Caro Historical Society.)

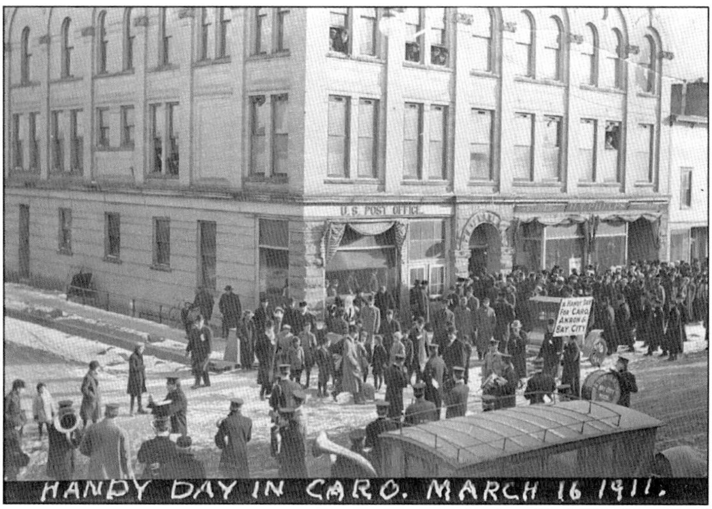

Handy Day, 1911. On March 16, 1911, the opening of the Detroit, Bay City & Western (DBC&W) Railroad was celebrated in Caro. The railroad was formed by the four Handy brothers of Bay City. The DBC&W operated four passenger trains per day until 1924. After that date, the railroad only hauled freight. (Courtesy of Watrousville-Caro Historical Society.)

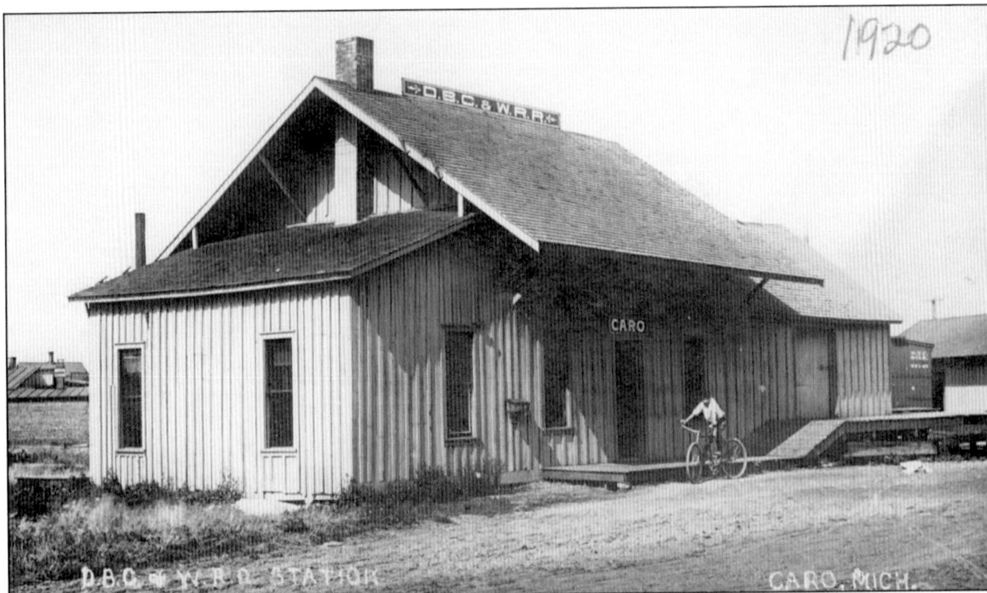

DBC&W Railroad Station, 1920. Located near the present-day TI Automotive south of the village, this station was the transfer point for many travelers. From business travel downstate, to leisure visits, and even excursion trips to Bay City theaters or society events, train travel was a blessing to area residents. (Courtesy of Watrousville-Caro Historical Society.)

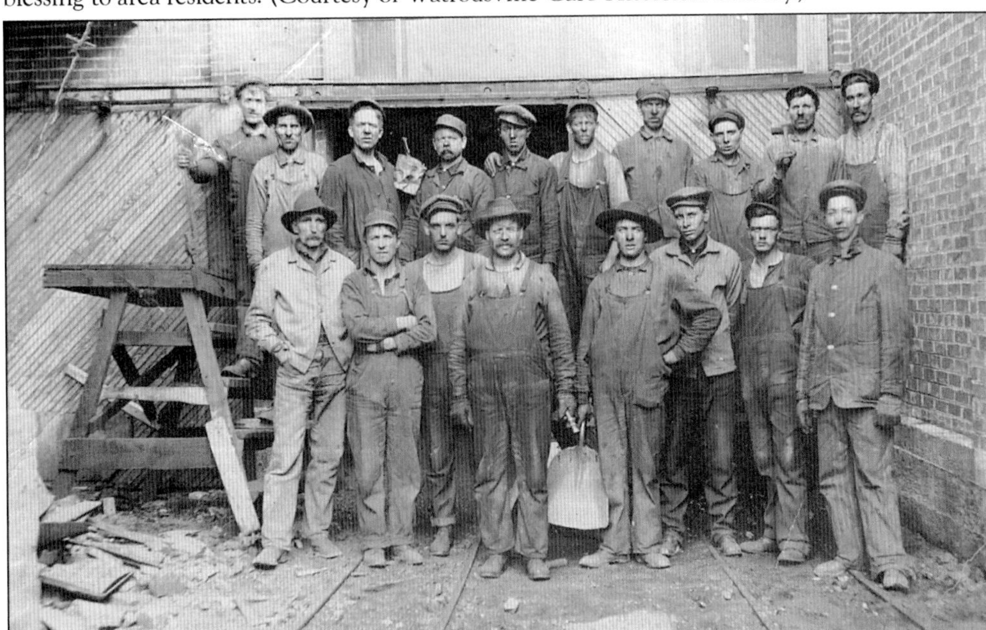

Crew Building Sugar Factory. As attention began to focus on sugar beets as a crop, Charles Montague and William A. Heartt agreed to sell land at a low enough price to enable a sugar refinery to be built near the Cass River. Charles Montague and John F. Seeley backed the project with their banks. In 1899, crews like this moved in and went to work building the refinery. (Courtesy of Watrousville-Caro Historical Society.)

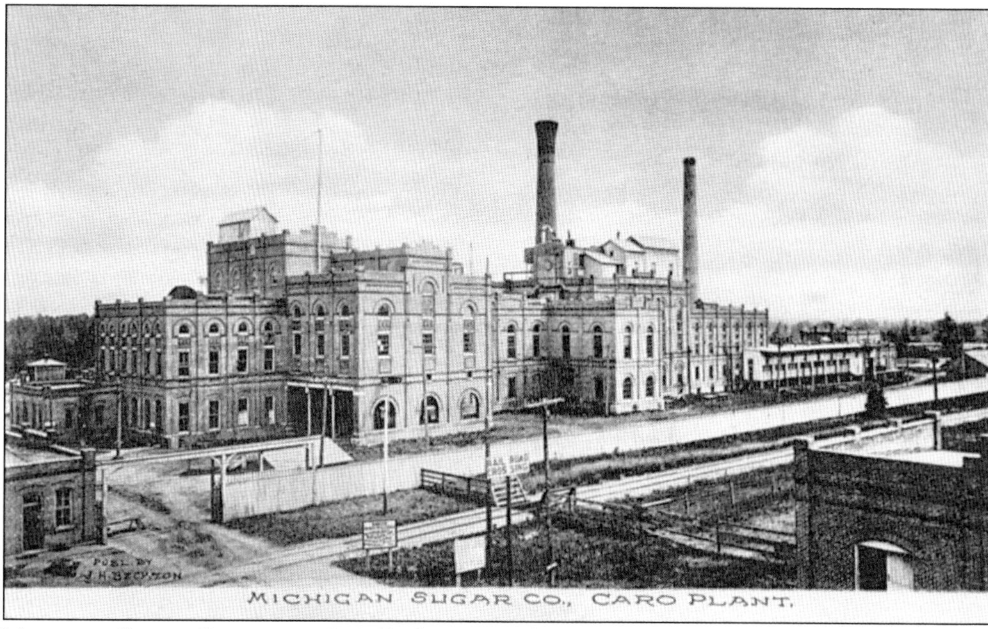

MICHIGAN SUGAR COMPANY, 1909. Deforestation brought the need for other land uses. Strong support from local bankers and investors facilitated the building of the Peninsular Sugar Refining Company in 1899, and local farmers began planting sugar beets. By 1900, 1,200 tons of beets were processed into 300,000 pounds of sugar, or eight to ten train car loads every 24 hours. In 1909, Peninsular became the Michigan Sugar Company. (Courtesy of Gloria Hall.)

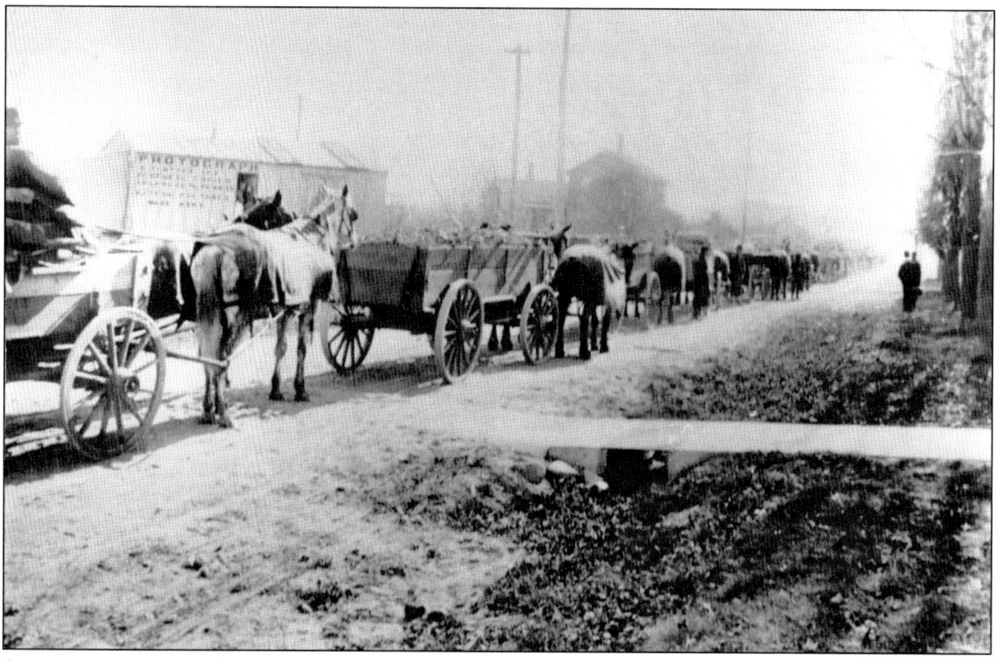

SUGAR BEET LINE UP. Farmers lined up with their wagons of sugar beets to be unloaded and processed at the refinery. In 1901, the first crop was processed, and in the early 1900s, this refinery became the second largest beet factory in the United States. Today, beets continue to be a very important crop and industry in the area. (Courtesy of Watrousville-Caro Historical Society.)

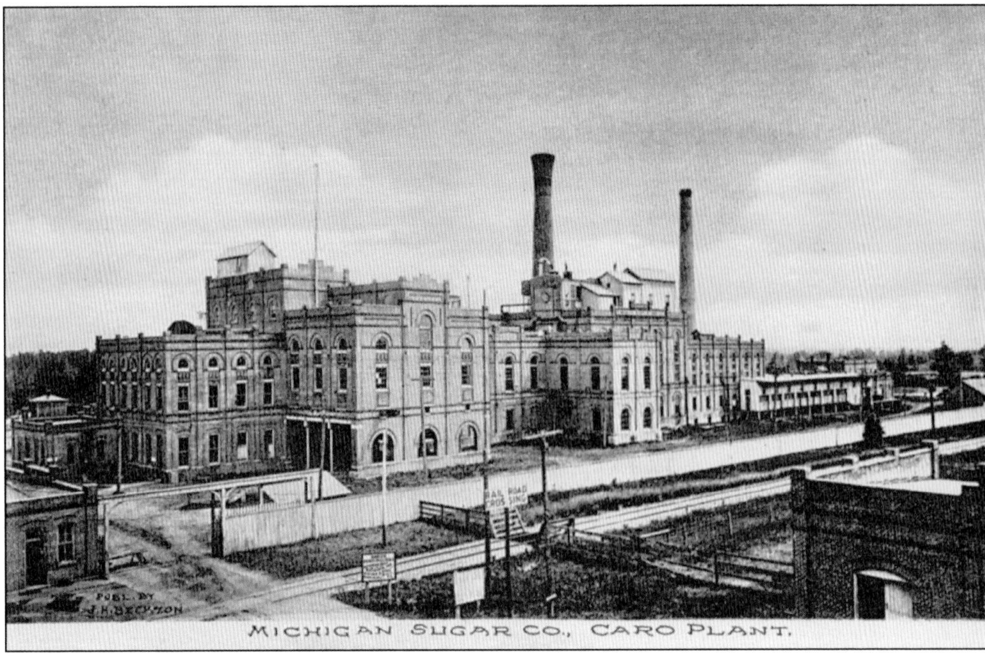

Peninsular Sugar Refining Company. This expansive view of the Peninsular Sugar Refinery reveals a plant that, by 1905, required 12,000 acres of beets be grown in a season. The work involved in cultivating and harvesting 12,000 acres of beets brought hundreds of seasonal laborers to the area annually. Sugar beets became the best paying crop on the farm. (Courtesy of Watrousville-Caro Historical Society.)

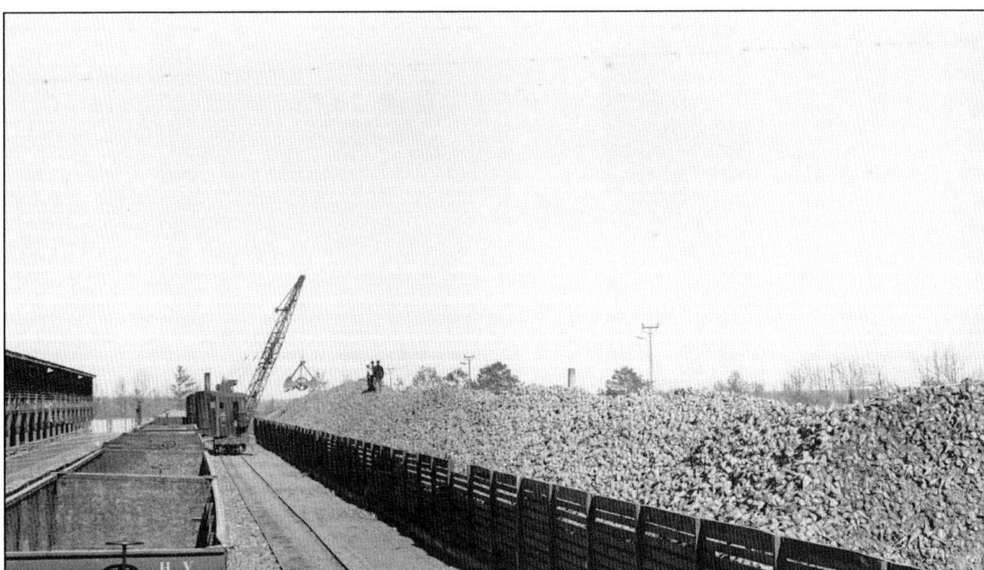

Sugar Beet Pile, 1915. This photograph was labeled, "3,600 tons of beets and a derrick at Caro. Charles Sieland and Charles Bills standing on beets." Freshly harvested beets are heavy, with an average stack estimated to weigh approximately 40,000 tons. The refinery runs 24 hours a day, seven days a week, from September through February or March, and the process is relatively unchanged since its beginnings a century ago. (Courtesy of Watrousville-Caro Historical Society.)

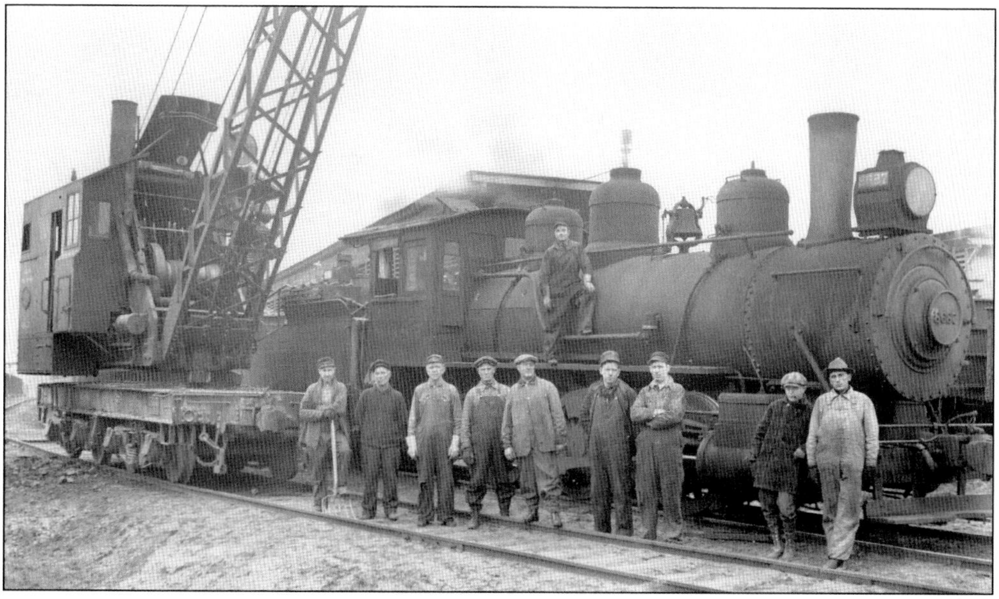

MICHIGAN SUGAR YARDS, 1915. This photograph shows the Michigan Sugar Company yards in November 1915, with crane operator Joe Hendrie and yard locomotive conductor George Wilson, although they are not specifically identified. No other workers in the photograph are identified. An enormous undertaking for its day, the heavy equipment and rail component were essential to running a successful campaign. (Courtesy of Watrousville-Caro Historical Society.)

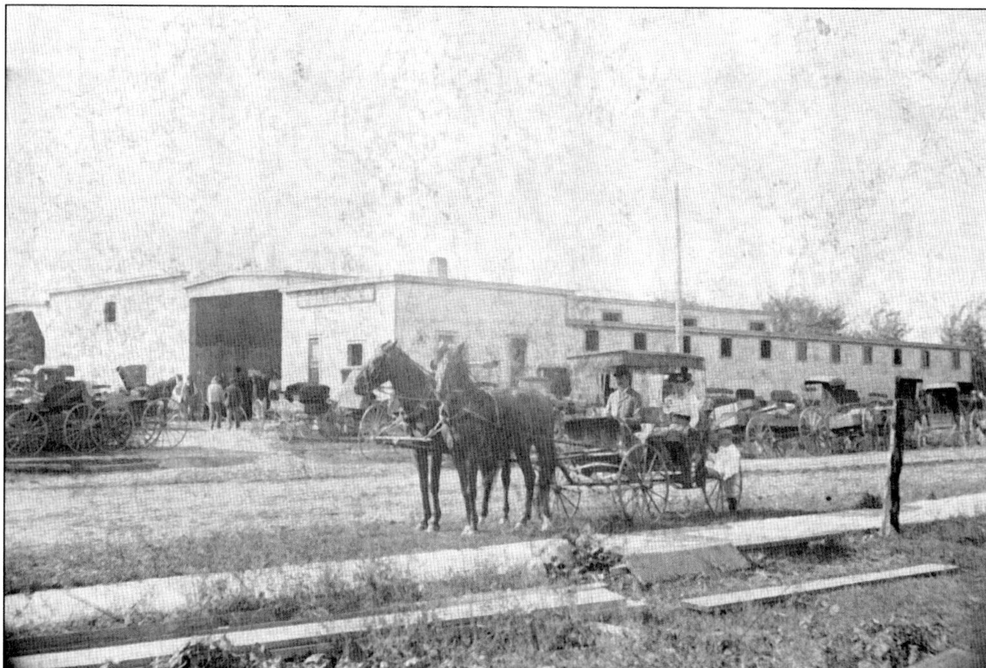

YORK 10-CENT BARN. Built in about 1885 by Walter T. York at the corner of West Frank and North Almer Streets, this 10-cent horse barn did a brisk business until the advent of the automobile. Basically a parking garage for horses and buggies, it was torn down in about 1936, a dozen years or so past its useful, intended life. (Courtesy of Gloria Hall.)

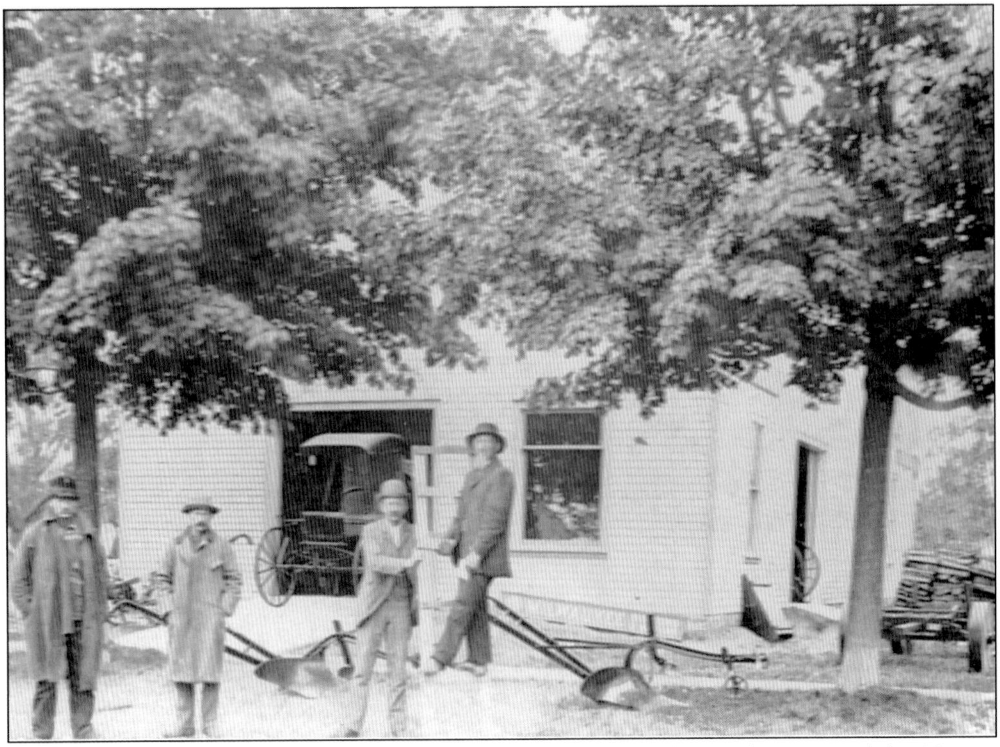

Walter York and Peter Bush. In this 1901 photograph, Walter York, owner of the 10-cent horse barn, is seen along with Peter Bush (on ladder), who was one of the village founding fathers. Frank Patrick is on the left and the other man is unidentified. As much local information and gossip could be learned at a 10-cent barn as at a barbershop. (Courtesy of Gloria Hall.)

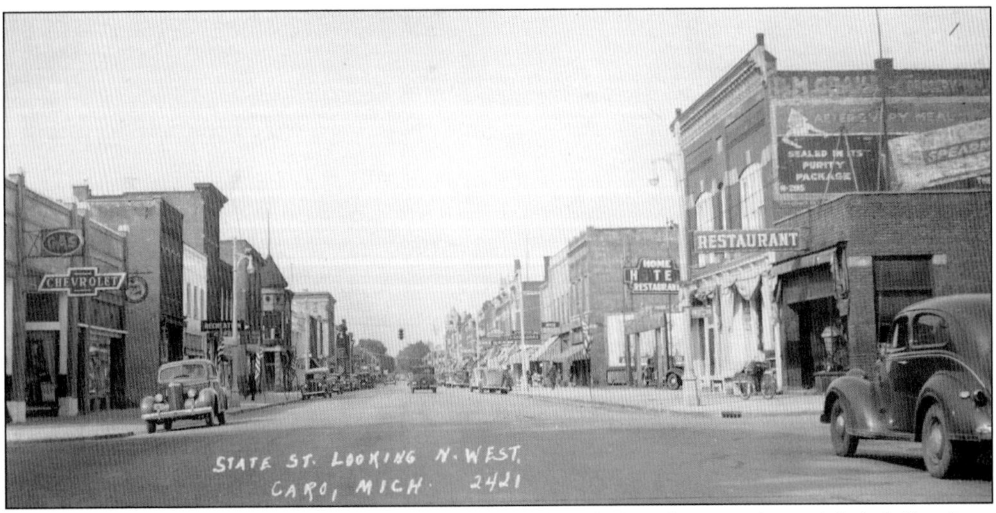

Looking Southwest Down State Street, 1935. Although this photograph was labeled, "Looking North West," it actually is a view looking southwest down State Street. This is an illustration of the confusing street layout of Caro, which persists to the present day. Also visible is the traffic light at State and Burnside Streets, a development that came with the automobile. (Courtesy of Watrousville-Caro Historical Society.)

Three

Village Life

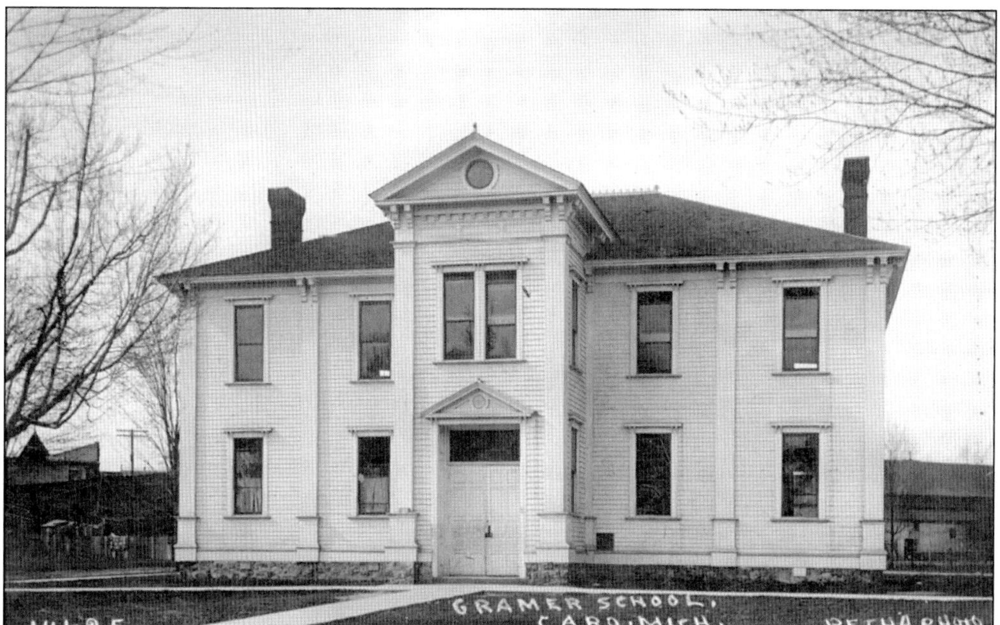

Early Caro School. This two-story, frame school was built on land donated by Peter D. Bush in 1868 at a cost of $4,000. Located at the corner of East Frank and Burnside Streets, it was known as the White Building. In 1887, a new brick high school was erected next to this building, which then became the grammar school. It was torn down in 1924. (Courtesy of Gloria Hall.)

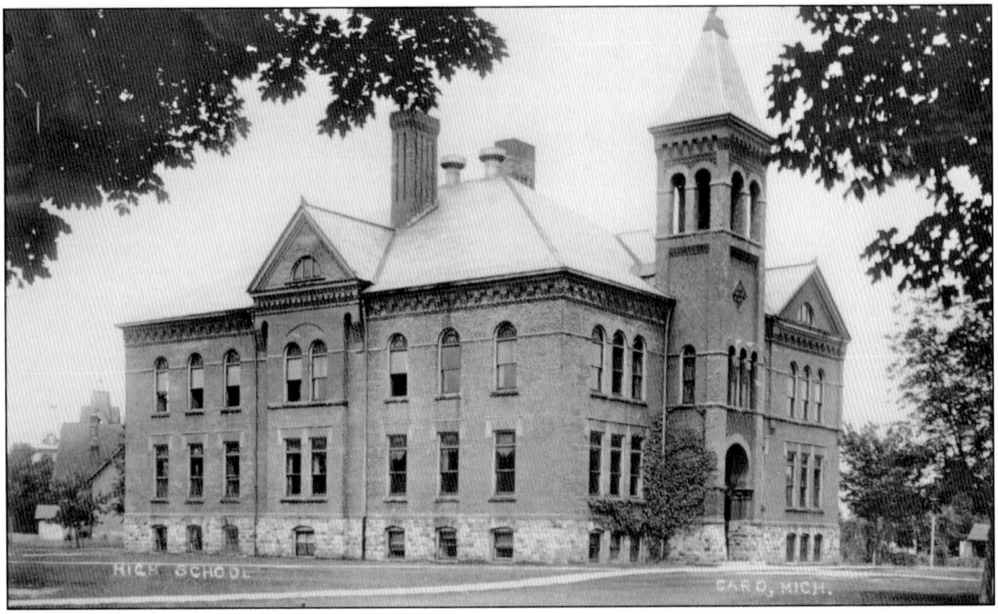

Caro High School. Built in 1887 to provide needed space for a growing student population, this two-story, brick school faced East Frank Street. The school had a shop classroom in the basement. From the fall of 1908 until June 1951, it was also the location of the Tuscola County Normal School. Known as the County Normal, the school trained hundreds of local rural teachers. (Courtesy of Watrousville-Caro Historical Society.)

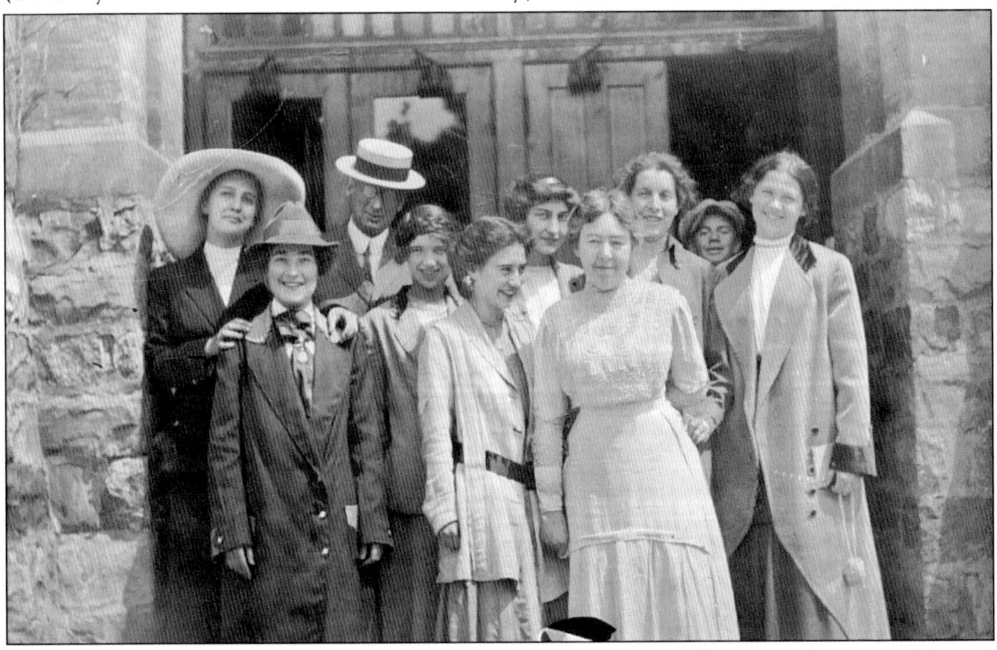

County Normal Class, 1913. This photograph is labeled as part of the Tuscola County Normal class of 1913. From left to right are (first row) Gertrude Martin, Bernice Tompkin, and teacher Miss Gilbert; (second row) Clara Hurford, superintendent of Caro schools Frank E. Schall, Mildred Tibby, Bess Winans, unidentified, and Emma Bearse. They appear to be a proud and happy group. (Courtesy of Watrousville-Caro Historical Society.)

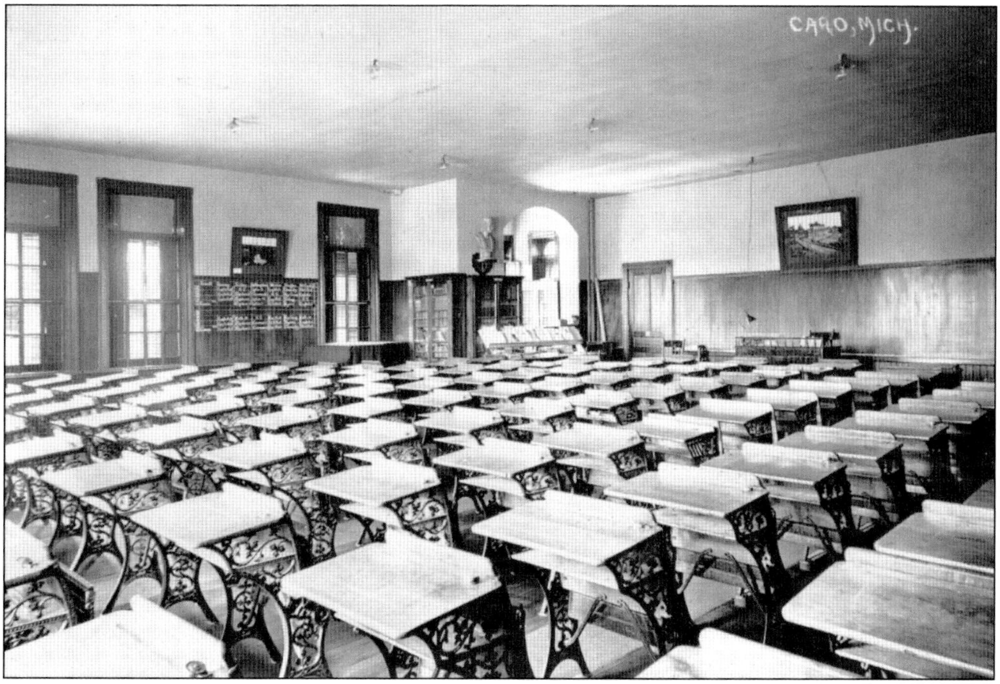

Assembly Hall, 1912. Pictured is the assembly room, or study hall, in the Caro High School. Each desk was attached to the desk in front of it by that desk's seat. There were shelves under the desktops for books, and inkwells were in the top right corners. The library is in the corner of the room (top, middle). (Courtesy of Watrousville-Caro Historical Society.)

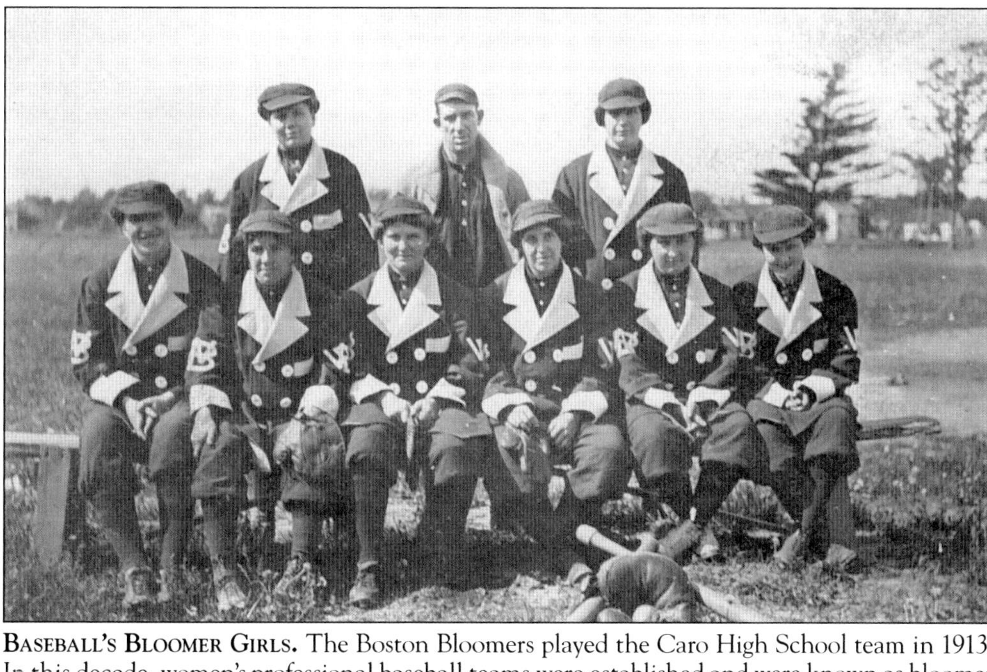

Baseball's Bloomer Girls. The Boston Bloomers played the Caro High School team in 1913. In this decade, women's professional baseball teams were established and were known as bloomer teams because of the trousers they wore. They crisscrossed the country, playing professional and non-professional teams. (Courtesy of Watrousville-Caro Historical Society.)

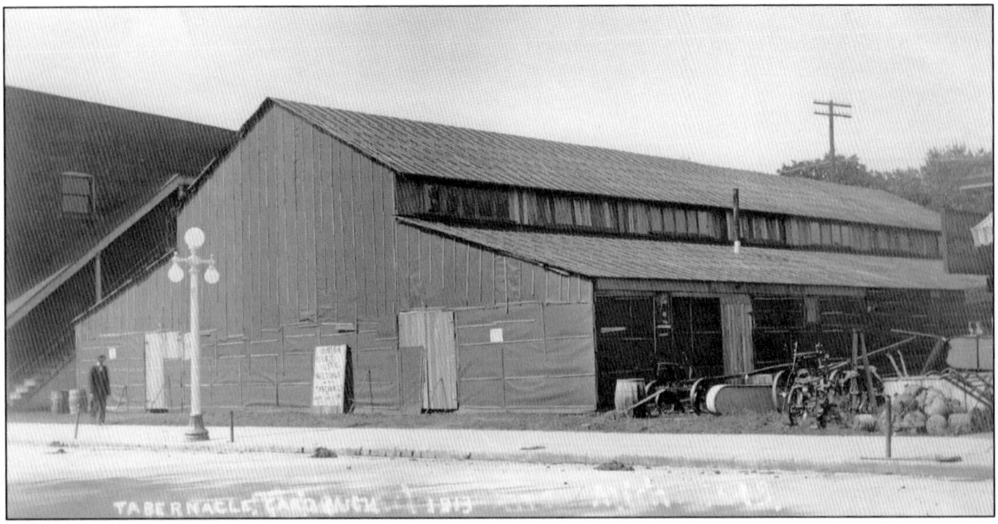

TABERNACLE, C. 1913. This sizeable building on State Street, across from the courthouse, was built in 1913 by a group of local Protestant churches for revival meetings. Evangelists Herbert C. Hart and A.S. Magann held a series of revivals and claimed 700 conversions in their tenure at the tabernacle. At left is the Carson-Ealy Bank. At right is a harness, implement, and repair shop. (Courtesy of Watrousville-Caro Historical Society.)

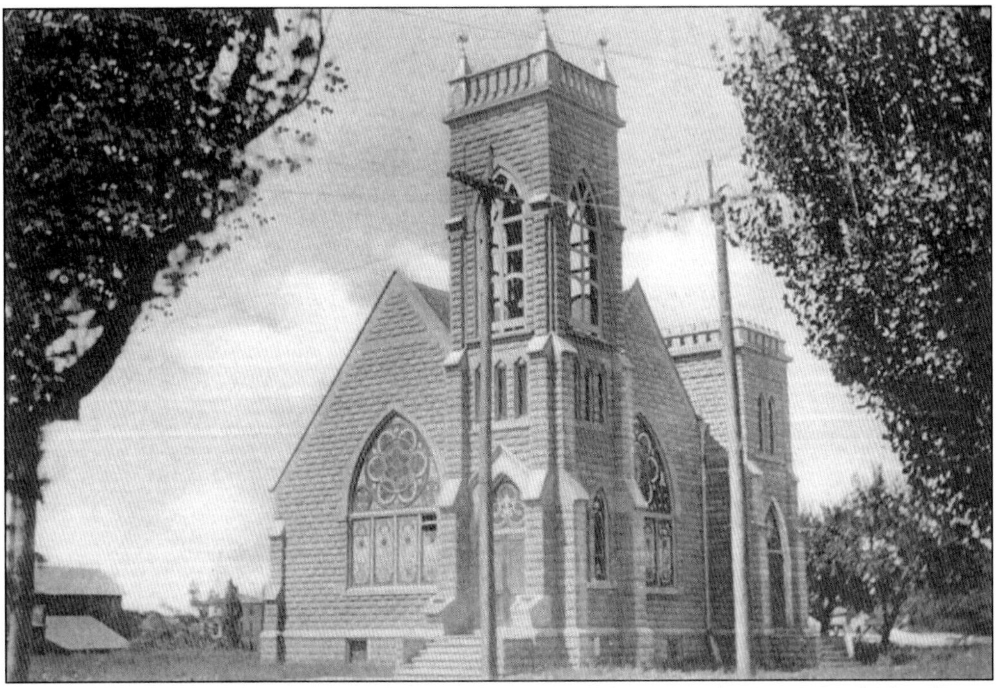

CARO EVANGELICAL UNITED BRETHREN CHURCH. Organized in 1872, the Evangelical Church met in private homes until 1887, when they purchased a frame church. This building, noted as being made of "artificial stone," was dedicated in December 1905 and was located at State and Washington Streets. The Evangelical merged with the United Brethren in 1946. When it was destroyed by arson in 1984, it was owned by the Caro Church of Christ. (Courtesy of Gloria Hall.)

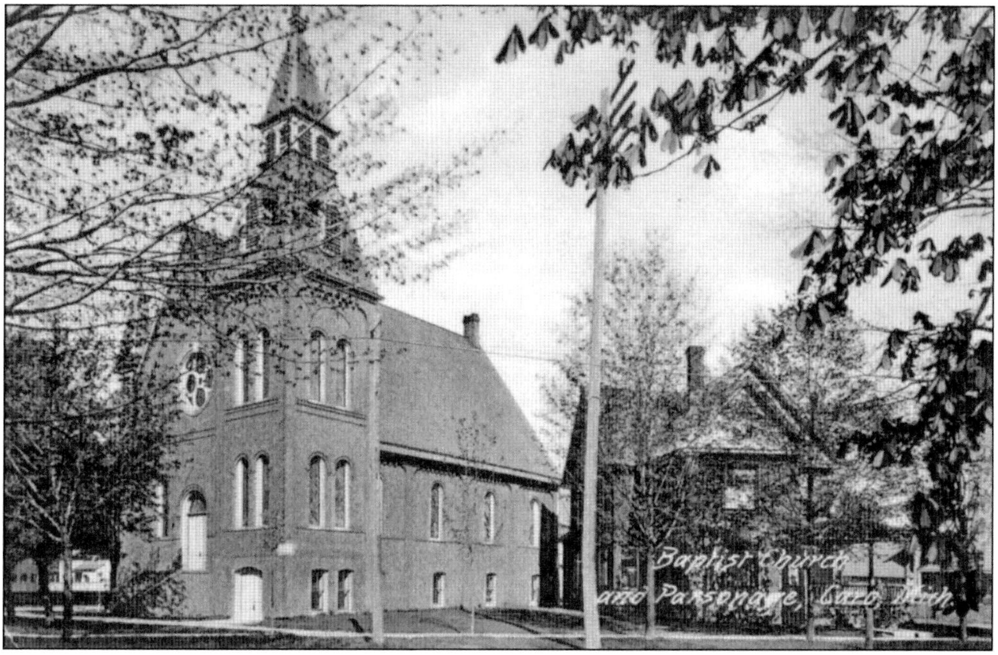

First Baptist Church. Organized in 1876, the church dedicated this brick building on the corner of West Lincoln and North Almer Streets in February 1877. The cost to build the church was about $10,000. The building has most recently been used by the New Creation Community Church. The parsonage next to the church was built in 1902 and is now a private home. (Courtesy of Watrousville-Caro Historical Society.)

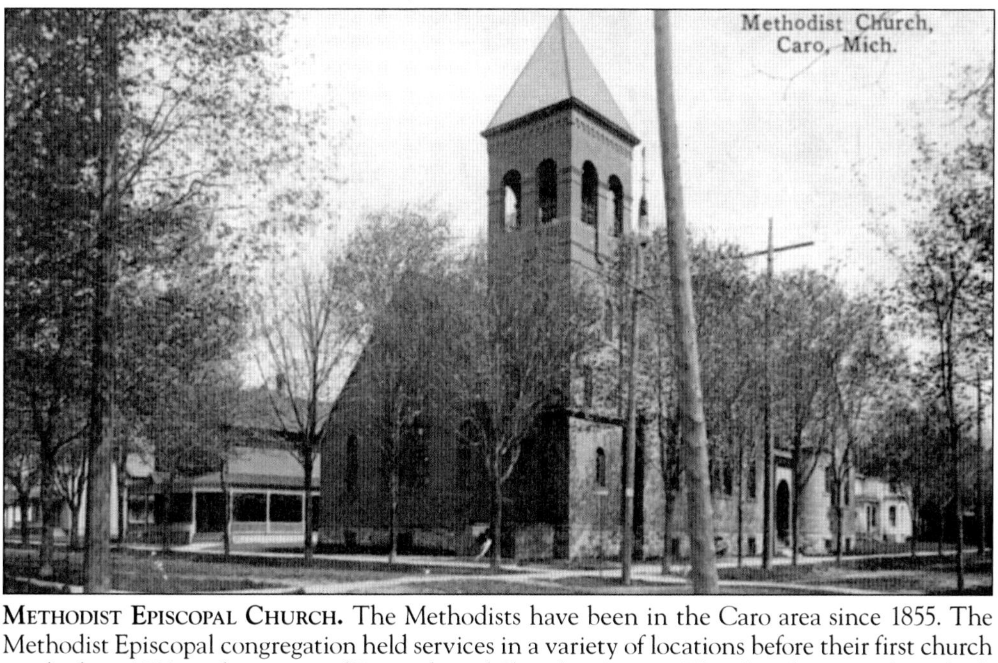

Methodist Episcopal Church. The Methodists have been in the Caro area since 1855. The Methodist Episcopal congregation held services in a variety of locations before their first church was built in 1870, at the corner of Burnside and Sheridan Streets. The church pictured was built on the same site in 1894. It was sold in 1974 when a new church was built on Gilford Road. (Courtesy of Watrousville-Caro Historical Society.)

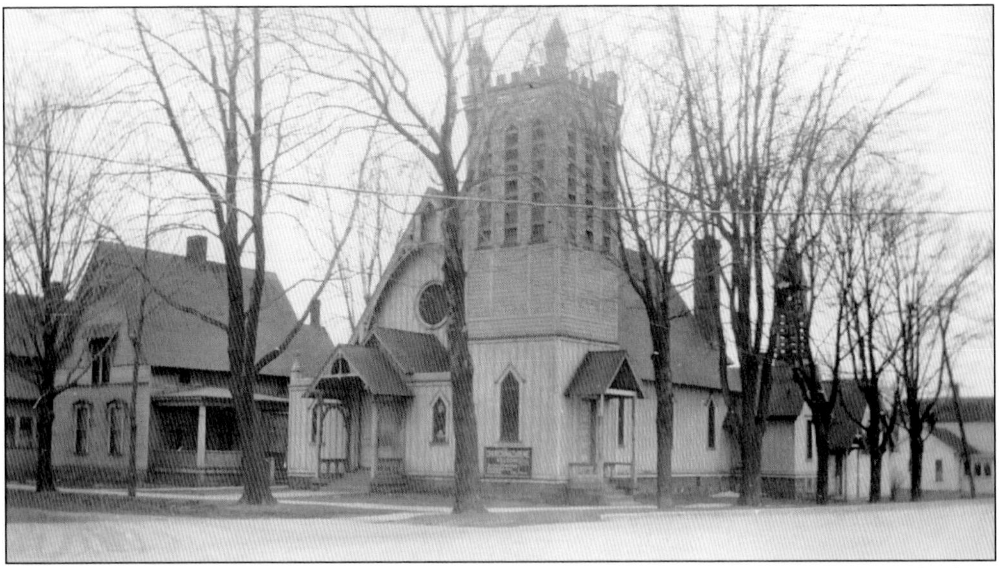

Trinity Episcopal Church. Organized in 1871, this Gothic Revival frame church was built in 1880. With the decline of the Episcopal congregation, the building was sold to the Church of the Nazarene in 1934. They occupied the church until 1974, and the building, now owned by the City of Caro, is used by the Thumb Area Center for the Arts. (Courtesy of Watrousville-Caro Historical Society.)

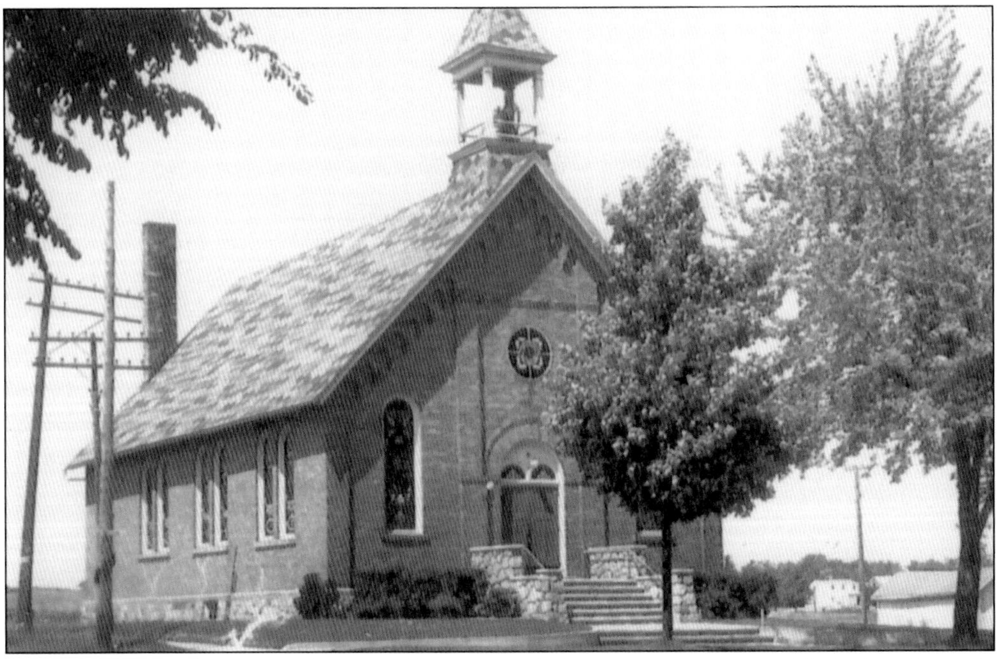

Sacred Heart Catholic Church. Roman Catholic services were established in Caro in 1879. This first Catholic church in Caro was built in 1902, at Frank and Hooper Streets. This was a mission church, sharing a priest with the Reese parish, until a rectory was built in 1932. The present Sacred Heart Church was erected in the early 1960s. (Courtesy of Sacred Heart Catholic Church.)

FIRST PRESBYTERIAN CHURCH. First organized in 1878, the Presbyterians built a frame church in 1880 on the corner of Pearl and Lincoln Streets. This limestone and brick church, located on the corner of Lincoln and Almer Streets, was dedicated on December 13, 1903, the 25th anniversary of the church's organization. It remains the First Presbyterian Church today. (Courtesy of Watrousville-Caro Historical Society.)

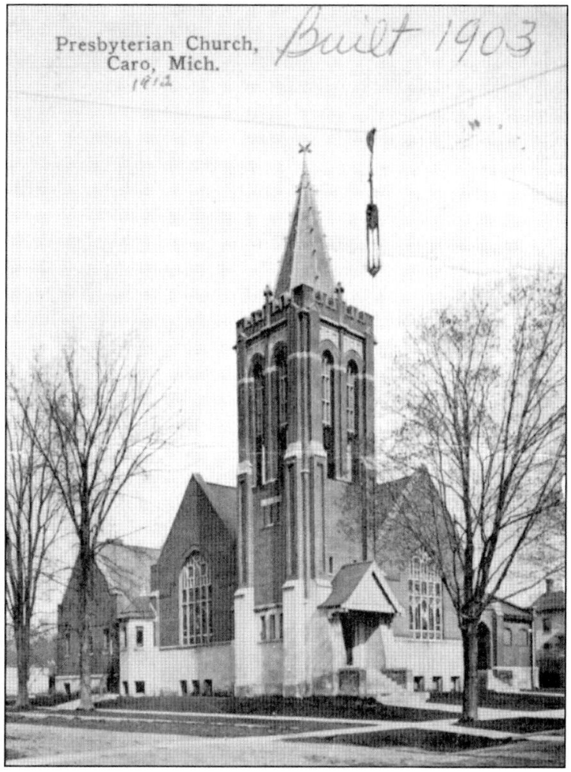

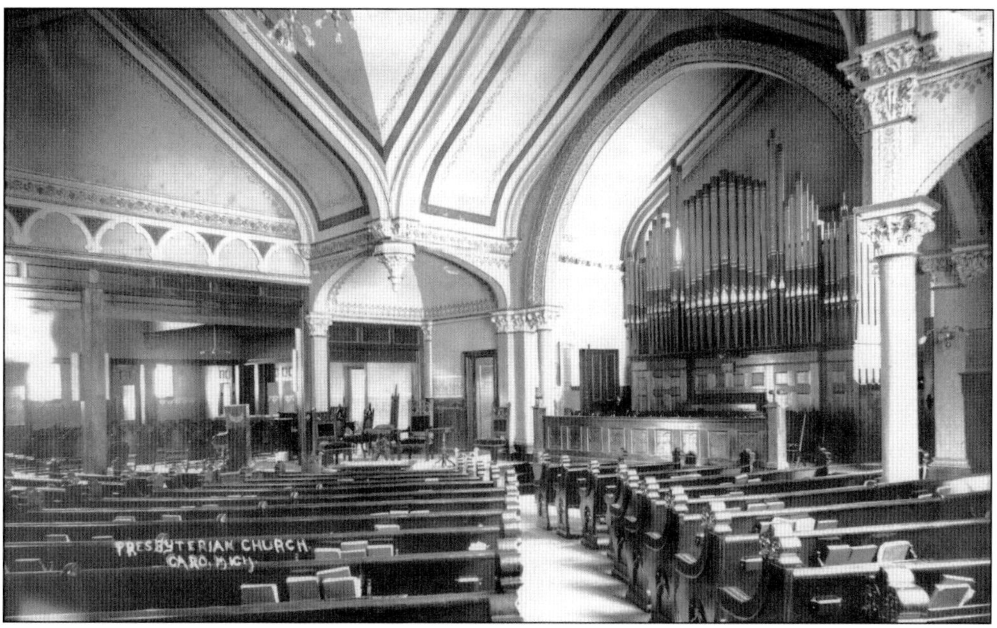

INTERIOR, PRESBYTERIAN CHURCH. Taken in 1912, this photograph shows the auditorium of the church with its mahogany pews and magnificent organ. The frescoing on the sides and ceiling of the room were green and buff trimmed in gold. A grapevine of plaster of Paris encircled the auditorium with its fruit done in purple and tinged with gold. The stained-glass windows were green and terra-cotta. (Courtesy of Watrousville-Caro Historical Society.)

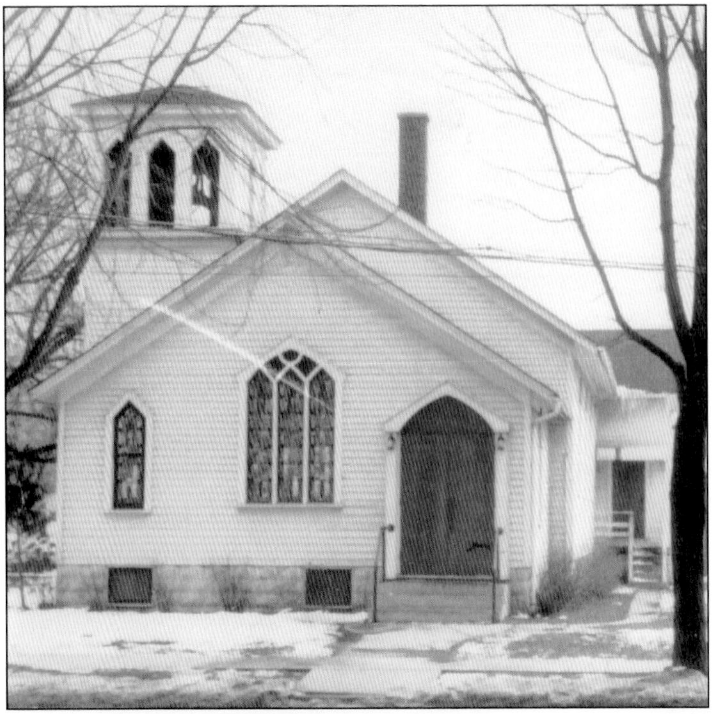

St. Paul's Lutheran Church. This congregation was organized in 1916, initially renting the Christian Science and the old Episcopal Churches. Known by many as the German Church because of their multilingual services, they built this frame church on South State Street in 1922 (shown after 1932 renovations). In 1983, original building components were auctioned before razing the building and erecting a new one close to the same location. (Courtesy of St. Paul's Lutheran Church.)

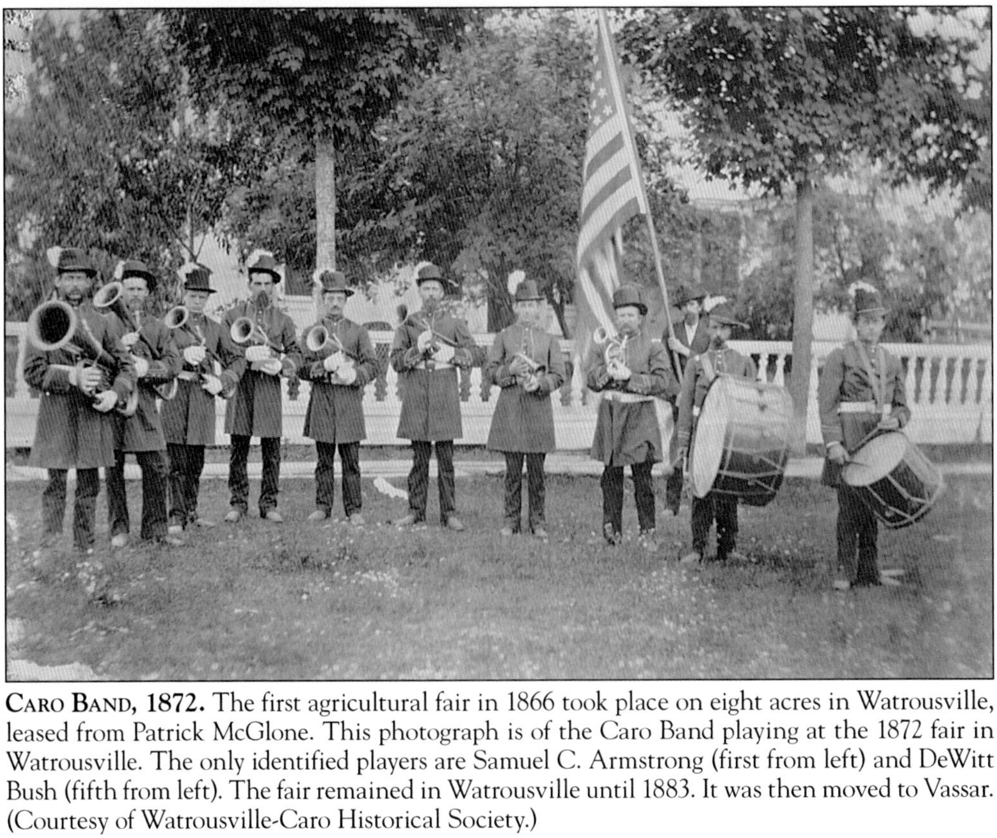

Caro Band, 1872. The first agricultural fair in 1866 took place on eight acres in Watrousville, leased from Patrick McGlone. This photograph is of the Caro Band playing at the 1872 fair in Watrousville. The only identified players are Samuel C. Armstrong (first from left) and DeWitt Bush (fifth from left). The fair remained in Watrousville until 1883. It was then moved to Vassar. (Courtesy of Watrousville-Caro Historical Society.)

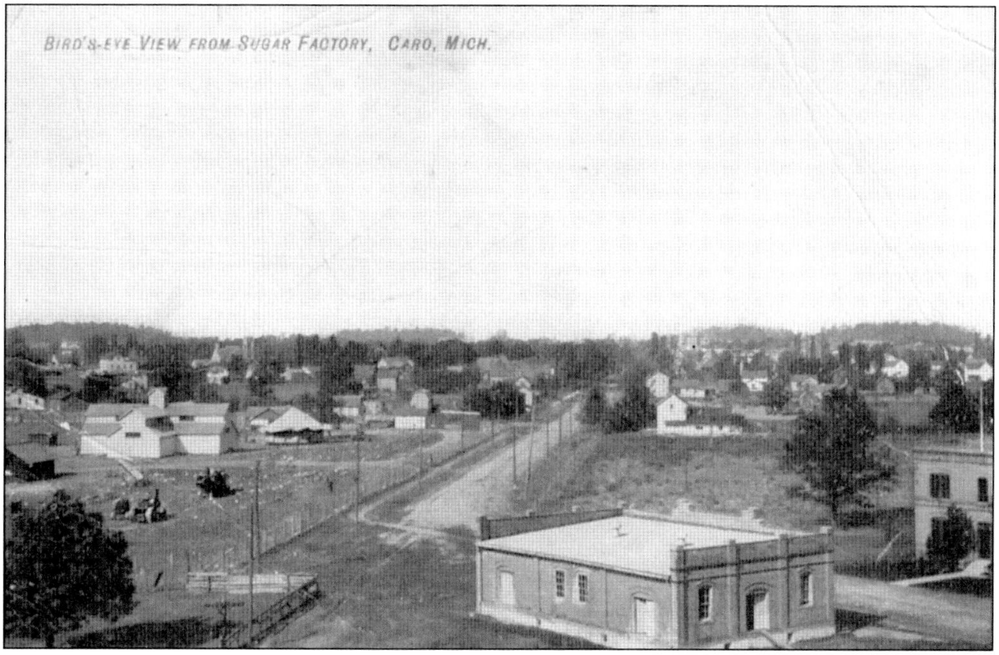

BIRD'S-EYE VIEW. This panoramic shot was taken in about 1910 by an intrepid photographer perched high atop the Michigan Sugar Company main building. It affords a sweeping view of South Almer Street and the south side of the village, including the fairgrounds buildings (left). (Courtesy of Watrousville-Caro Historical Society.)

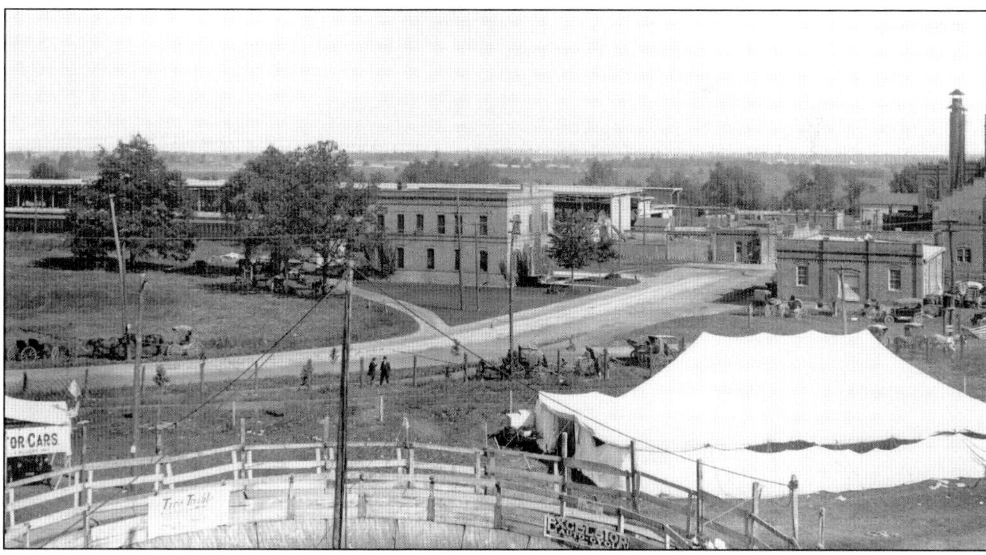

A VIEW FROM THE FAIR. This photograph was taken in August 1915, just as the fair was about to get underway. The background shows the Michigan Sugar Company plant office, seed house, and beet sheds, while the foreground shows the fair setup, including merchants such as Louie Luder and his car sales tent. (Courtesy of Watrousville-Caro Historical Society.)

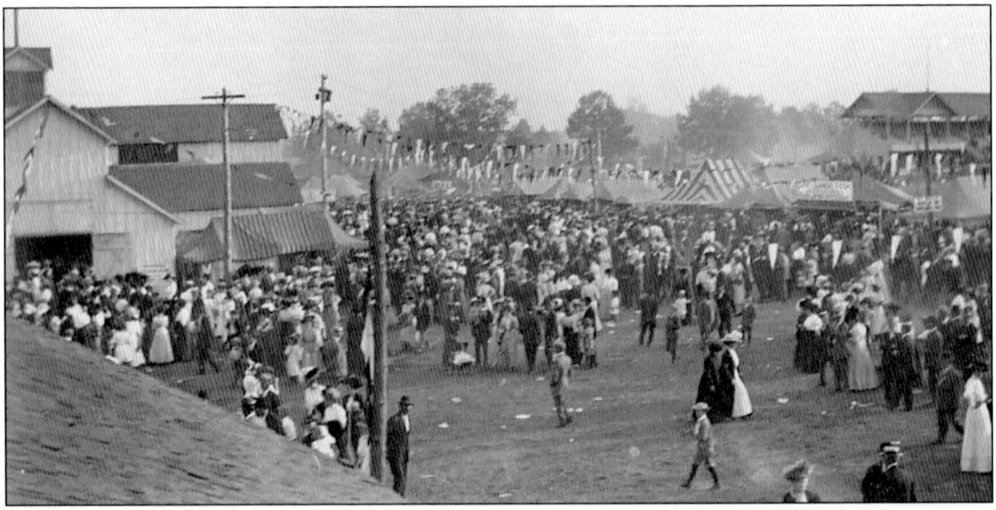

A Crowd at the Fair. The first fair held in Caro was in September 1882. The clay track for harness racing was built in 1892, and the first grandstand was completed in 1894. This photograph illustrates how popular the fair was. The grandstand is visible in the upper right of the photograph. (Courtesy of Watrousville-Caro Historical Society.)

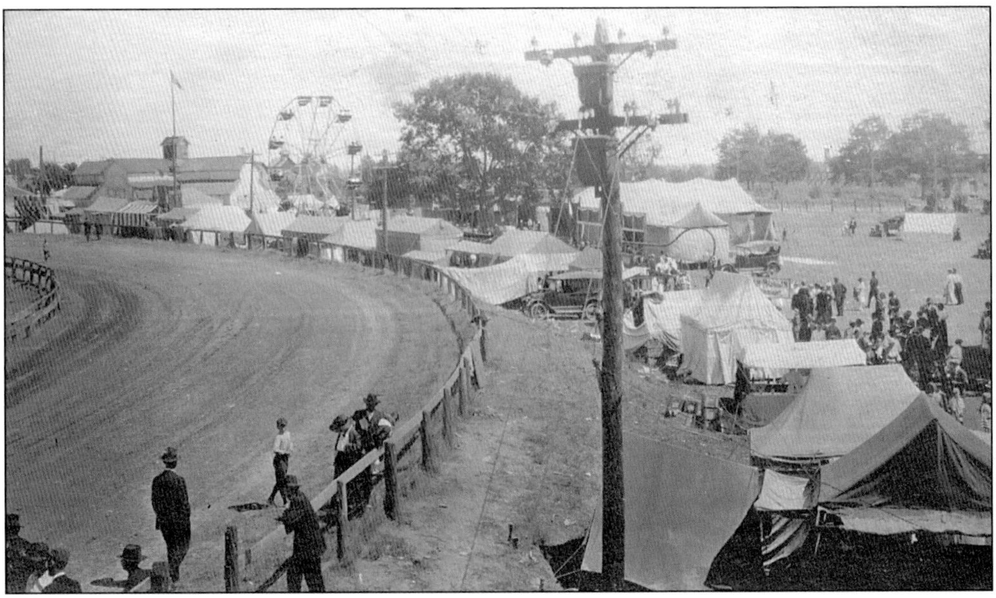

Caro Fairgrounds, 1918. This is a view of the clay track used for harness racing. It was built in 1892 at a cost of $1,000, using 7,000 yards of dirt that was primarily sand. This was topped with 3,000 yards of clay, all of which was brought in by horse and wagon. (Courtesy of Watrousville-Caro Historical Society.)

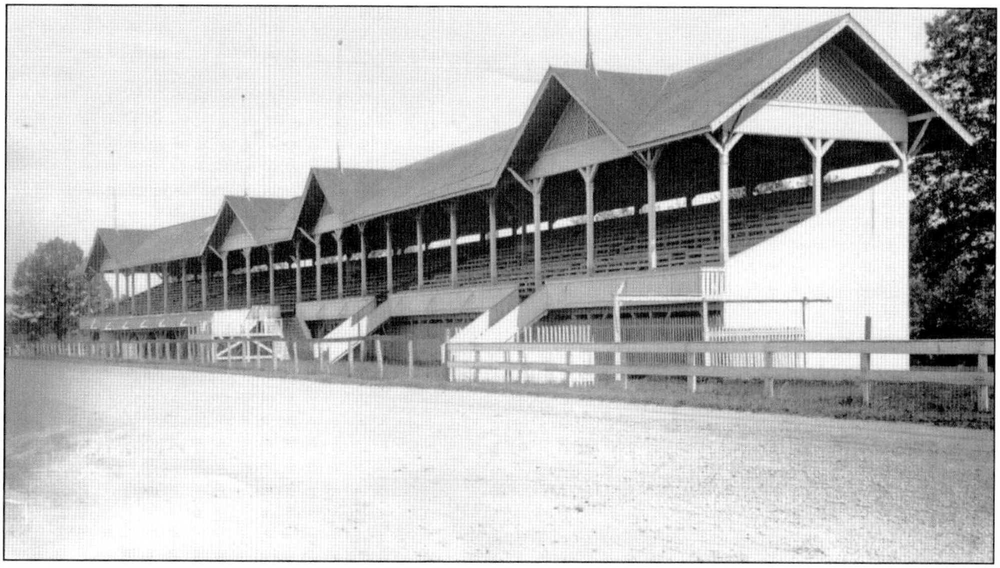

Fairgrounds Grandstand, 1926. The first wooden grandstand was completed in 1894 and seated about 1,500 people. Later, a stage was built with cement-block dressing rooms in the basement. Many entertainment acts appeared at the fair over the years. This grandstand burned in July 1937. A new wooden grandstand was erected in six weeks for the upcoming 1937 fair. That grandstand burned in 1979. (Courtesy of Watrousville-Caro Historical Society.)

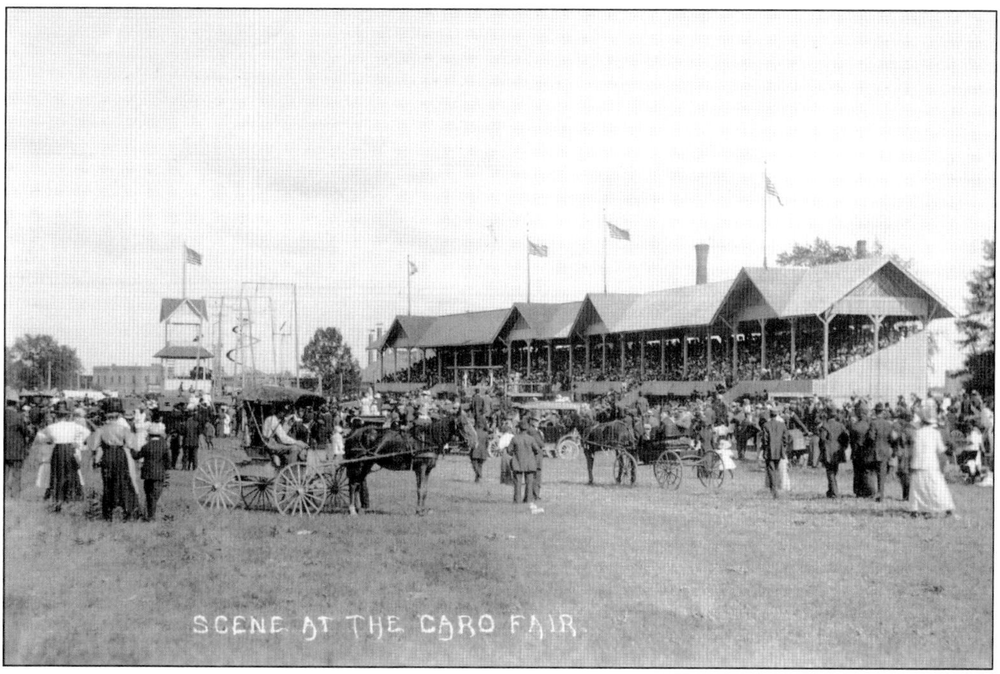

Full Grandstand. Here is a view of the grandstand fully occupied. In the early years, the Michigan Sugar Company's power plant supplied electricity. The railroad tracks leading to the plant were used to bring in entertainment acts such as early pilot Katherine Stinson, known as the "Flying Schoolgirl." Her plane was delivered by rail and assembled in the fairgrounds track infield. (Courtesy of Laureen Joslin.)

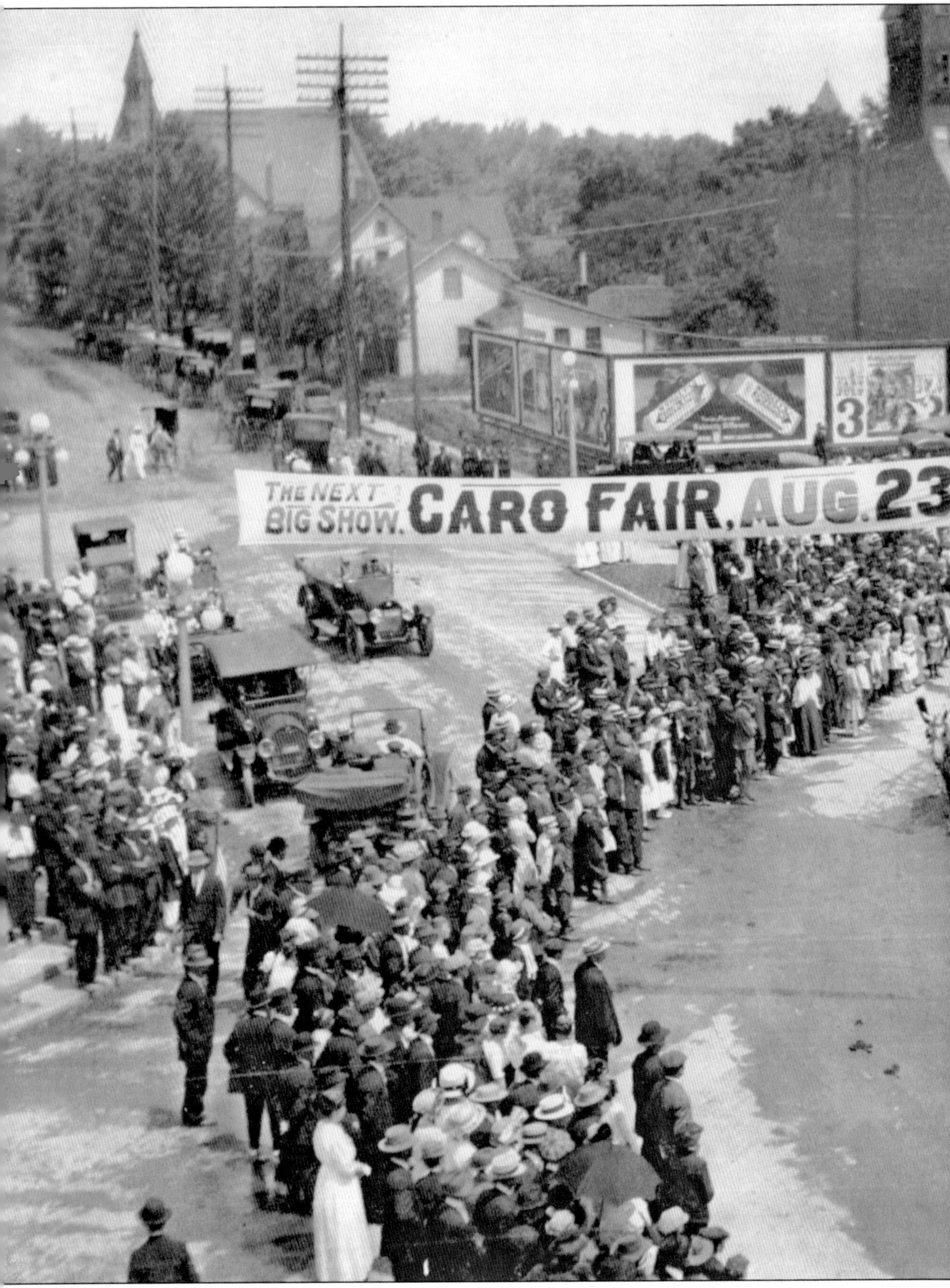
THE NEXT BIG SHOW.
CARO FAIR, AUG. 23

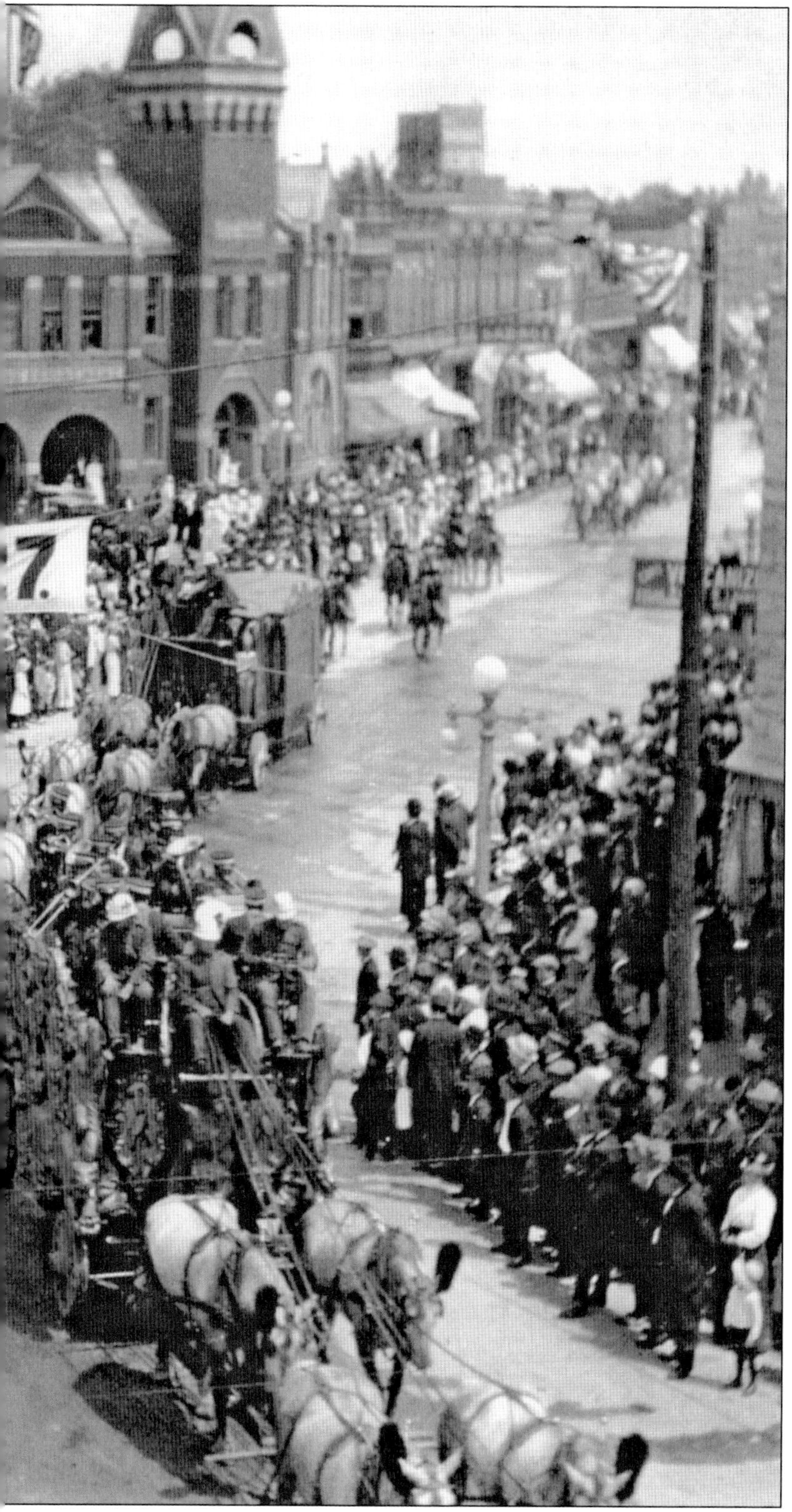

GRAND PARADE. This wonderful photograph shows a grand parade down State Street as it turns onto South Almer Street on its way to the fairgrounds. The banner advertising "The Next Big Show" at the Caro Fair seems to indicate a circus, as do the plumed horses and the coaches. This photograph also offers a unique perspective on the village triangle and the village beyond. It was taken after 1913, as the new streetlights are in evidence. The photographer was Herbert Leon Cope, who was also a speaker and humorist known as the "Bob Hope of World War I." Living on West Frank Street, he captured many wonderful images of the area throughout his career. This photograph was found in the late 20th century in a trunk of glass negatives at the former Cope home. (Courtesy of Tim Romain/ Cope collection.)

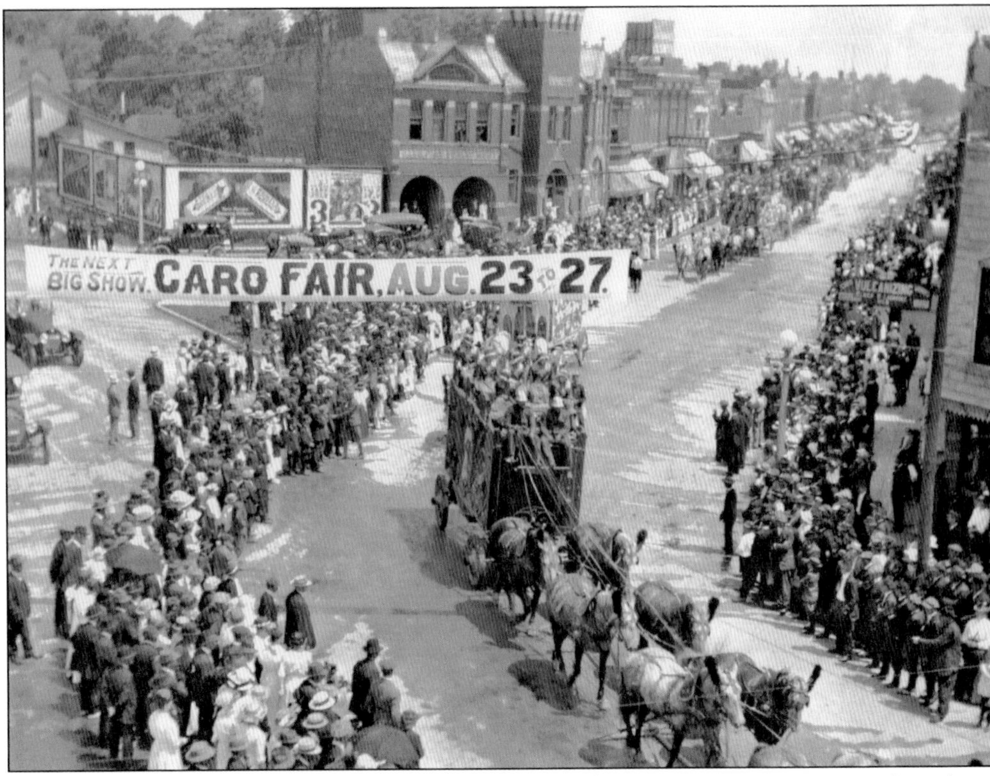

A Closer View. This close-up of the same parade from the previous pages appears to have been taken from the top of the two-story Moreland Implement warehouse on the corner of South Almer and State Streets. The Caro Fair Association ran the fair until 1938, when it became the Tuscola County Fair Association by an act of the Michigan legislature. (Courtesy of Tim Romain/Cope collection.)

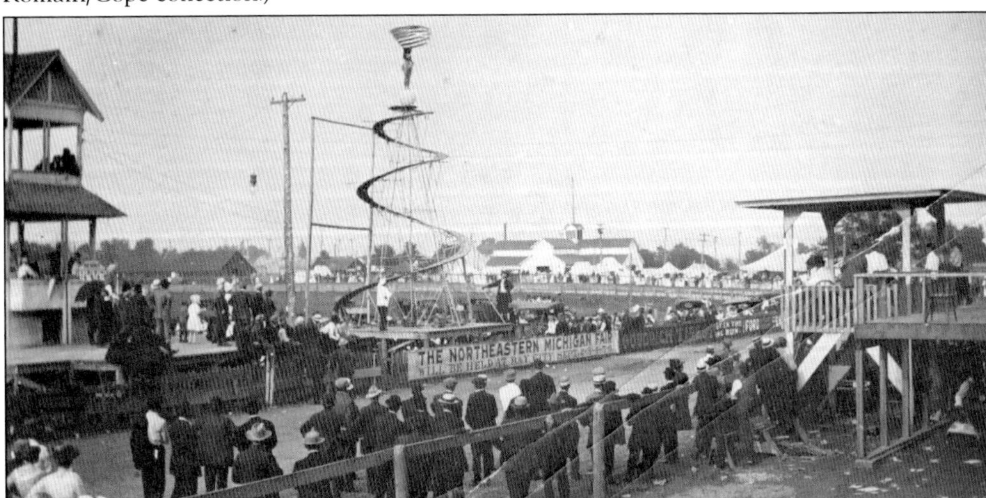

Fun at the Fair. This photograph from about 1912 shows a spiral attraction at that year's fair. The signs on the fence advertise the upcoming Northeastern Michigan Fair in Bay City, Goodrich Tires, and Ford. A judging stand is on the far right. (Courtesy of Watrousville-Caro Historical Society.)

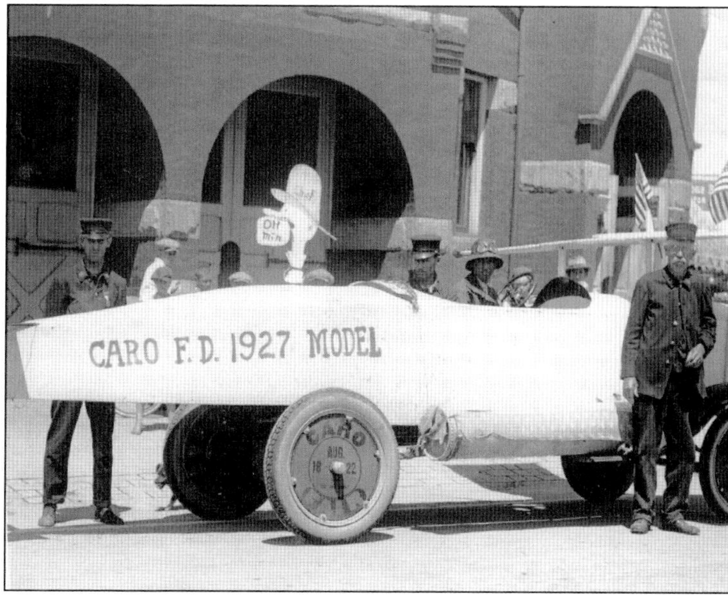

Caro Fire Department Model, 1927. This was built by the fire department as a fun contribution to the 1927 Caro Fair. Standing on the far left is Charles E. Middaugh and on the far right is Chief Frank D. Riddle. Chief Riddle helped organize the department in 1883 and was chief until 1938 when he retired. He was succeeded by Middaugh. (Courtesy of Watrousville-Caro Historical Society.)

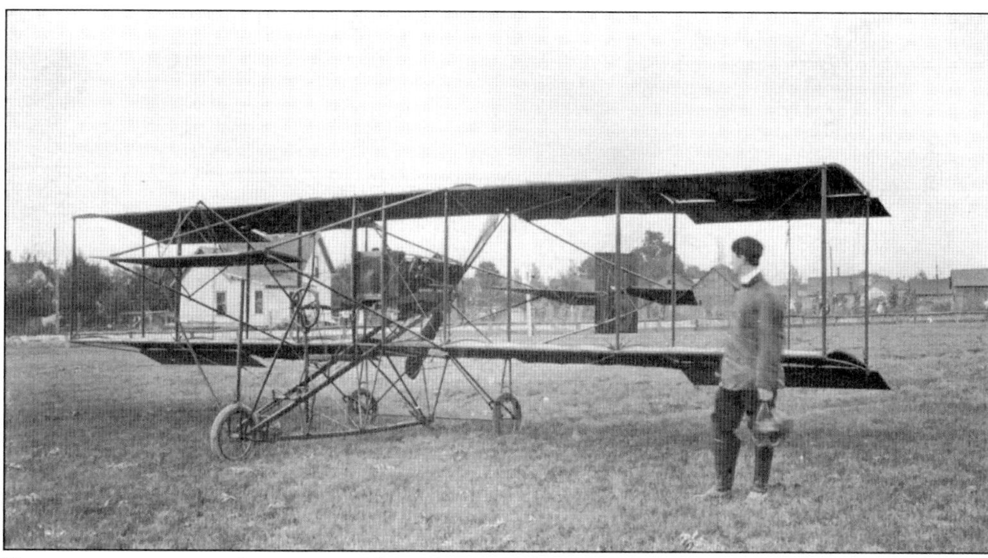

Barnstorming, c. 1910–1912. This photograph appears to have been taken at the Caro Fairgrounds and is labeled, "Bud Morris barnstorming." There was an early aviator in the United States named Bud Morriss, and the plane in the photograph appears to be a Glenn Hammond Curtiss Farnum biplane, which was flying at this time in aviation history. (Courtesy of Watrousville-Caro Historical Society.)

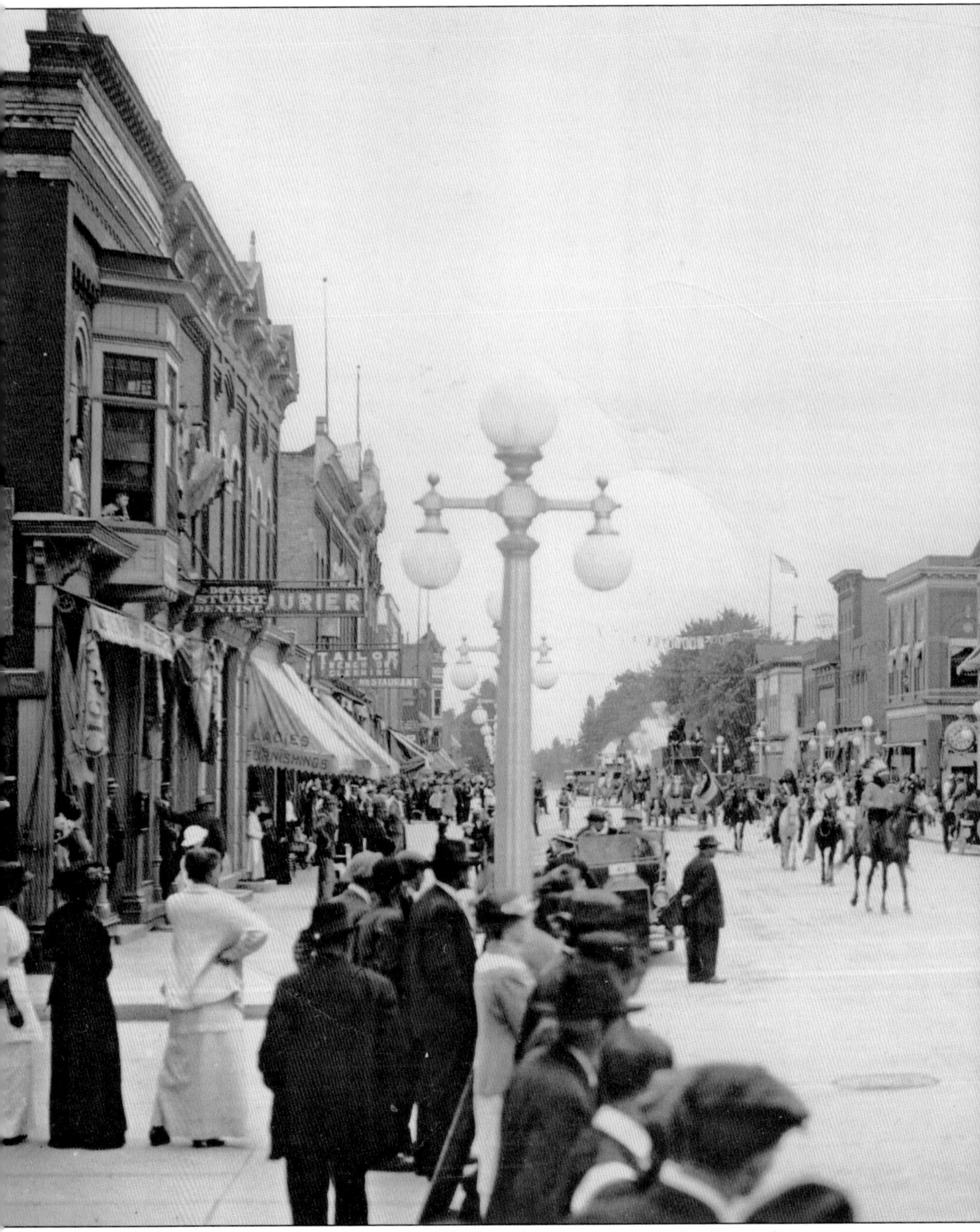

Wyoming Bill's Wild West Show. Wild West shows were a popular form of entertainment in the late 19th and early 20th centuries. Wyoming Bill's Wild West Show debuted in Philadelphia in April 1913 and came to Caro in 1914. The poster for this show advertised "an almost endless procession of delightful sights and sensations with entrancing miles of pomp and splendor. A

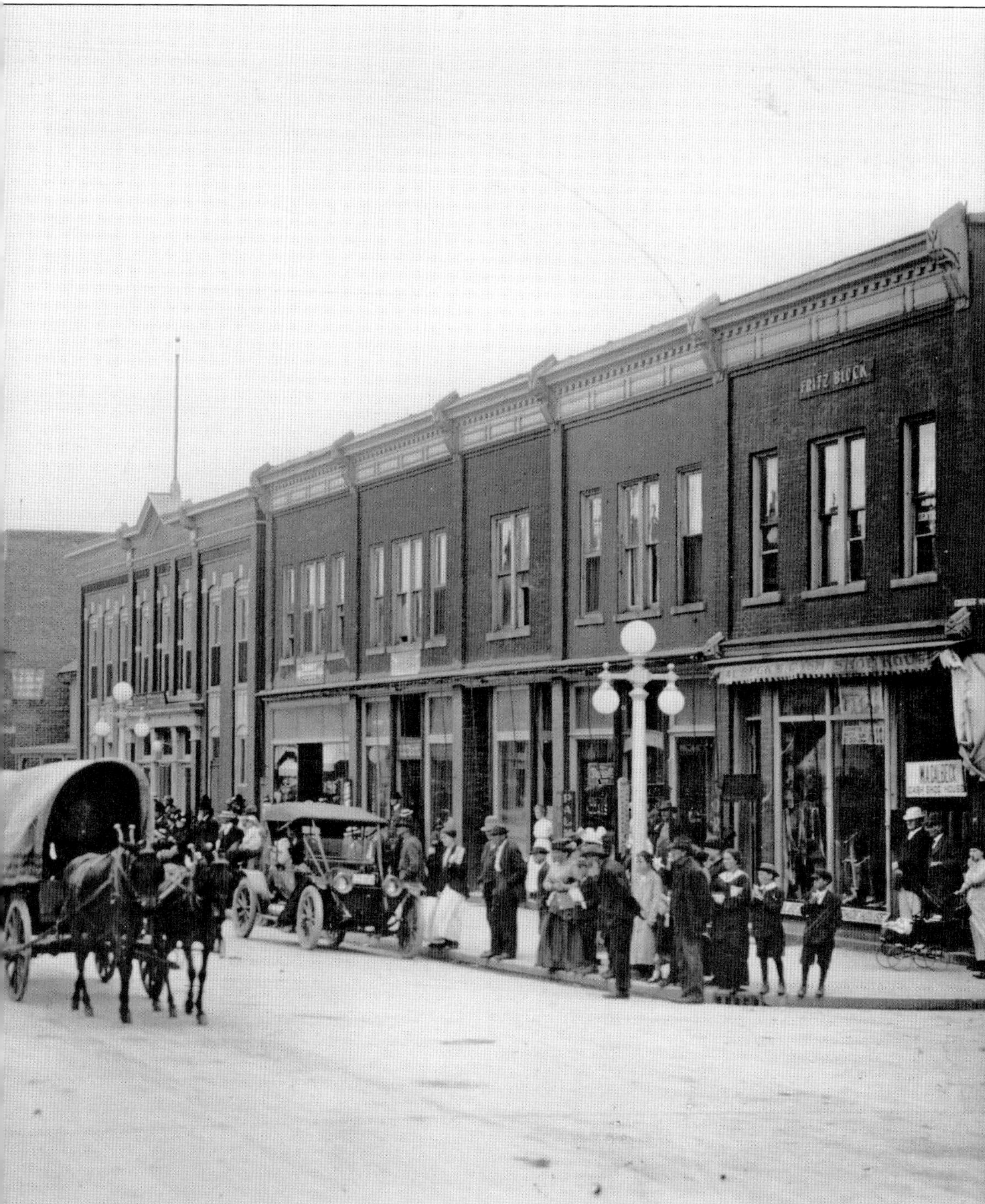

teeming world in moving panoramic pictures of animated life presenting a colossal gathering of martial bands, native tribes, traits, trails and trains of all nations in peace and war." The show was in existence for just one year, 1913–1914. Much of Caro appears to be enjoying the spectacle. (Courtesy of Watrousville-Caro Historical Society.)

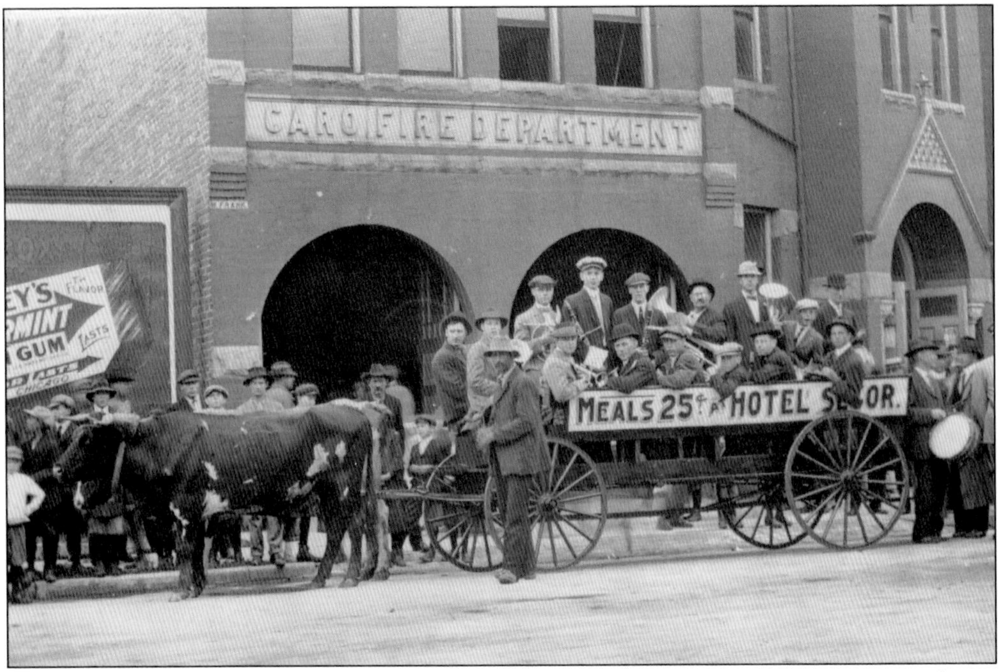

EARLY 20TH-CENTURY ADVERTISING. The Hotel Secor advertises 25¢ meals by way of an ox-driven wagon, complete with a band. They have stopped in front of the city hall, located at State and Frank Streets, sometime after 1913 and were presumably part of a parade. (Courtesy of Watrousville-Caro Historical Society.)

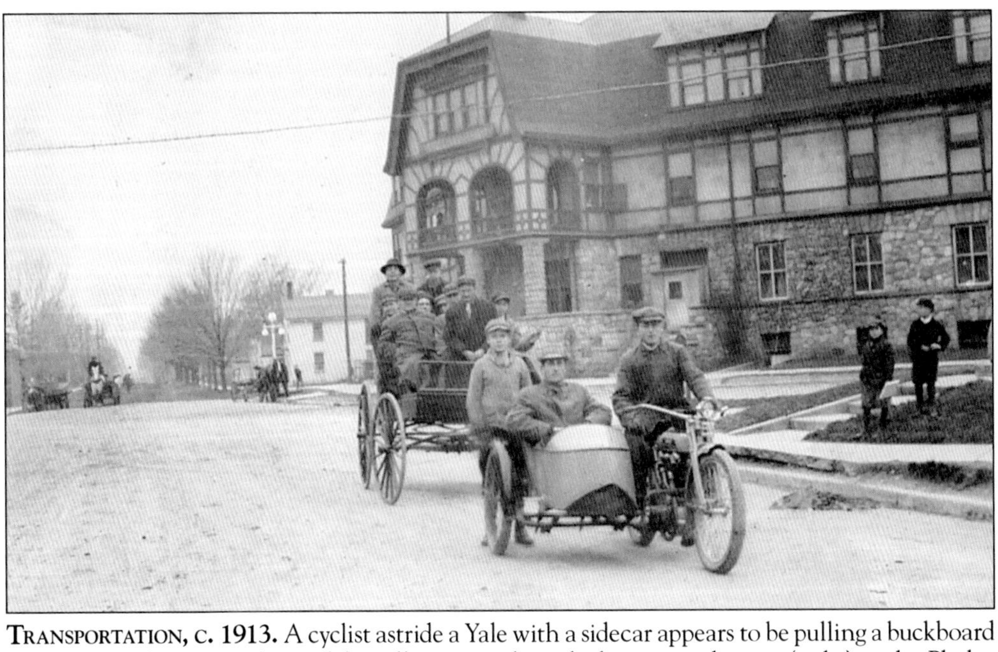

TRANSPORTATION, C. 1913. A cyclist astride a Yale with a sidecar appears to be pulling a buckboard full of men. They are in front of the village triangle with the approach steps (right) to the Phelps Fountain. Looming behind is the Hotel Montague. (Courtesy of Tim Romain/Cope collection.)

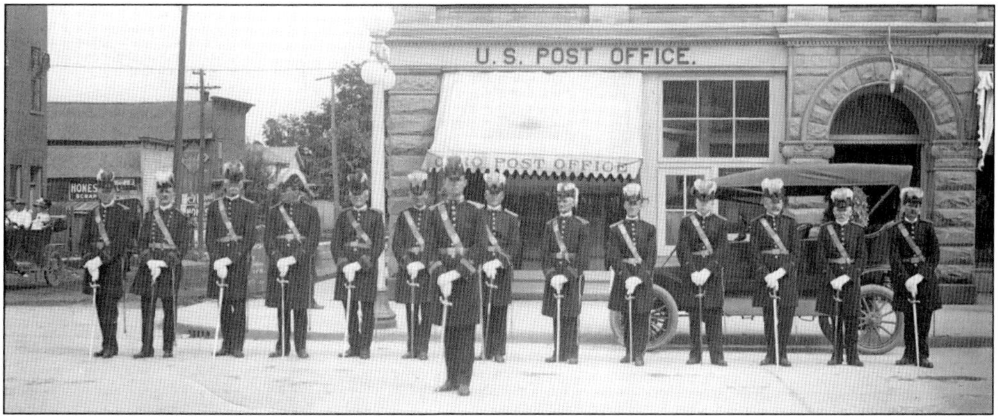

CARO CANTONS, 1914. Affiliated with the International Order of Odd Fellows, the Cantons pose in parade formation in front of the Caro Post Office (McNair Building) on June 14, 1914. From left to right are Frank Bowles, Henry Johnson, J.J. England, unidentified, Dey Naarmore, unidentified, Captain William Webb, Gordon Knowles, William Imerson, Frank Goodwin, Otto Clough, Oscar O'Kelly, Sam Ennis, and James Slaght. (Courtesy of Watrousville-Caro Historical Society.)

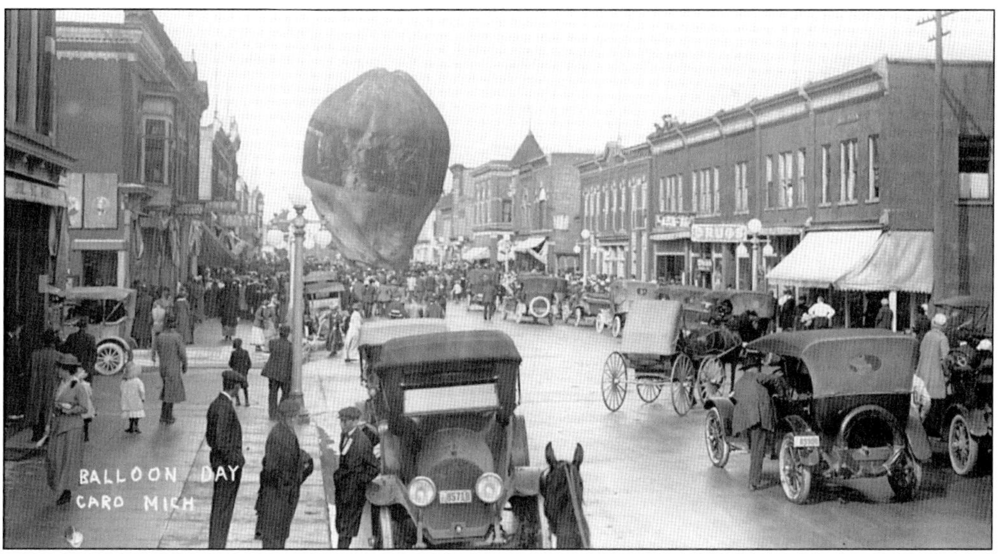

BALLOON DAY, 1916. On June 10, 1916, there was much ado about something, but aside from Earl Beyette's photograph, no one ever documented the reason why. This balloon was eventually launched with a man dangling below from a rope, to the interest of the crowd. Spectators even gathered on the rooftop (right). (Courtesy of Watrousville-Caro Historical Society.)

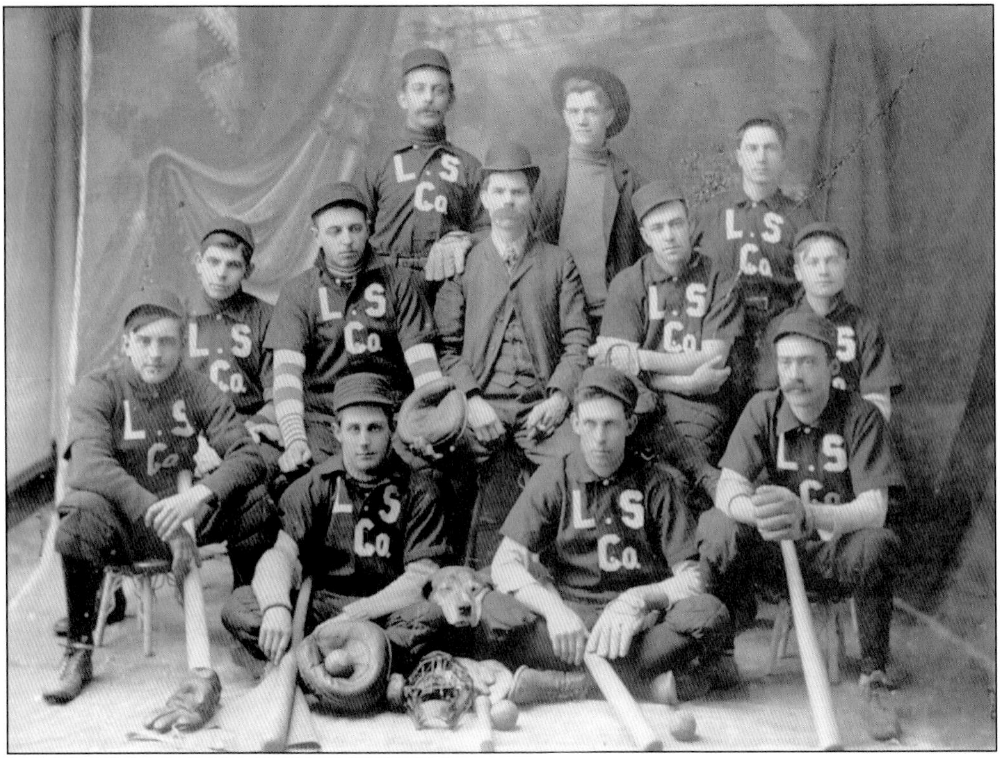

Lacey Shoe Company Baseball Team, 1903. The Lacey Shoe Company was a controversial manufacturing venture in Caro. It set up operation in 1902 and was out of business by 1906 when the company's treasurer and chief salesman left town with all the company's funds. (Courtesy of Watrousville-Caro Historical Society.)

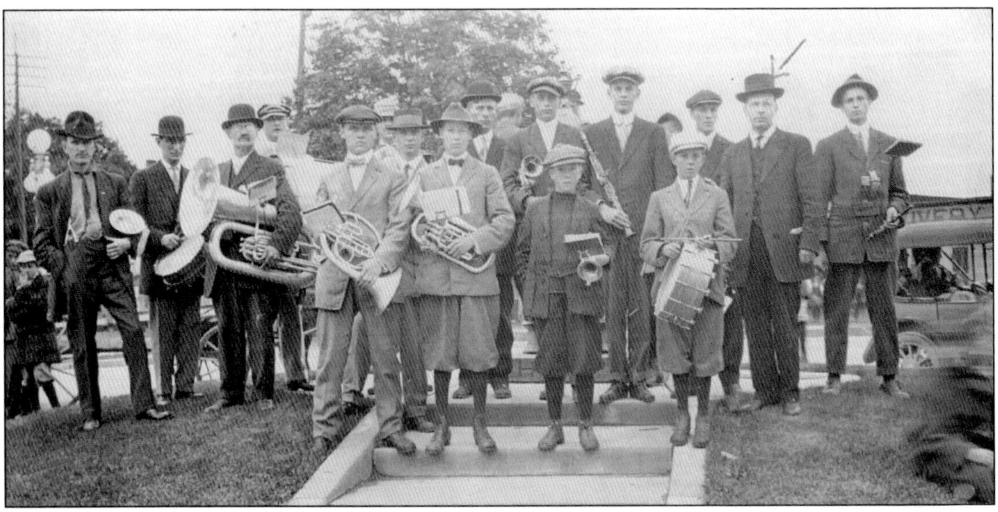

Caro Community Band. This 1914 photograph shows the Caro Community Band posed in front of the Phelps Fountain at the village triangle. Bandleader Harvey Campbell is second from right, drummer Ed St. Mary is second from left, and Bill Berry, with the tuba, is third from left. The rest of the players are unidentified. (Courtesy of Watrousville-Caro Historical Society.)

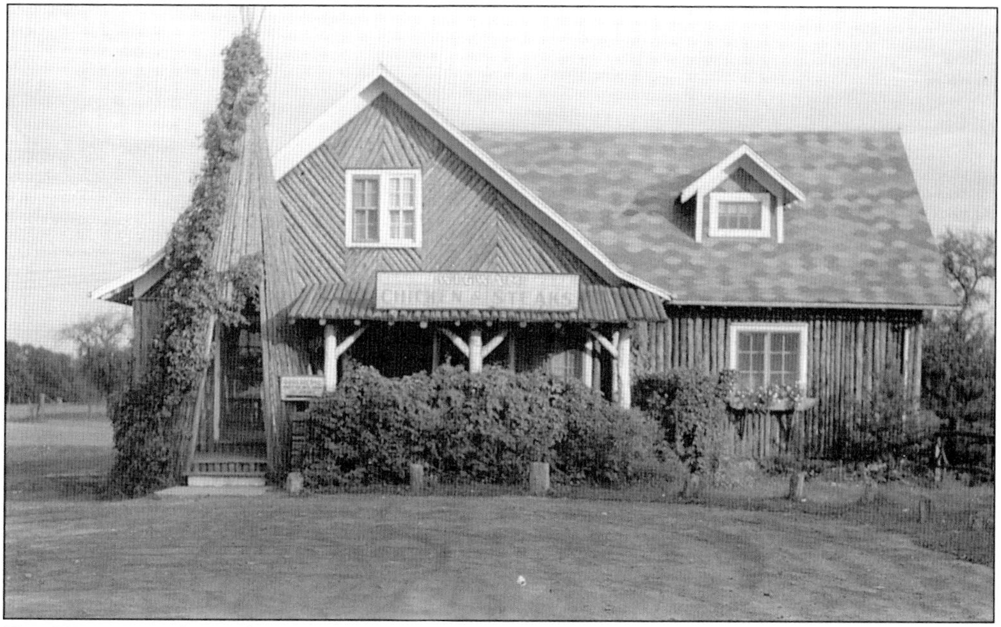

The Wigwam. This is the Wigwam night club at the Caro Golf Club. The name came from the wooden tepee over the entrance. Specially selected birch logs were used inside and out to give a rustic appearance. The building was destroyed by fire in the 1940s, as it was outside the village limits and without nearby water mains. (Courtesy of Watrousville-Caro Historical Society.)

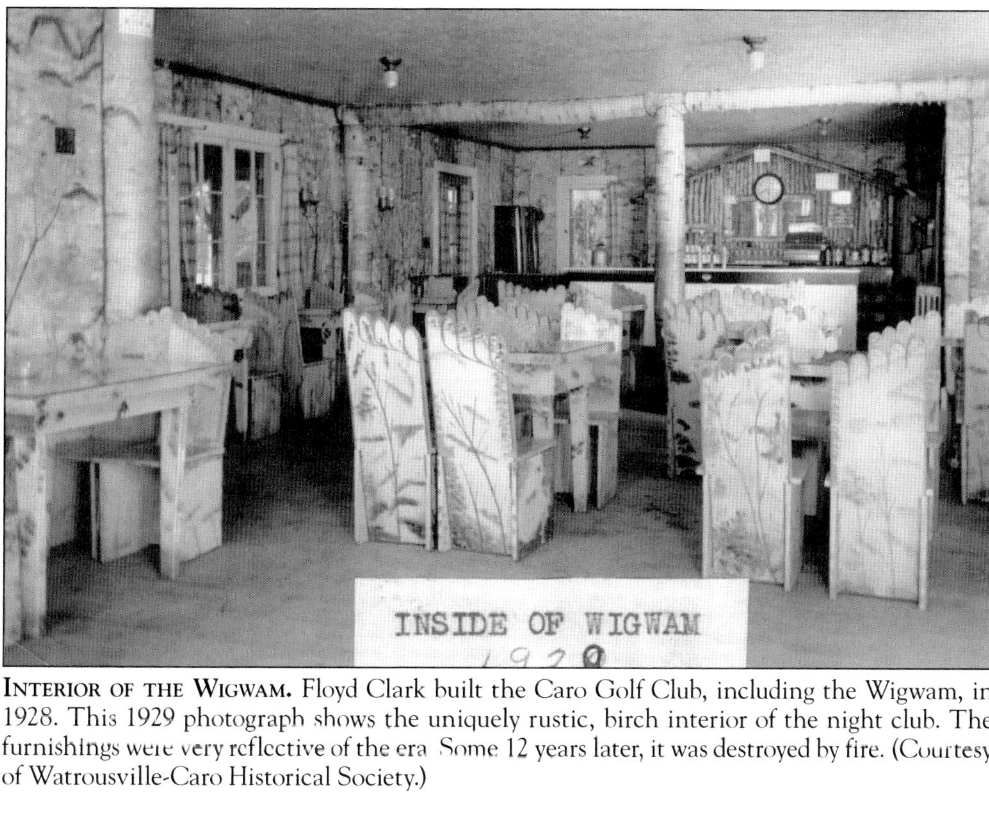

Interior of the Wigwam. Floyd Clark built the Caro Golf Club, including the Wigwam, in 1928. This 1929 photograph shows the uniquely rustic, birch interior of the night club. The furnishings were very reflective of the era. Some 12 years later, it was destroyed by fire. (Courtesy of Watrousville-Caro Historical Society.)

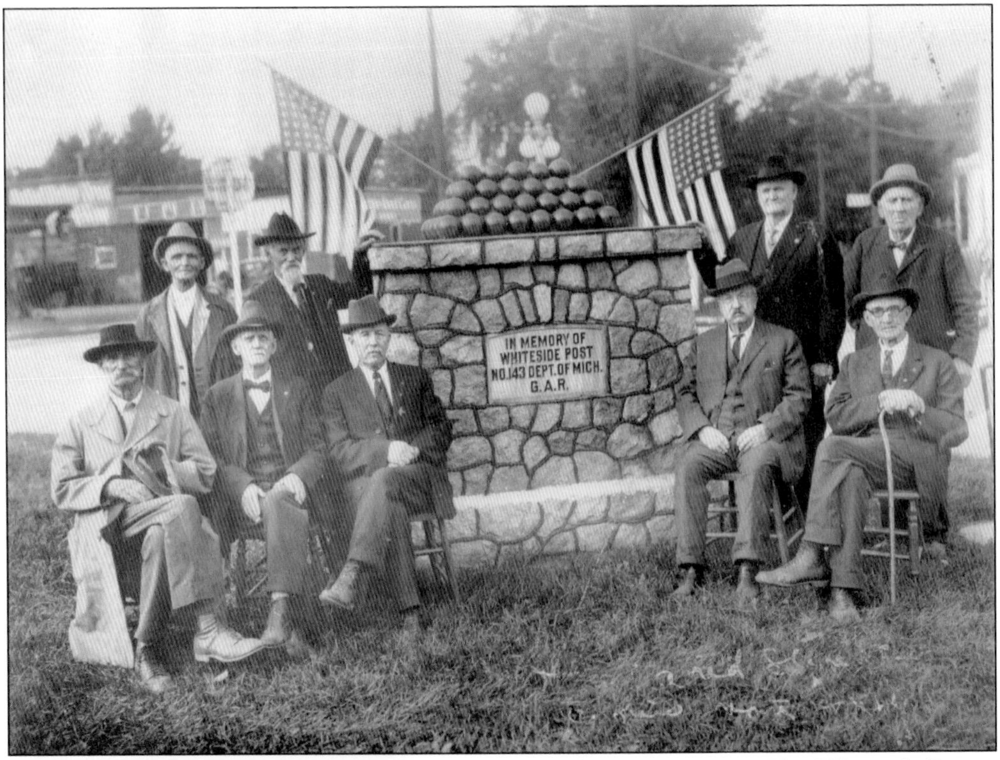

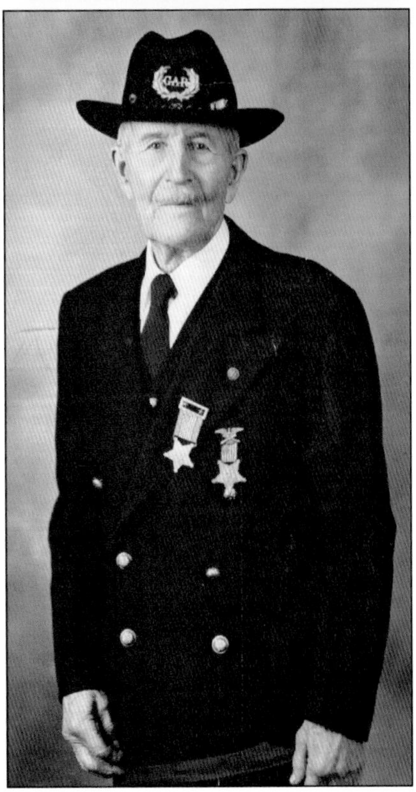

CIVIL WAR MEMORIAL, 1926. The Whiteside Post No. 143 of the Grand Army of the Republic (GAR) was established in 1883 and closed with the death of Orlando LeValley in 1948. Shown from left to right are (first row, seated) William Westbrook, Charles Amsden, Orlando LeValley, Lyman C. Grady, and John L. Myers; (second row) Orrin Barber, Charles Bills, D.S. Arnold, and Norman V. Romain. (Courtesy of Watrousville-Caro Historical Society.)

ORLANDO LEVALLEY. Born in September 1848, LeValley was 99 years old when he died in April 1948. He was in command of the GAR's Department of Michigan from 1945 until his death. He was the last surviving Civil War veteran in Michigan. (Courtesy of Gail Lesoski.)

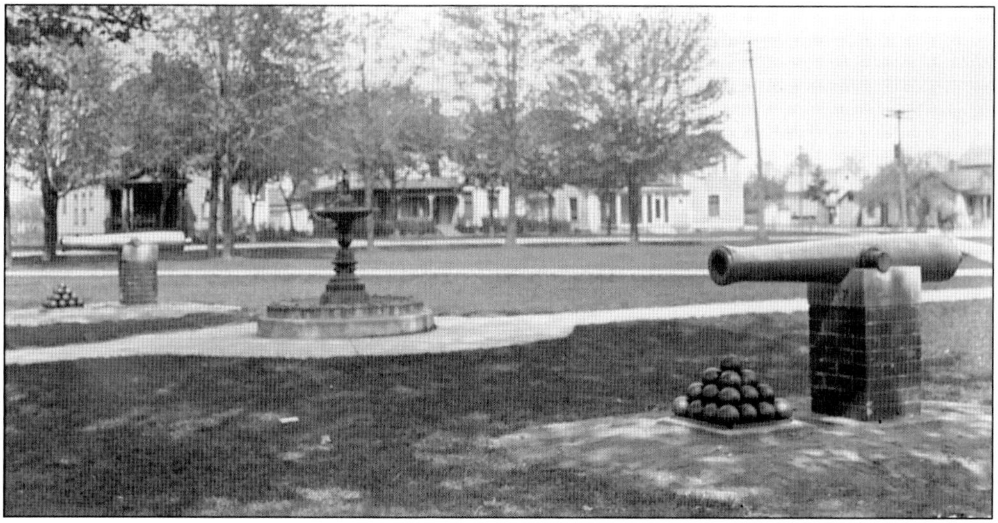

Cannon on Courthouse Lawn. In 1917, this cannon stood on the lawn of the courthouse as a memorial to Tuscola County's veterans and fallen heroes. Through the years, there have been many monuments displayed in various locations and many active veteran organizations. (Courtesy of Watrousville-Caro Historical Society.)

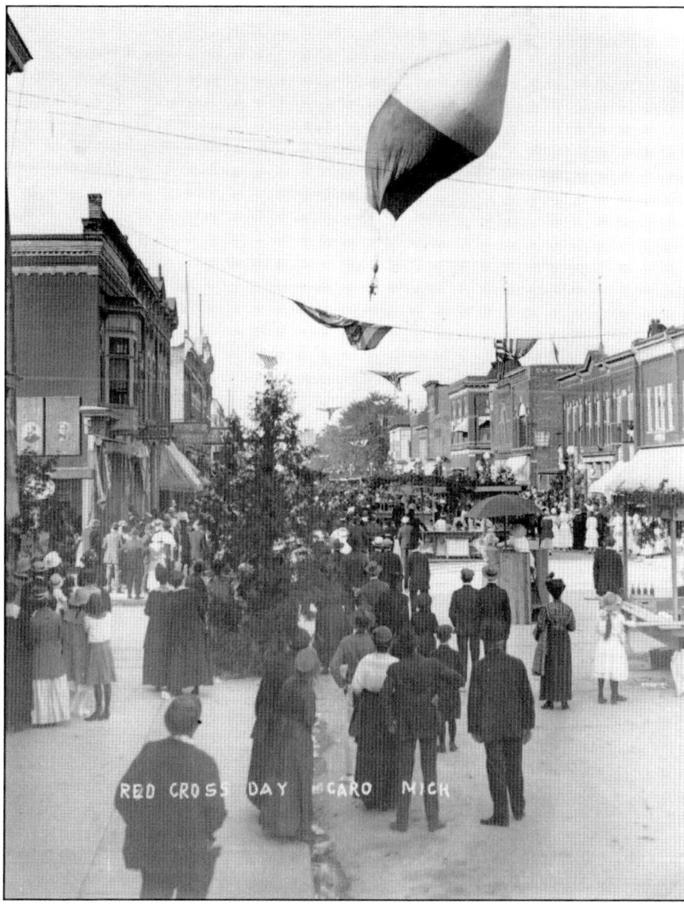

Red Cross Day, 1917. July 4, 1917, saw Red Cross Day celebrated in Caro. When America declared war against Germany in 1917, the Red Cross mobilized to contribute. They helped so much that in 1917, the Red Cross won the Nobel Peace Prize for its efforts in serving American and Allied forces as well as the civilian victims of the war. (Courtesy of Watrousville-Caro Historical Society.)

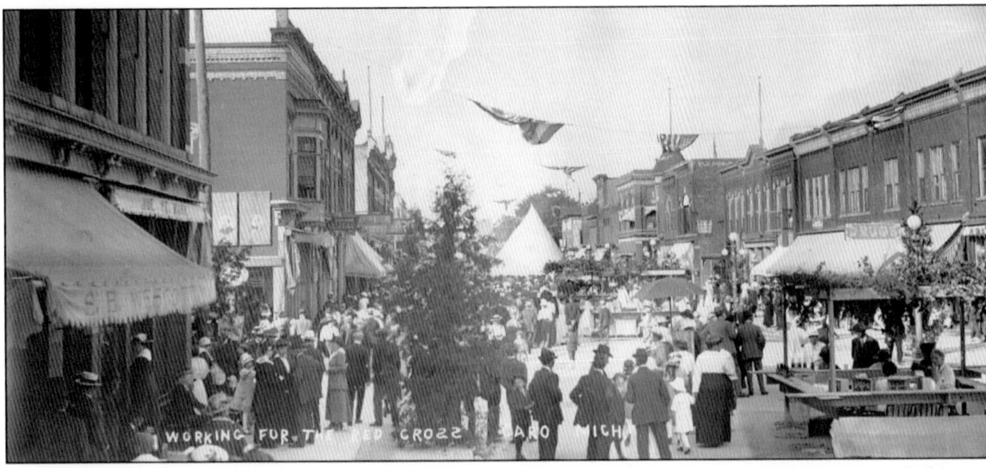

Supporting the Red Cross. Residents of Caro and surrounding areas turned out to work for and support the Red Cross on July 4, 1917. With the United States entering World War I on April 6, 1917, patriotism was at a fever pitch, and communities all over the country rushed to establish local Red Cross chapters. (Courtesy of Watrousville-Caro Historical Society.)

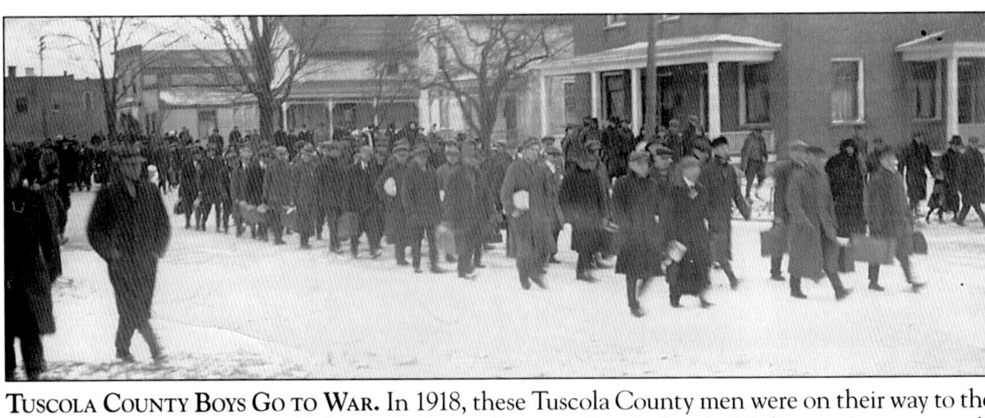

Tuscola County Boys Go to War. In 1918, these Tuscola County men were on their way to the train station where they would depart for Camp Custer in Battle Creek, Michigan. Approximately 90,000 troops went through Camp Custer, and Tuscola County contributed its share. (Courtesy of Watrousville-Caro Historical Society.)

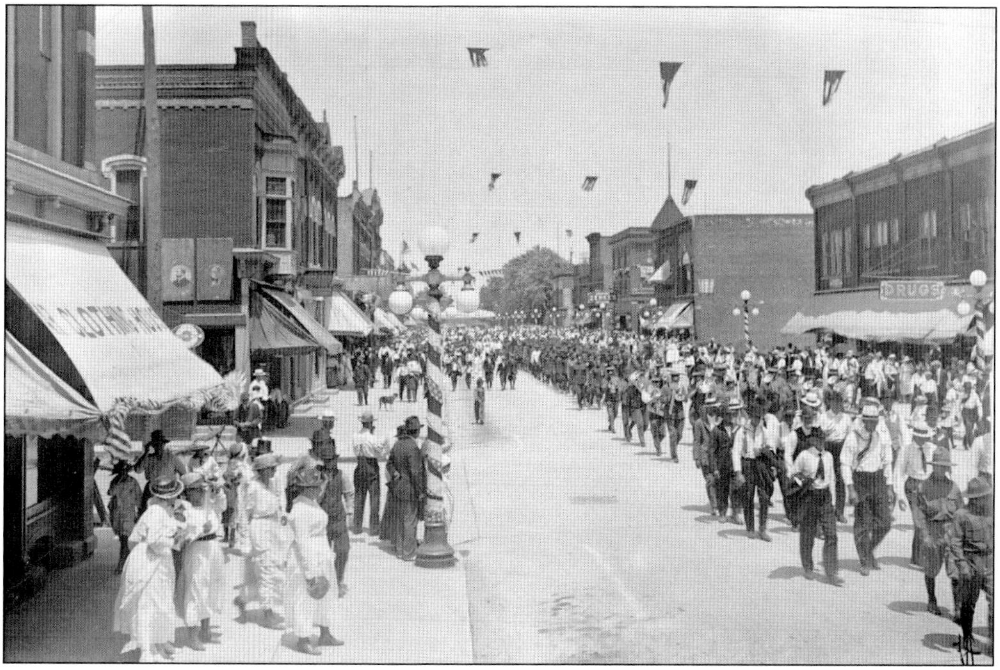

World War I Veterans Parade. On July 4, 1919, returning soldiers and sailors paraded in full uniform through downtown Caro. Civil War veterans also paraded in shirts and ties (right foreground). This grand welcome-home celebration was sponsored by the Tuscola County Red Cross. This view was taken at Lincoln and State Streets in front of the St. Mary's Clothing House. (Courtesy of Watrousville-Caro Historical Society.)

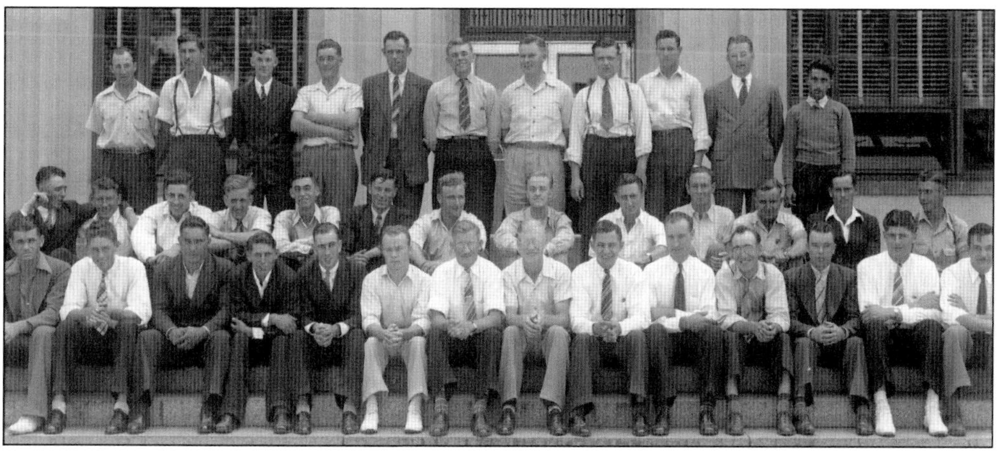

World War II Draftees. The men in this photograph are not identified. They sit on the courthouse steps, and the date given is August 1941. Once again, young men from Tuscola County went off to war and hopefully returned home when it was over. (Courtesy of Watrousville-Caro Historical Society.)

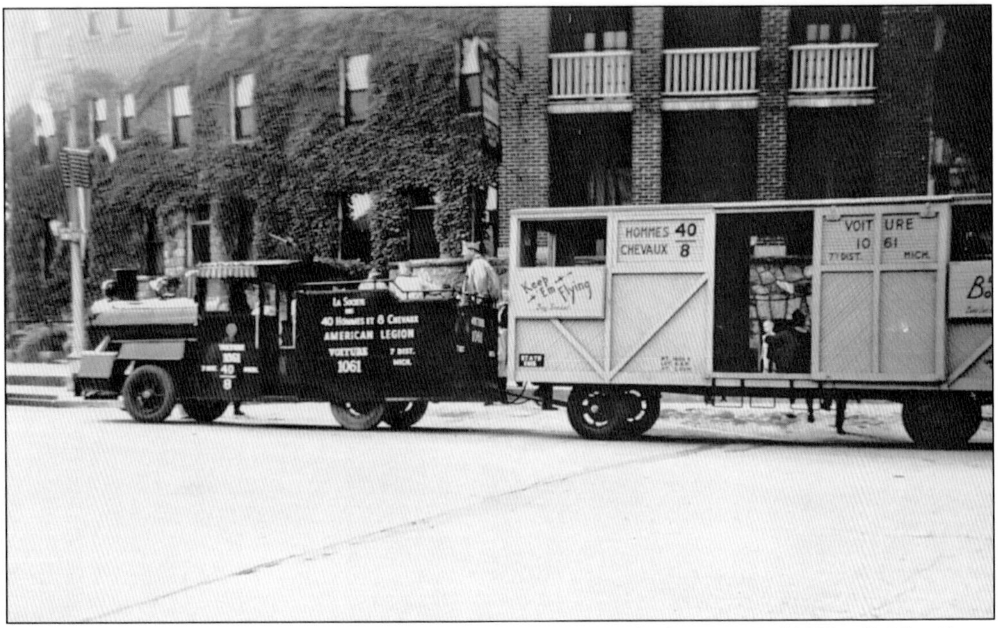

THE FORTY & EIGHT. This unit was part of a patriotic parade during World War II. The Forty & Eight were founded after World War I by American veterans. The name refers to the French boxcars that carried Americans to the battlefront. A boxcar could carry either 40 men or eight horses. (Courtesy of Watrousville-Caro Historical Society.)

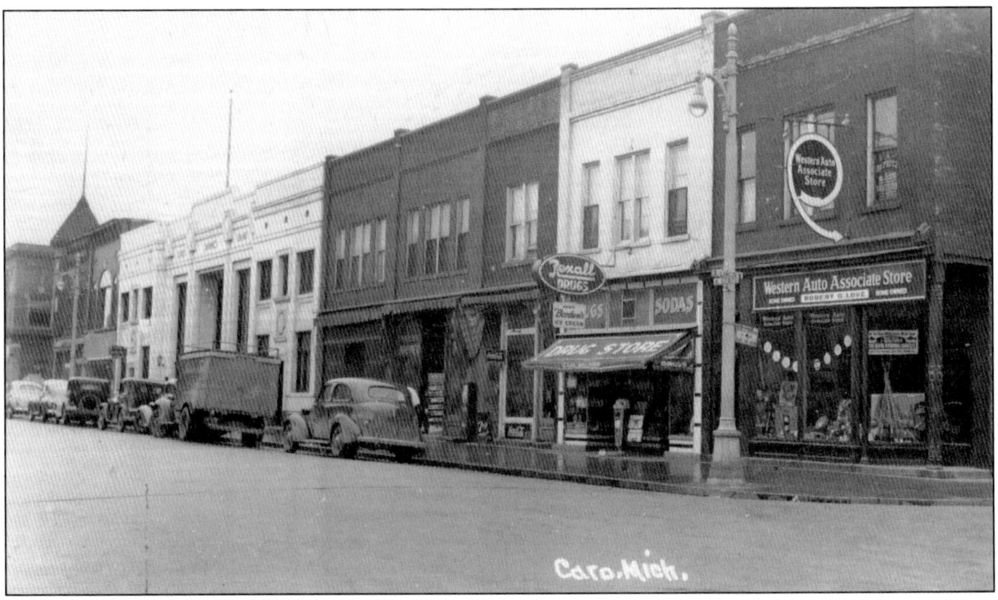

STATE STREET, c. 1940. This view looking east from Lincoln Street finds Western Auto occupying the corner building and the Fritz Dental office above. Next are Palmer's Rexall Drugstore, Kremer's, and an empty building. The large, white building is the State Savings Bank. (Courtesy of Watrousville-Caro Historical Society.)

Four

A Walk through Caro

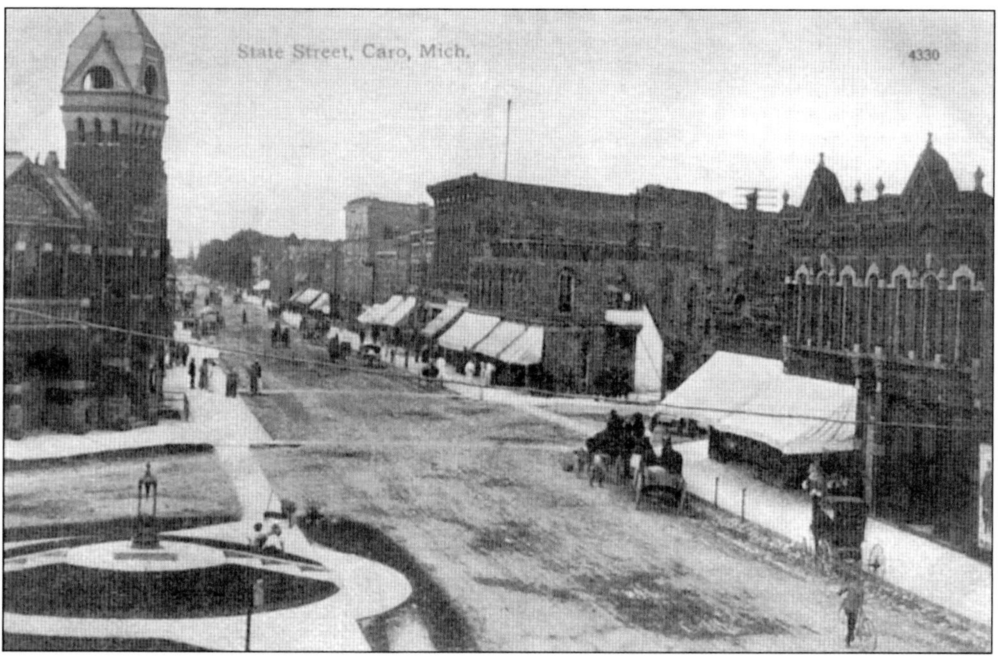

Phelps Fountain. This pre-1913 postcard view highlights the village triangle with the Phelps Fountain (lower left), which was named for George W. Phelps, who constructed the village's water works system. This fountain provided relief to man and beast in hot weather as well as a playground for the village children. (Courtesy of Gloria Hall.)

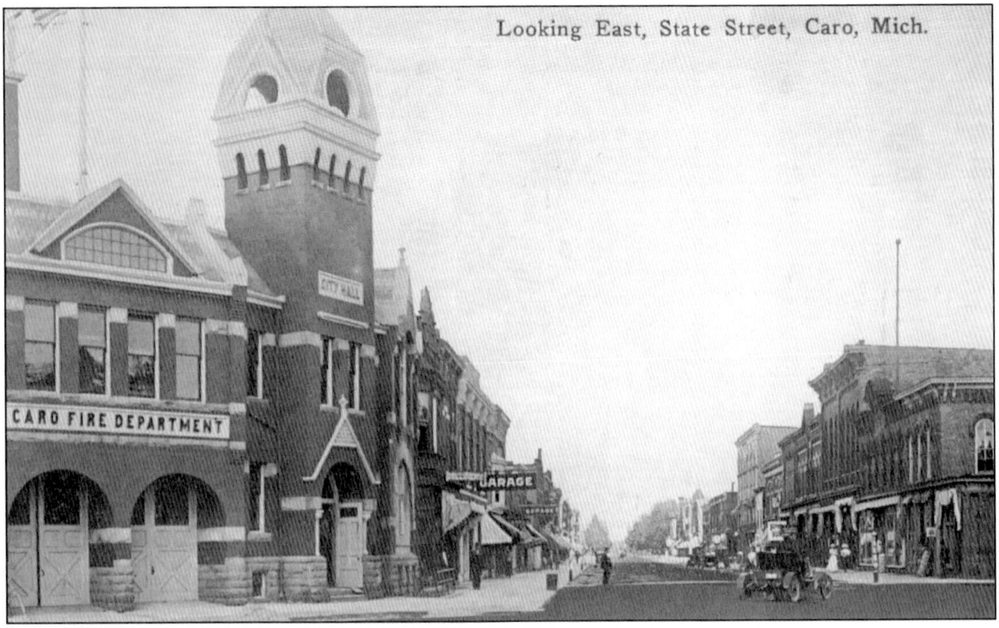

City Hall, 1914. Here is a close view of the Caro City Hall and Fire Department erected in 1887. The building was a source of civic pride, representing all the growth and progress Caro had achieved since its founding. (Courtesy of Watrousville-Caro Historical Society)

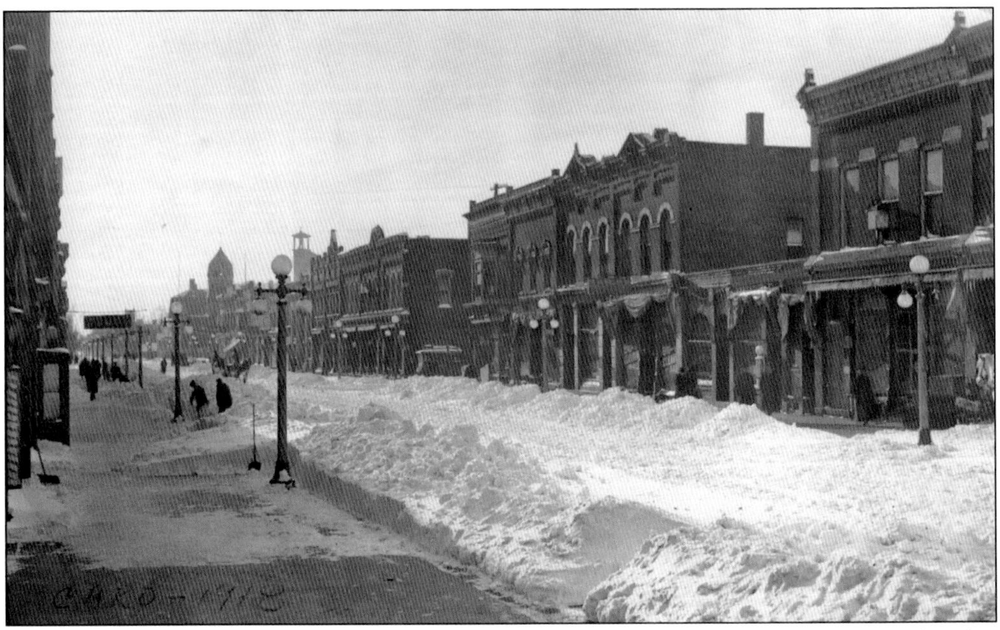

Snowstorm. Caro entered 1918 with a sizeable snowstorm choking the streets and roads. This photograph of downtown Caro was taken on January 14, 1918, and shows residents digging out. Silhouetted in the background against the western sky is the tower and bell of the city hall and the roof of the Hotel Montague. (Courtesy of Watrousville-Caro Historical Society.)

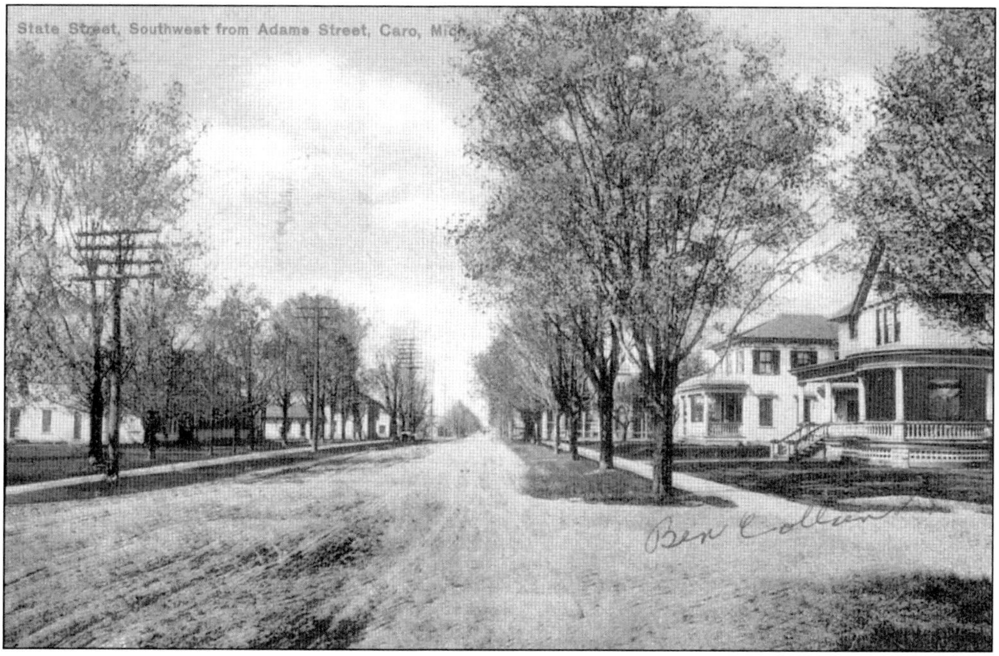

View Down South State Street. This view looking west down South State Street from Adams Street is much more bucolic than the same view today. The first home on the right was the home of H.H. Smith and is now the Collon Funeral Home. Next to the Smith home is the home of Dr. John Handy, which was destroyed by fire in 1932. (Courtesy of Watrousville-Caro Historical Society.)

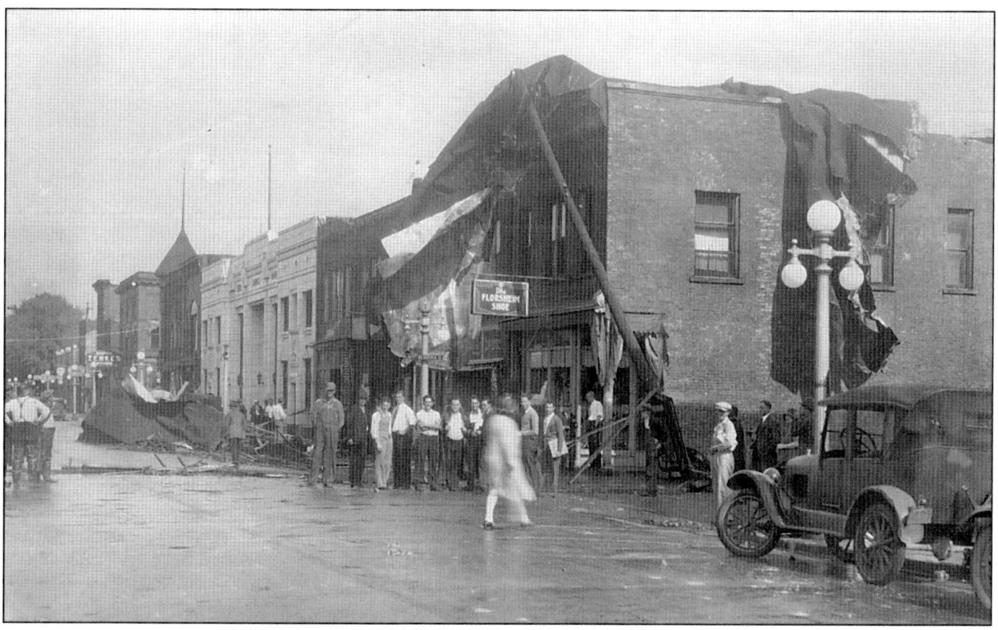

Tornado Damage. Several roofs in downtown Caro were removed by a tornado in September 1930. Looking east on State Street, the shoe store and the Palmer Drugstore were badly damaged, as was the St. Mary brothers' Star clothing store on the other side of the street. (Courtesy of Watrousville-Caro Historical Society.)

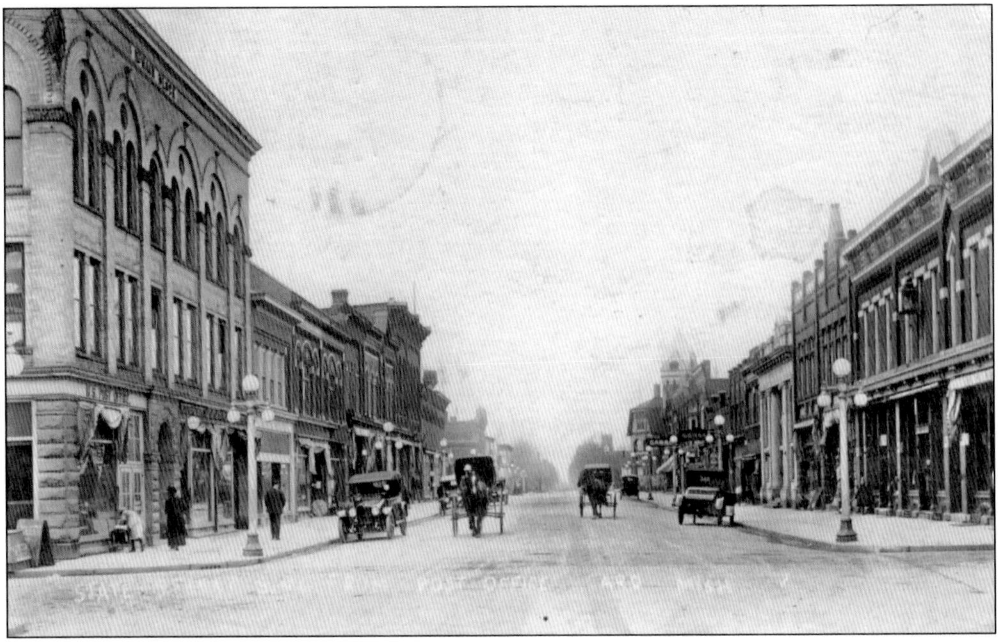

BUSINESS ON STATE STREET. Looking west, buggies and automobiles share a prosperous State Street in about 1921. The Caro Post Office is on the near left and St. Mary's Clothing Store is across the street on the near right. The Hotel Montague and the city hall are visible in the distance (right). (Courtesy of Gloria Hall.)

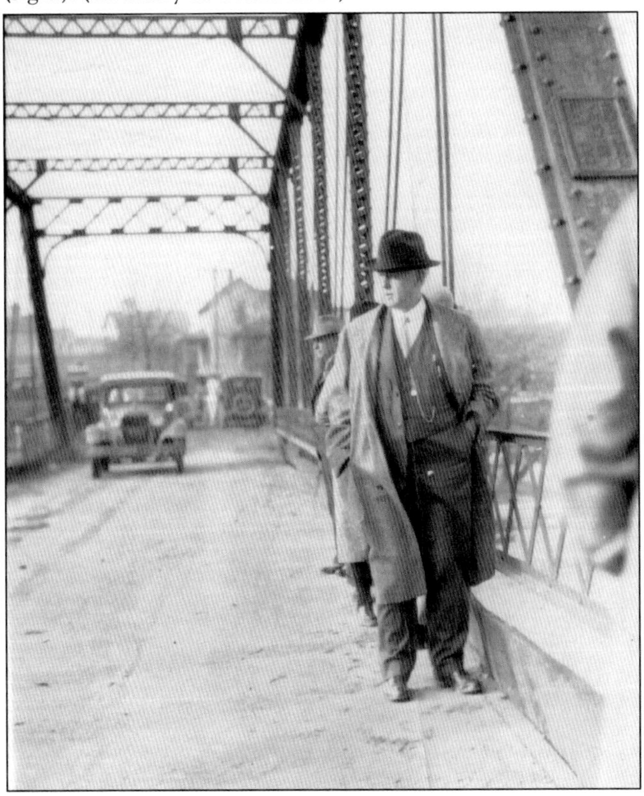

ARTHUR D. GALLERY. A.D. Gallery was the owner and editor of the *Tuscola County Advertiser*. In a mid-life career change, Gallery bought the newspaper in 1904 and proceeded to become a top-rate newspaperman as well as a trusted and influential community leader. He is shown crossing the Lower Bridge on the Cass River. (Courtesy of Watrousville-Caro Historical Society.)

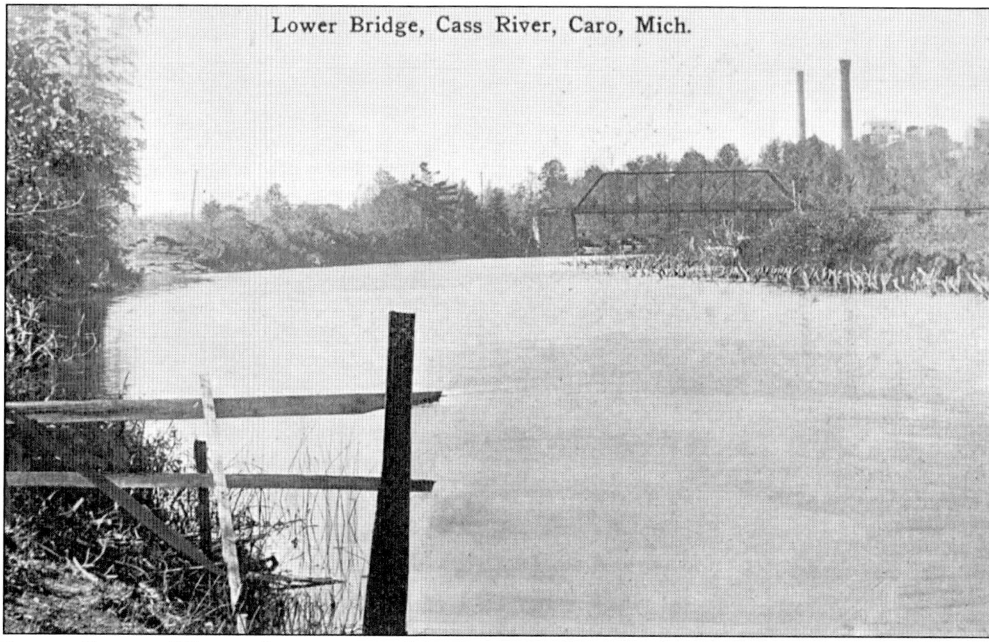

LOWER BRIDGE. This is a longer view of the Lower Bridge over the Cass River. There is currently a footbridge where the Lower Bridge was. The smokestacks of the Michigan Sugar Company are visible on the right. Starting around 1910 and for several seasons, a motor launch headquartered at the Lower Bridge took passengers on river trips. (Courtesy of Gloria Hall.)

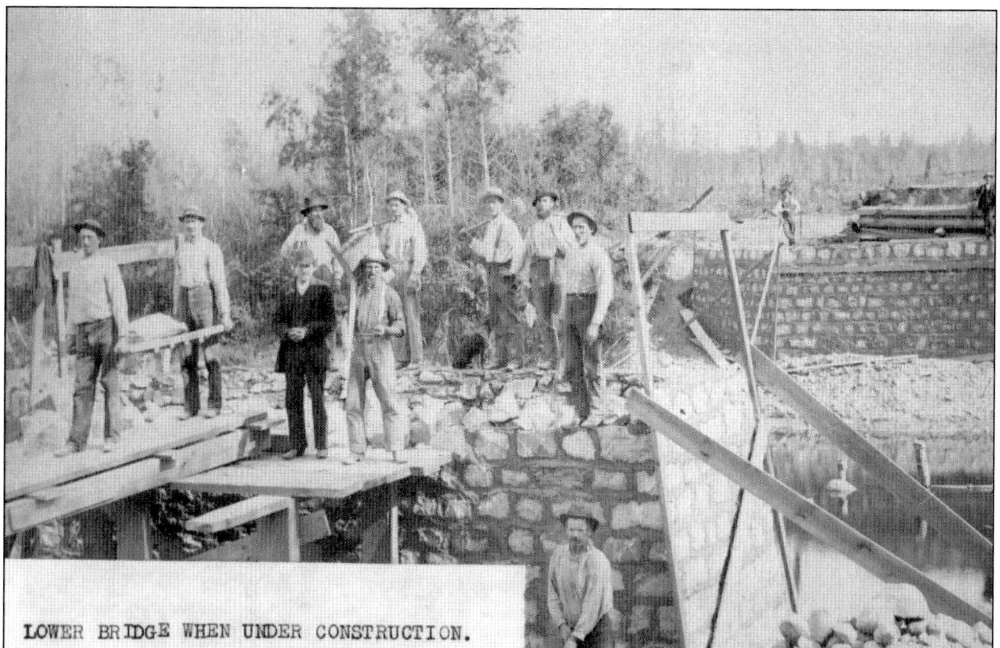

MANPOWER. The hard manual labor necessary to build the Lower Bridge over the Cass River is evident in this photograph. There was plenty of employment available in the prosperous, growing village. (Courtesy of Watrousville-Caro Historical Society.)

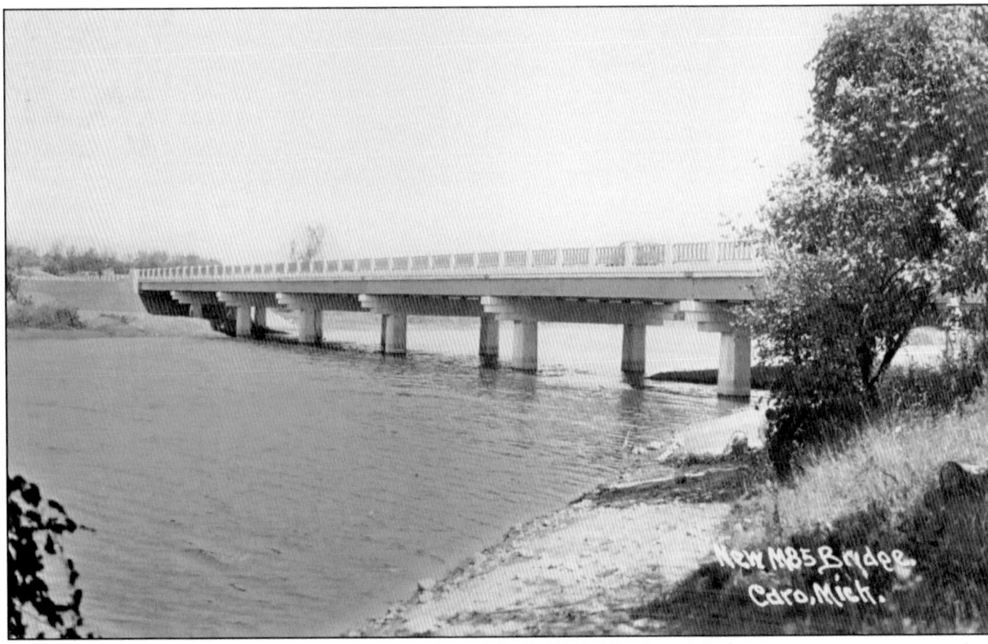

M-24 Bridge. Although this photograph is labeled M-85, that Michigan state route number was only used in 1930–1941. In 1942, that state route number was changed to M-24. In 1997, an extension took M-24 north to Unionville, where it ends at M-25. (Courtesy of Gloria Hall.)

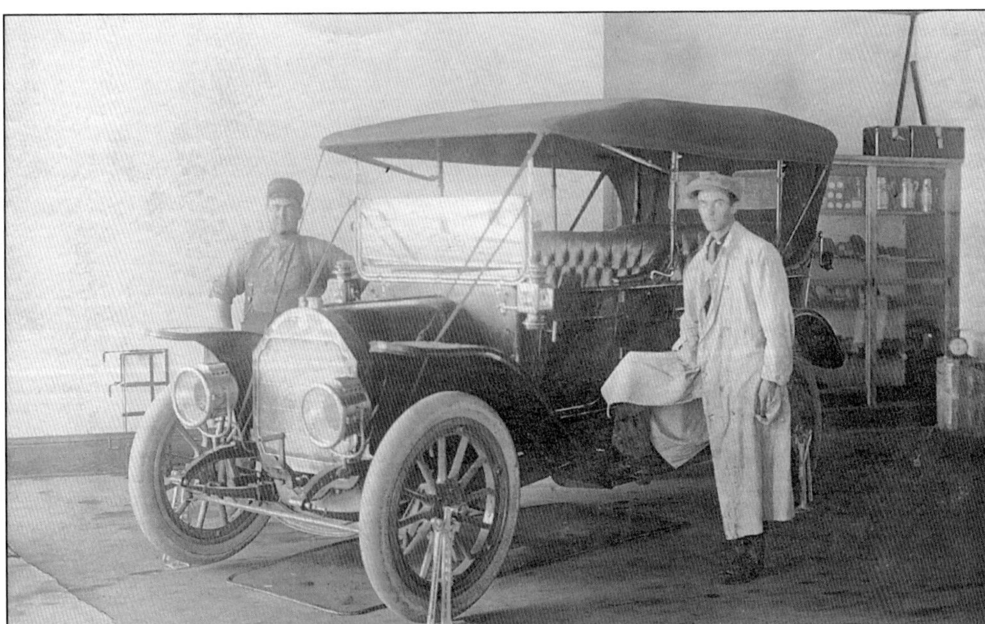

Early Automobiles. This photograph is labeled "Clyde Montague, c. 1910." Clyde and brother Clarence Montague worked as mechanics in the early 1920s for the Cooper Garage at the corner of State and Grant Streets. Later, Clarence and third brother, Carl, owned a garage on Columbia Street for many years. (Courtesy of Watrousville-Caro Historical Society.)

YOUNG MEN ABOUT CARO. These young Caro men are identified as (order unknown) Malen Hartley, Louis Deming, and Irv Wright, in about 1909. The long topcoats were needed for warmth while riding in buggies or early automobiles. Deming was a longtime Caro businessman. (Courtesy of Watrousville-Caro Historical Society.)

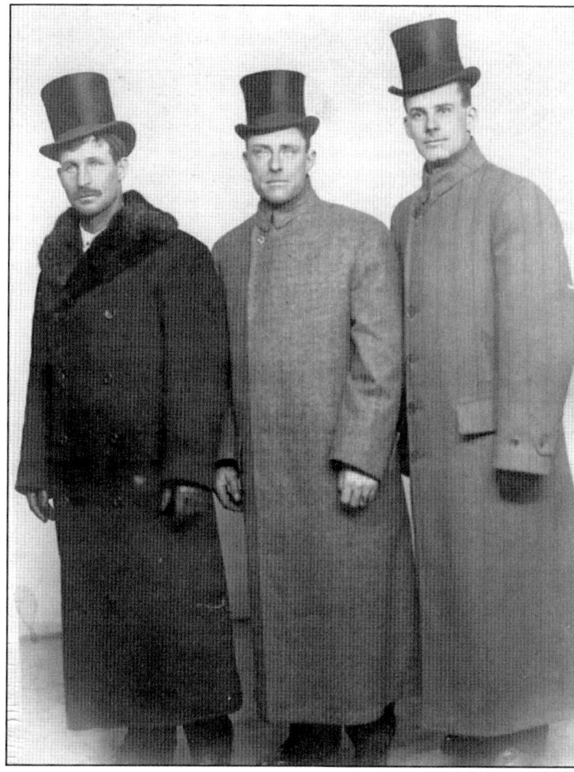

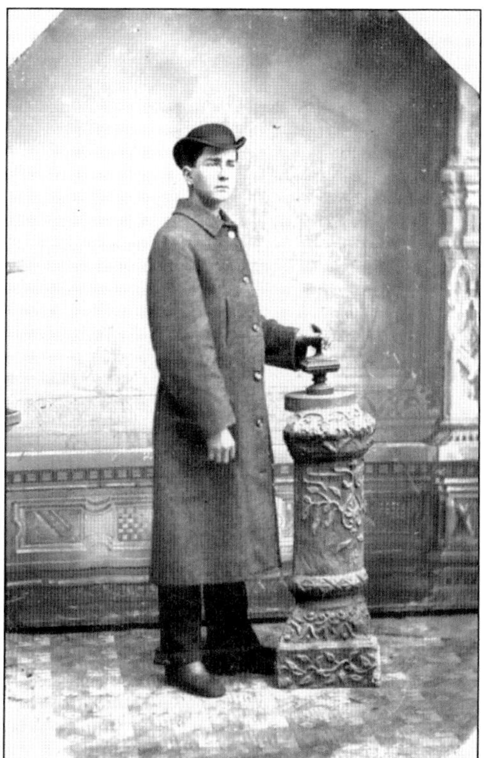

JOHN GREENFIELD. This tintype portrait identifies the young man pictured as John Greenfield. It appears to have been taken in the late 1800s. No information has been found by the authors about John Greenfield, but the Greenfield name was an early one in Caro. (Courtesy of Watrousville-Caro Historical Society.)

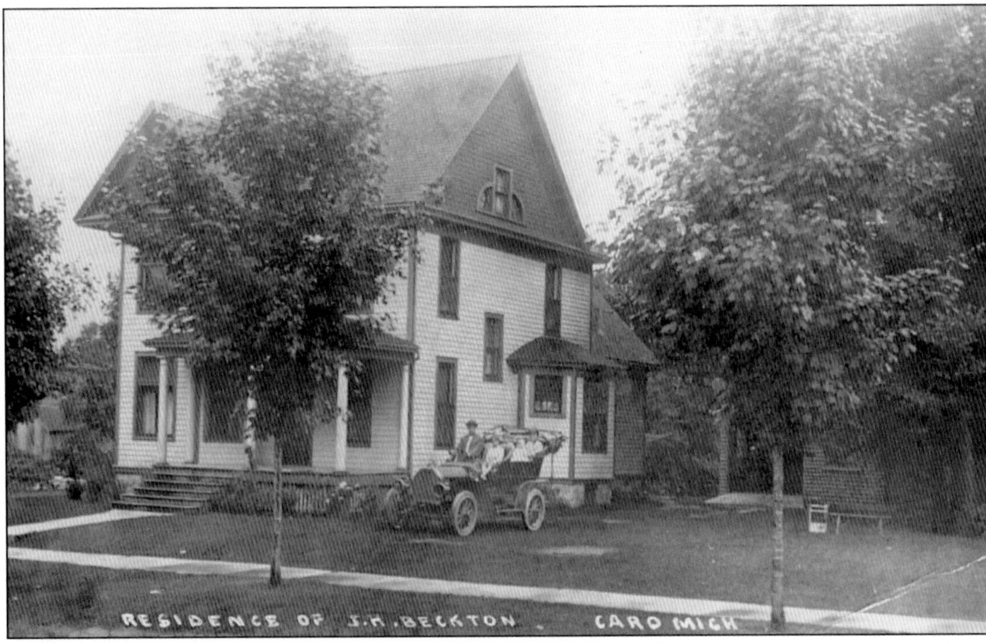

BECKTON FAMILY HOME. In 1911, this was the home of Joseph H. Beckton and his family. Born in Scotland in 1866, Beckton came to Caro in 1894 and operated a drugstore until 1913. He was also an active community leader. Here, he and his family sit in their automobile. The home and carriage house still stand at 205 West Bush Street. (Courtesy of David and Jane Neese.)

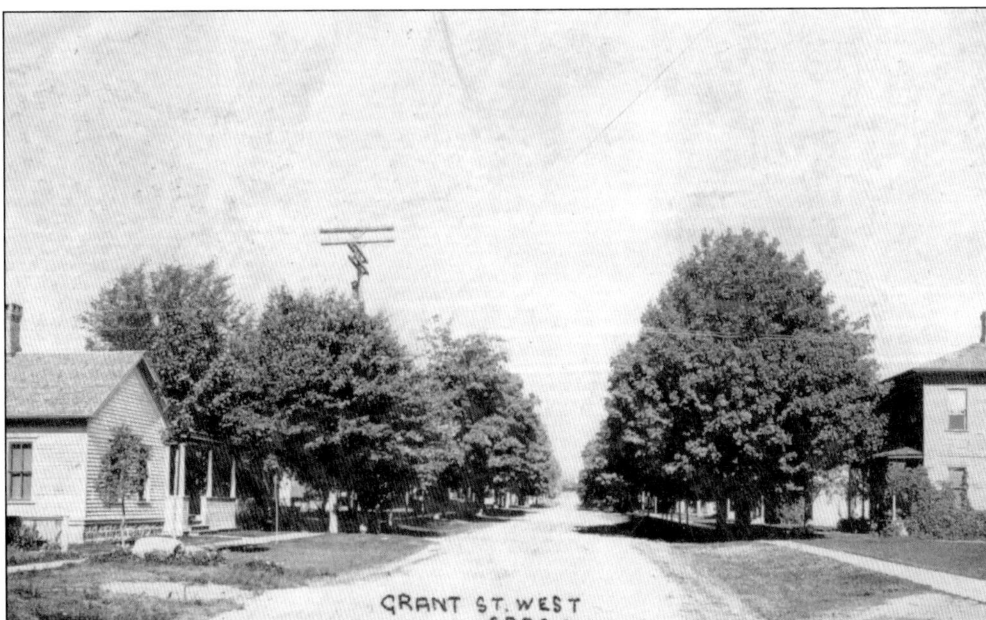

GRANT STREET WEST. Pictured is one of the many tree-lined neighborhoods in Caro around 1910. This is Grant Street looking west from State Street. The person who sent this postcard mentions having recovered from a three-week bout of typhoid fever as well as having attended the county fair the previous week. (Courtesy of Gloria Hall.)

A Summer Day. This is an unidentified home in the village with an elderly couple and their dog enjoying a lovely day. Several homes still exist in Caro with similar fretwork at their peaks and similar bay windows, but no perfect match could be found. It is possible that this house, like so many others, yielded to progress and this photograph is all that remains. (Courtesy of Tim Romain/ Cope collection.)

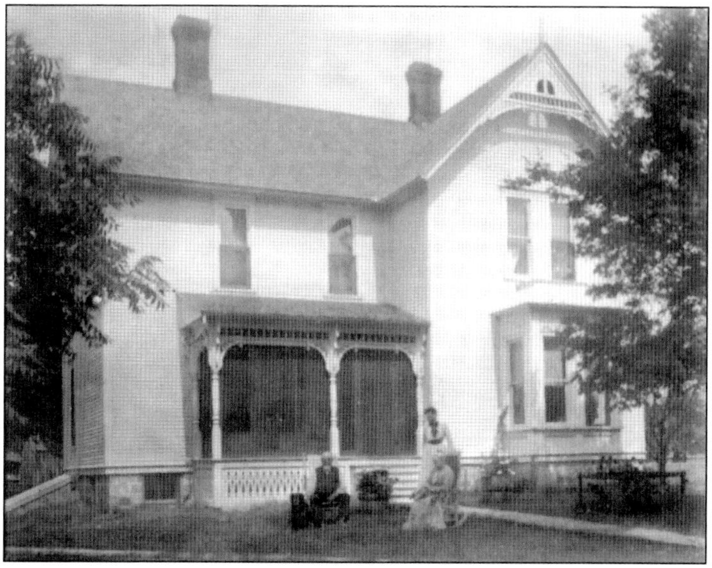

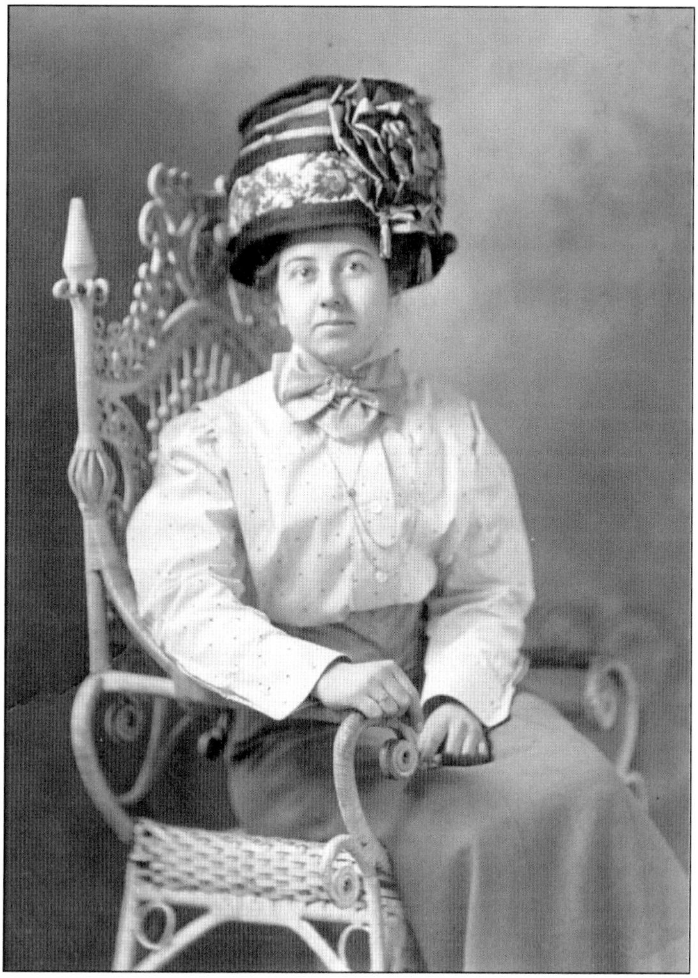

Portrait of a Young Lady. This young woman sat for her portrait wearing a hat in a style that was very popular in the early 1900s. She may possibly be Analena Lethbridge, but the photograph is not labeled. (Courtesy of Clara Korte/ Watrousville-Caro Historical Society.)

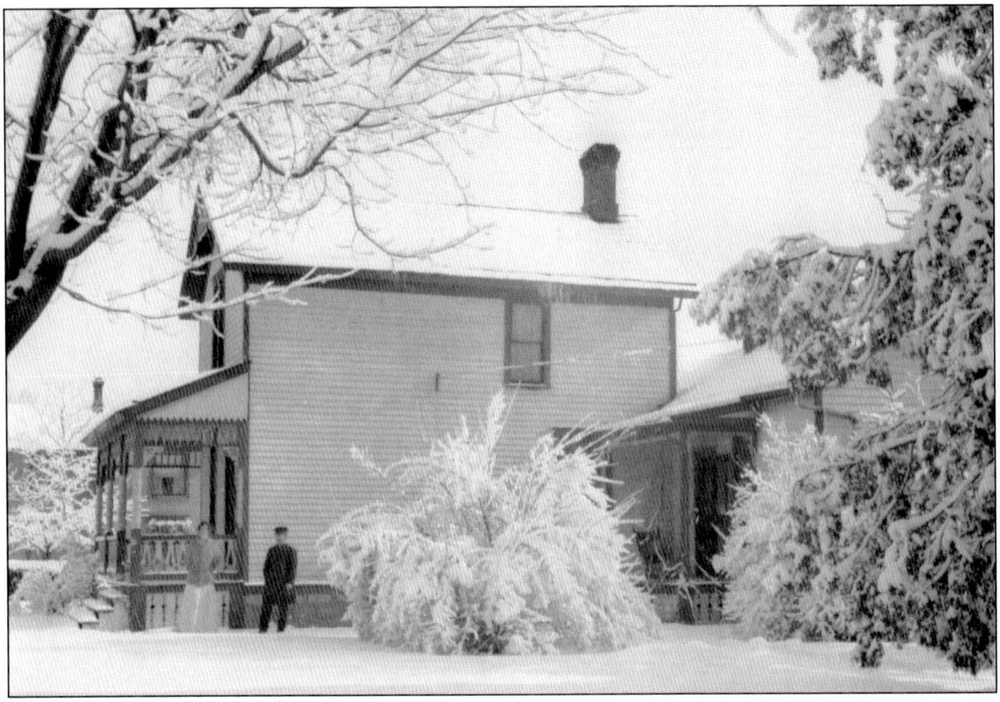

Snow Scene. Here is a Michigan winter scene of a home at the corner of Pearl and Lincoln Streets after a heavy snowfall. This photograph is from a glass negative found in a trunk at the former home of the Cope family on West Frank Street. (Courtesy of Tim Romain/Cope collection.)

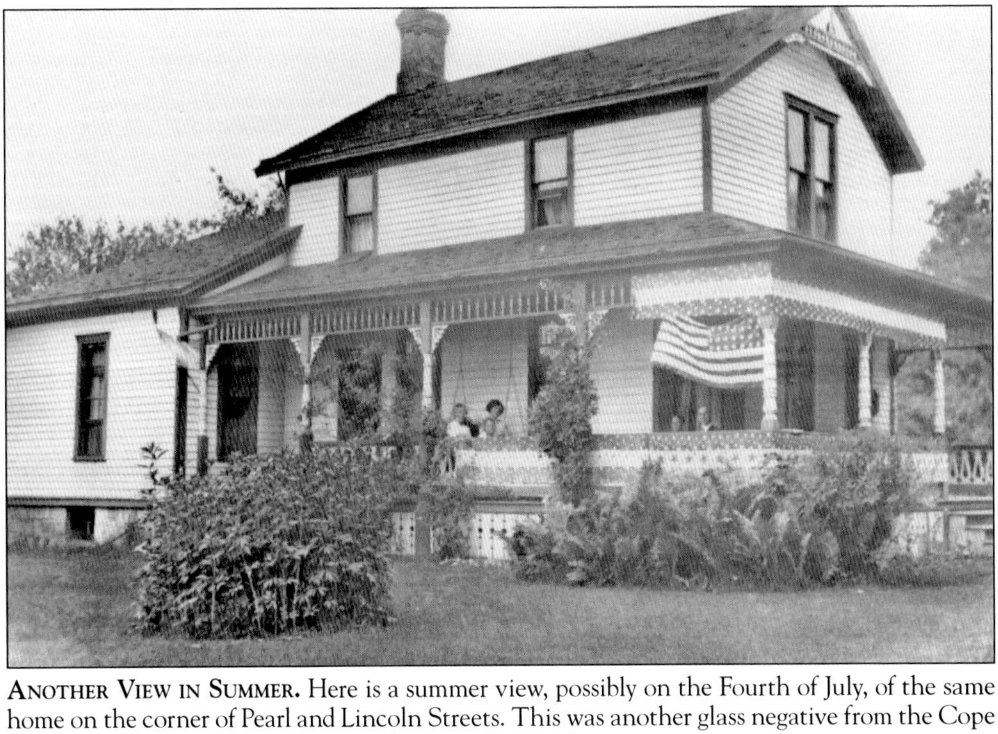

Another View in Summer. Here is a summer view, possibly on the Fourth of July, of the same home on the corner of Pearl and Lincoln Streets. This was another glass negative from the Cope collection. (Courtesy of Tim Romain/Cope collection.)

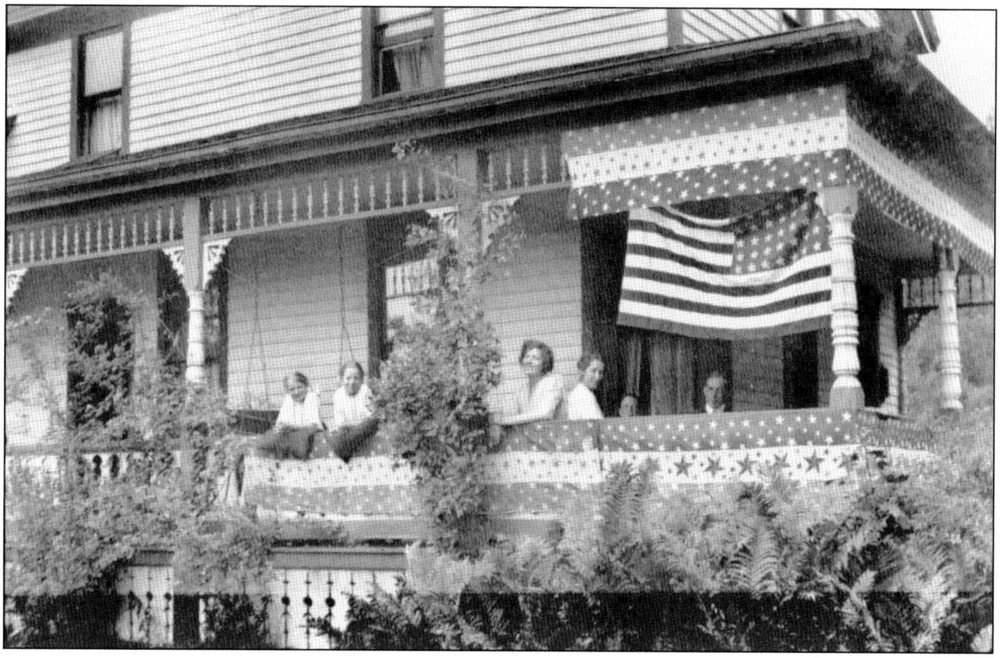

HAPPY CELEBRATION. Pictured on a festive front porch at Pearl and Lincoln Streets, this group is enjoying a Fourth of July celebration. The image seems to capture the best of small-town, American life in times gone by. (Courtesy of Tim Romain/Cope collection.)

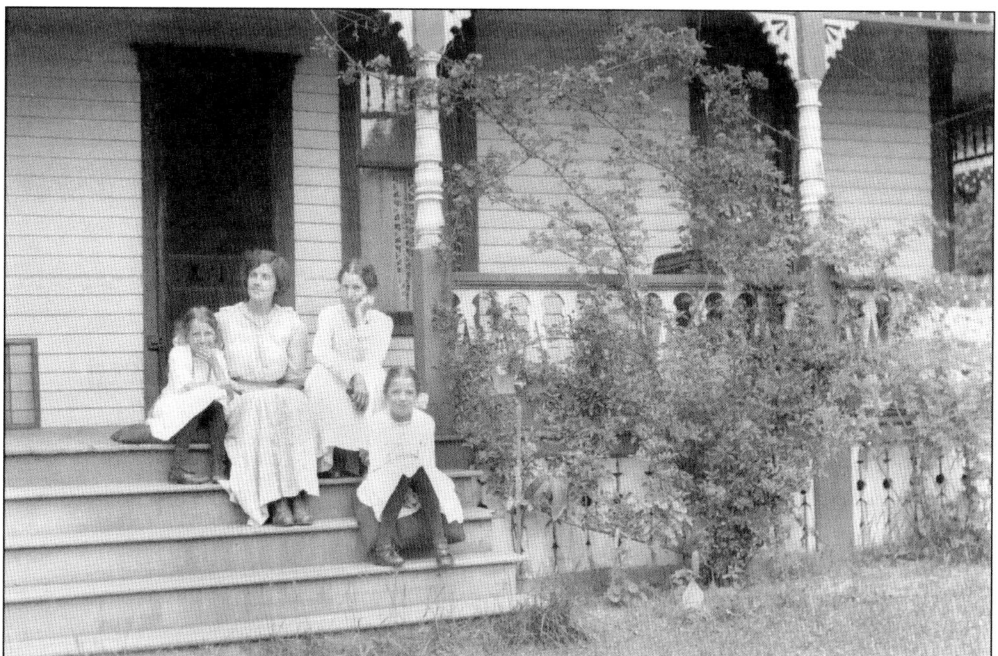

MOTHER AND CHILDREN. This photograph completes the group of photographs of the family at their Pearl and Lincoln Street home on the Fourth of July. The photographer of these scenes is assumed to be Caro native Herbert Leon Cope, who was also an internationally recognized speaker and humorist. (Courtesy of Tim Romain/Cope collection.)

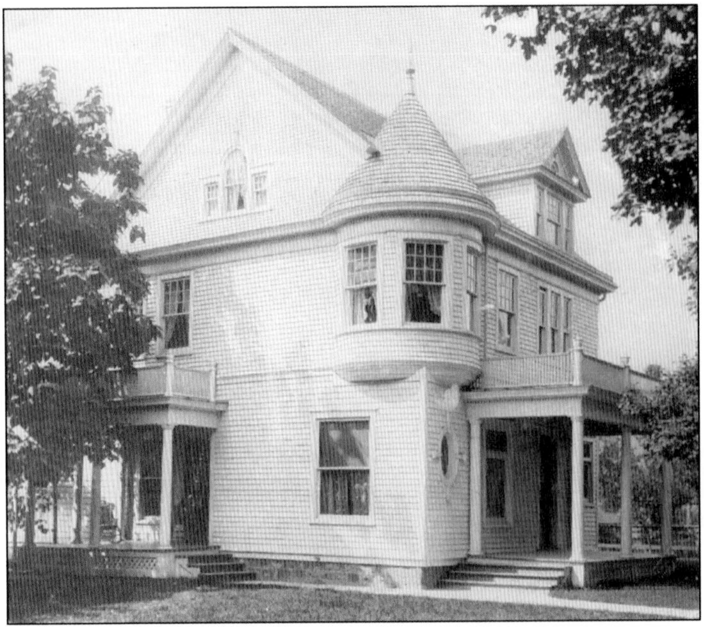

Dr. Chase Home. This home, located at 217 West Burnside Street, was built in 1888 by Dr. Sherman F. Chase, who was a highly respected homeopathic physician. It served as his family home, office, and base of operations for his rounds throughout the countryside. By 1920, it was owned by automobile dealer Fred C. Striffler. (Courtesy of Watrousville-Caro Historical Society.)

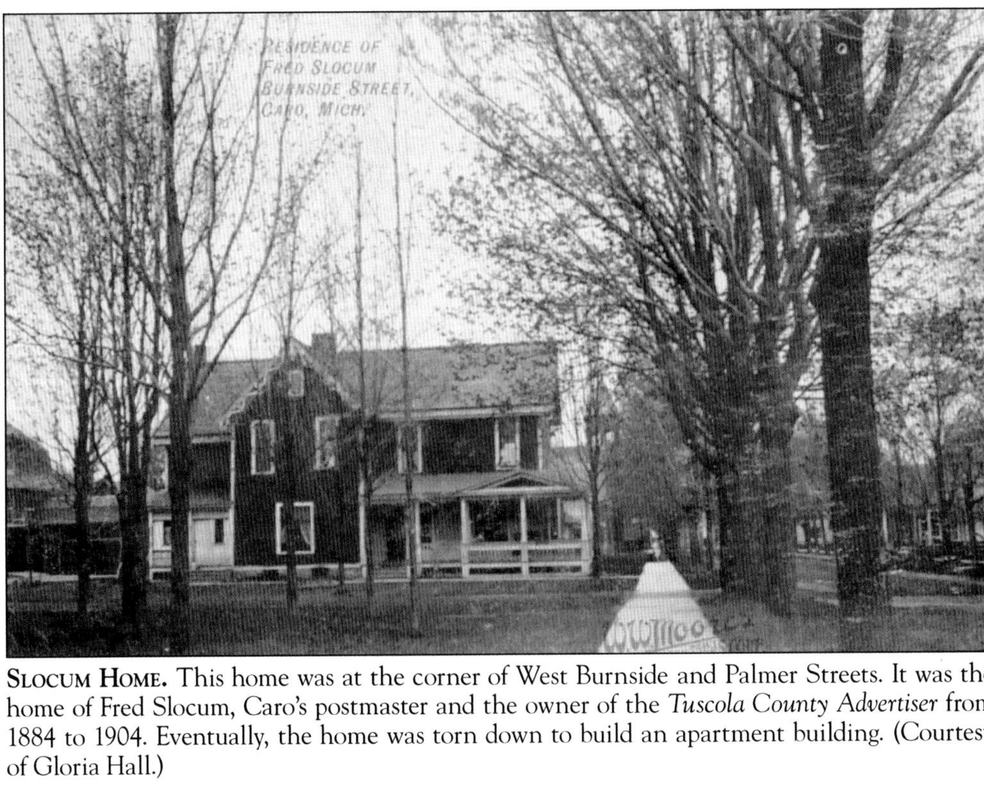

Slocum Home. This home was at the corner of West Burnside and Palmer Streets. It was the home of Fred Slocum, Caro's postmaster and the owner of the *Tuscola County Advertiser* from 1884 to 1904. Eventually, the home was torn down to build an apartment building. (Courtesy of Gloria Hall.)

William A. Heartt. Heartt arrived in the Caro area in 1853. Seeing enormous potential, he quickly set up operations at Wahjamega, eventually building a sawmill on the Cass River. His logging operation thrived until the 1880s, when the area was essentially logged out. As a community leader, he championed railroads and agricultural development. (*History of Tuscola and Bay Counties.*)

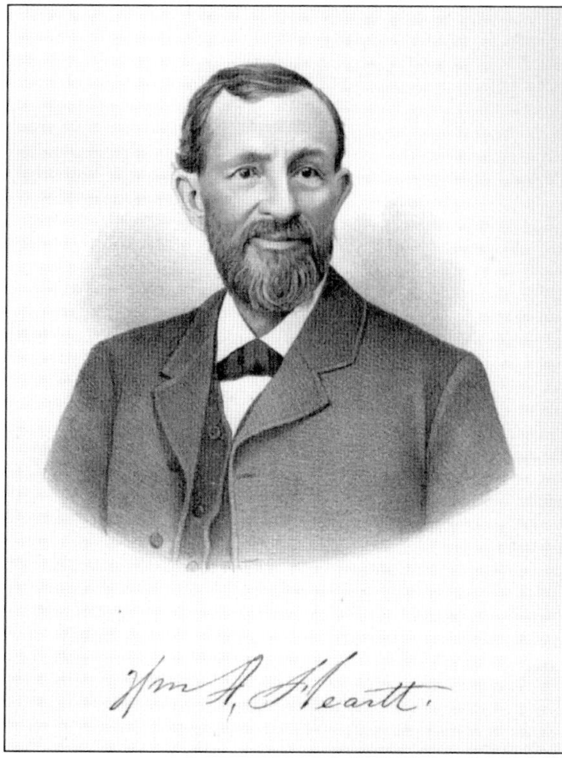

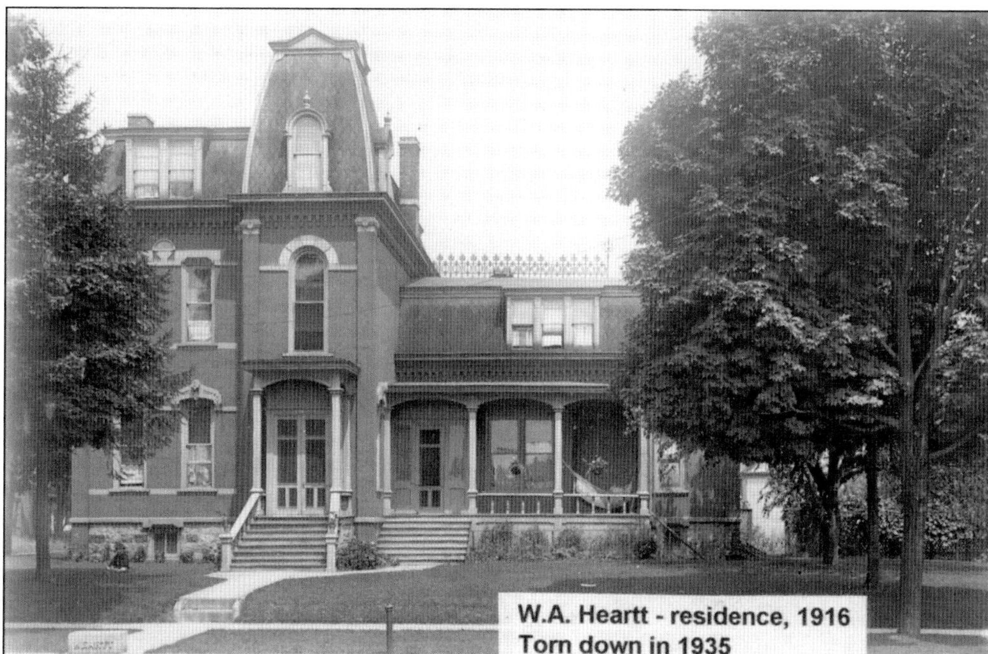

Heartt Home. Built in the early 1880s by Andrew C. Young, this home stood on the corner of West Burnside and Pearl Streets. In 1888, after a series of setbacks, Young sold the home to pioneer lumberman William A. Heartt. It was torn down in 1935. In later years, Mary and Hub Purdy lived on this site. (Courtesy of Watrousville-Caro Historical Society.)

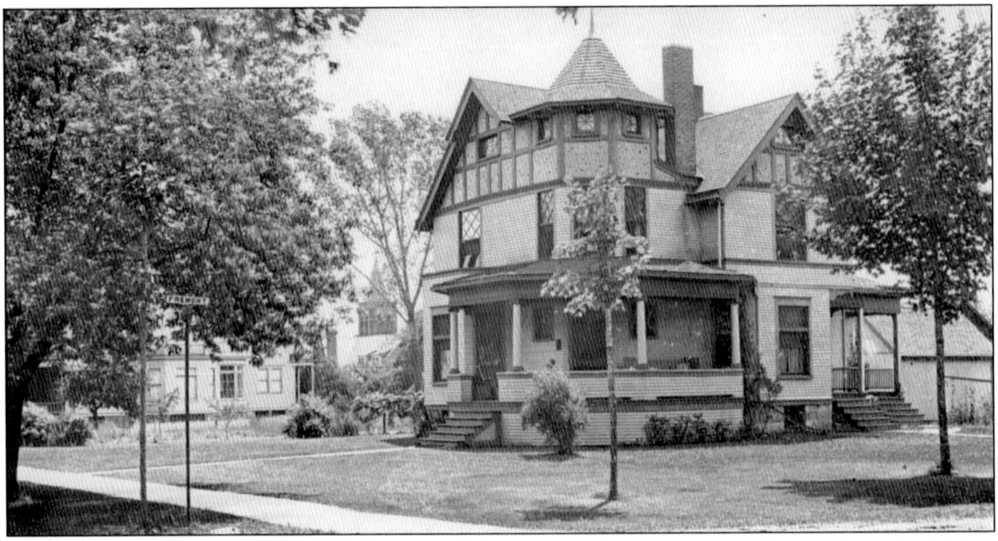

Wixson Home. This home is at the corner of West Burnside and Fremont Streets. Built by Walter S. Wixson, a prominent Caro attorney, the upper story is stucco embedded with broken colored glass. The glass has a story behind it: Mrs. Wixson was a strong believer in the Temperance movement, while Mr. Wixson, who enjoyed a nip, had some of his colored whiskey bottles broken and put into the stucco. (Courtesy of Watrousville-Caro Historical Society.)

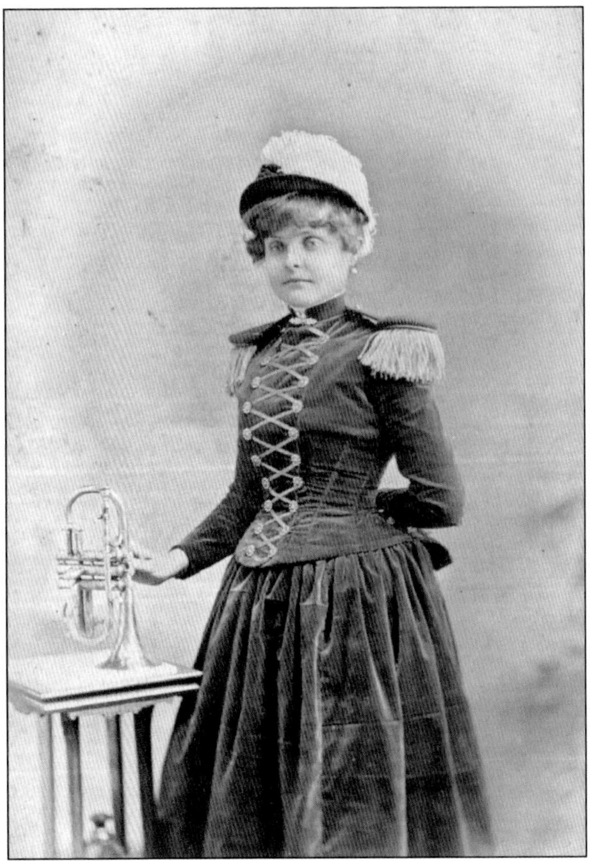

Young Lady with Cornet. In the late 19th century, Caro had a Young Ladies Cornet Band. This young woman was a member of that band. At that time, ladies literary societies and women's clubs began to appear and flourish. The Ladies Historical and Literary Society started around this time and was later known as the Wixson Club. (Courtesy of Almona Pierce Bradley.)

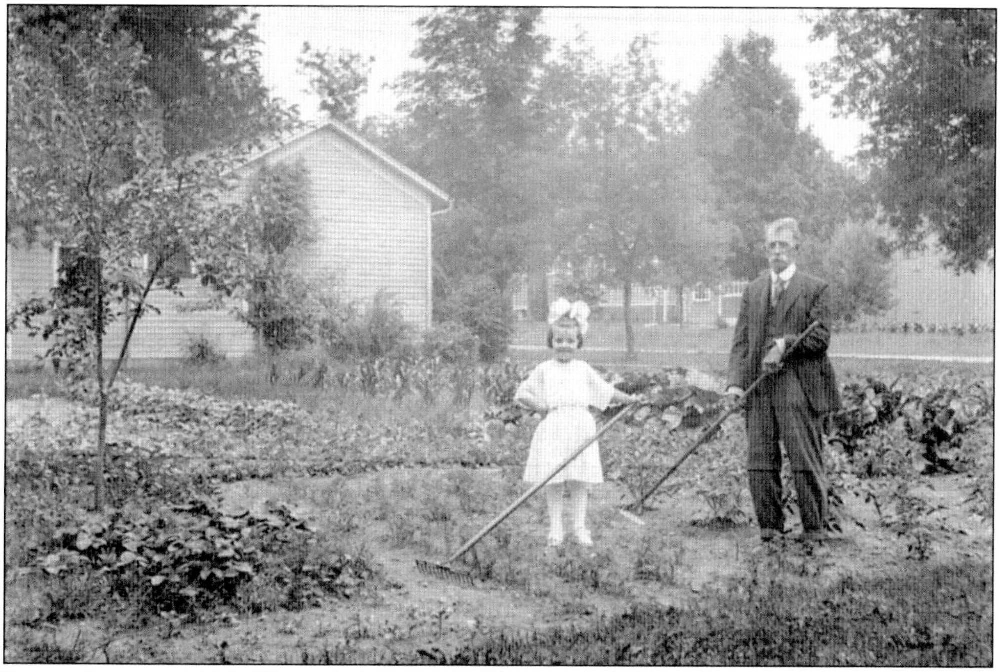

Little Rita, c. 1923. This is believed to be Rita Campbell Hitchings in the garden behind her family's West Frank and Fremont Streets home. Her fellow gardener is unidentified. Family gardens were undoubtedly a common sight throughout the tidy neighborhoods of the thriving village. (Courtesy of Tim Romain/Cope collection.)

Woman and Cat. An unidentified woman appears to be reading her newspaper in her rustic lawn swing. Until 1918, there were two newspapers in Caro, the *Tuscola County Advertiser* and the *Courier*. Arthur Gallery had folded the *Courier* into the *Advertiser* by 1918. (Courtesy of Tim Romain/Cope collection.)

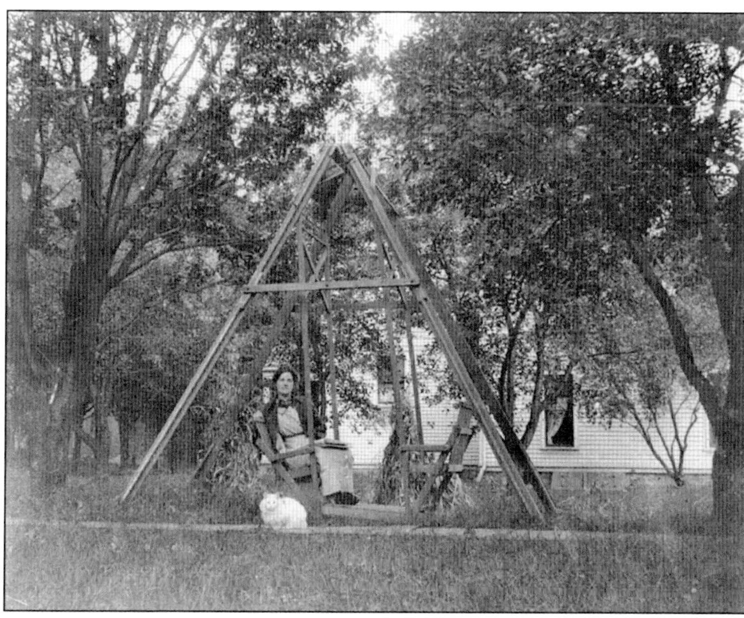

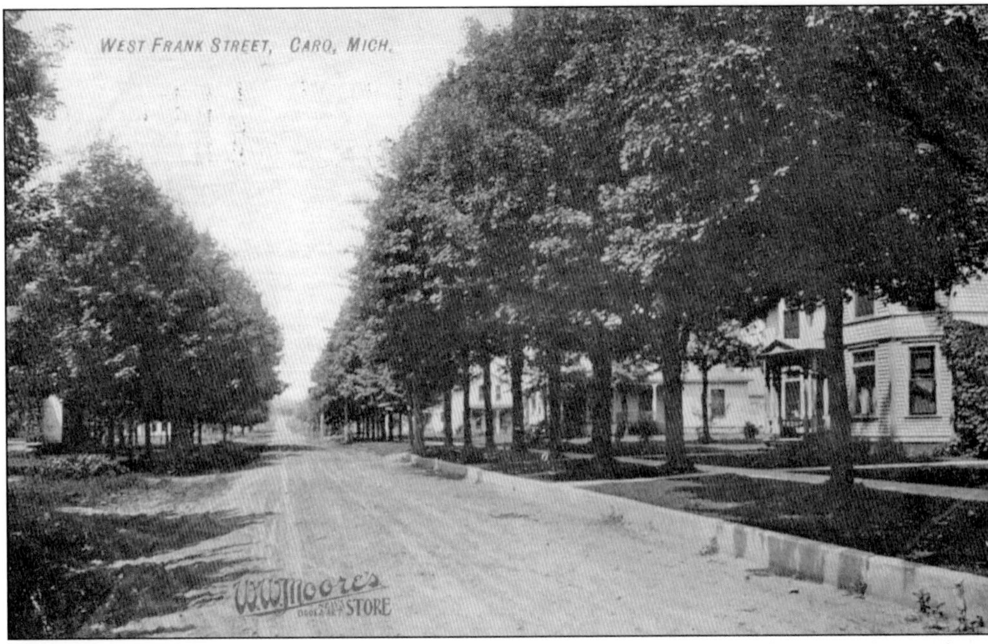

WEST FRANK STREET, C. 1908. This view down West Frank Street toward Hooper Street shows an unpaved thoroughfare, with the large homes of bankers John F. Seeley (far right) and his son Lewis G. Seeley (second from right) behind a row of beautiful trees. (Courtesy of Gloria Hall.)

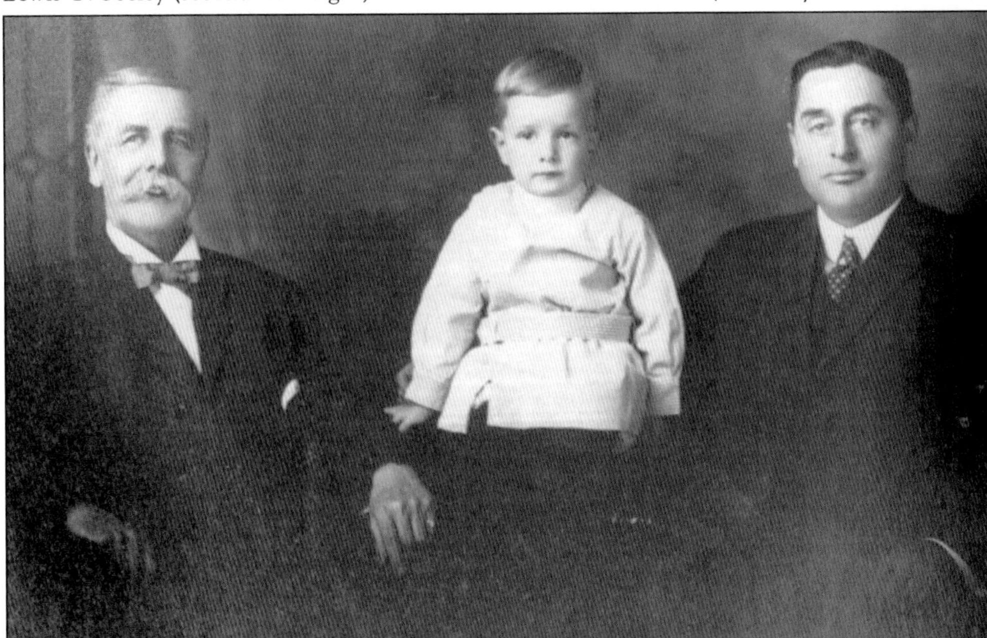

THE SEELEY MEN. Pictured are three generations of Seeley men in 1913. From left to right are John F. Seeley, John C. Seeley, and Lewis G. Seeley. John F. Seeley founded the Tuscola County Bank in 1878. The name of the bank was later changed to the Commercial Savings Bank, and in the 1920s, it was merged with the State Savings Bank. (Courtesy of Watrousville-Caro Historical Society.)

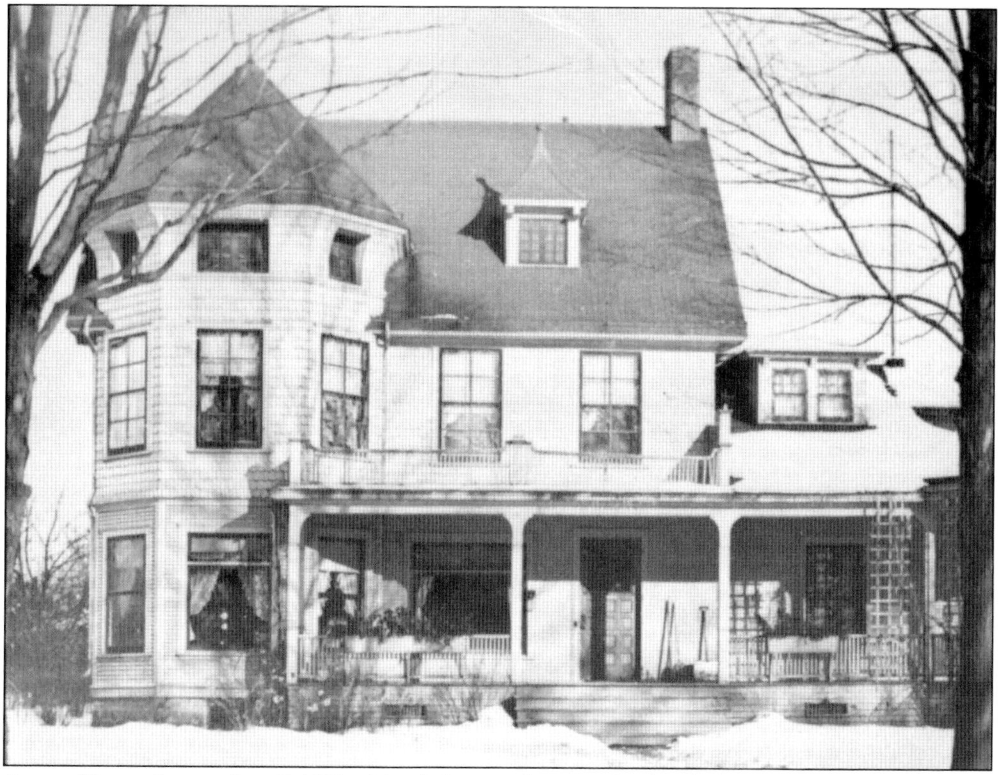

Seeley Home. Located at 636 West Frank Street, this was the family home of Lewis G. Seeley. It was resplendent with beveled glass windows, a stately tower, and ornate woodwork. In later years, it became known as the John C. Seeley home, having passed into the care of Lewis Seeley's son John C. (Courtesy of Watrousville-Caro Historical Society.)

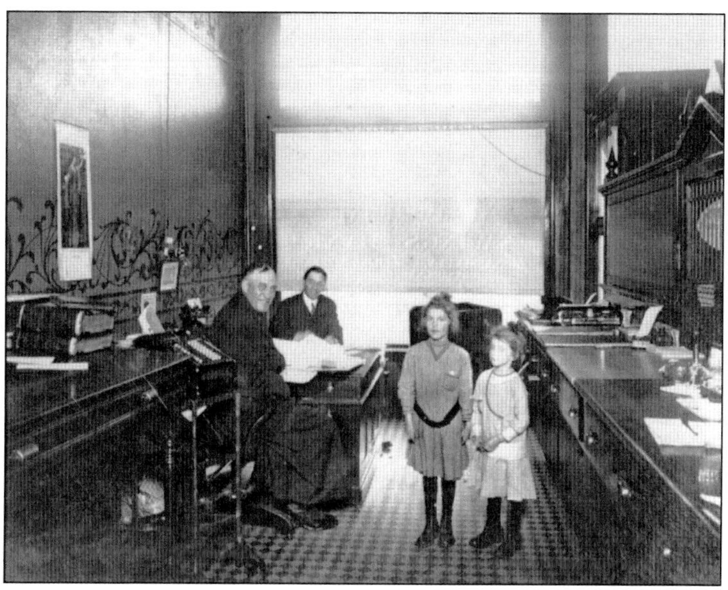

Interior, Commercial Savings Bank. From left to right are Rev. Osgood Fuller (of the Episcopal Church), Lewis G. Seeley, and the Seeley daughters Lucy and Margaret. Besides banking, Seeley was involved in fire insurance and real estate and was a noted local tennis player. (Courtesy of Watrousville-Caro Historical Society.)

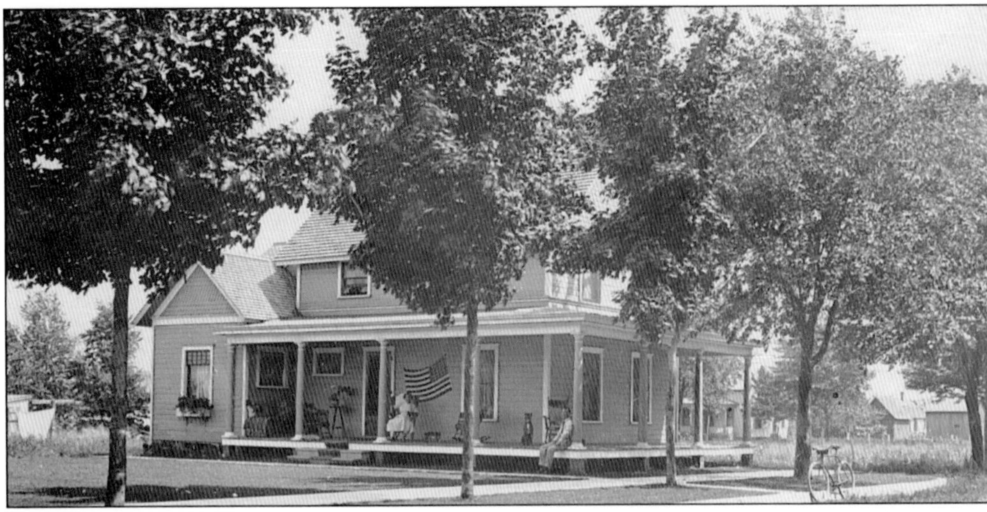

St. Mary Home. This vignette of turn-of-the-century America is the home of Joseph St. Mary and his family, located on South Almer Street between Norman and Wells Streets. St. Mary and his sons owned and operated the Star Clothing Store in Caro for many years. (Courtesy of Watrousville-Caro Historical Society.)

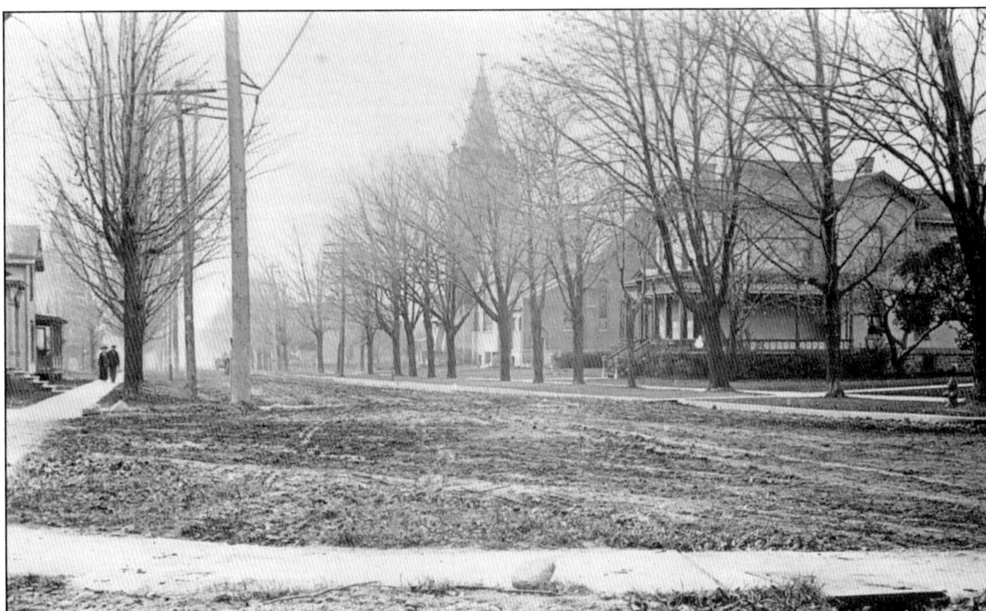

North Almer Street. This view looking south down North Almer Street was taken prior to 1921 when Almer was paved. The First Presbyterian Church tower is visible on the right in the center of the photograph. Also visible on the right is the Staley home. The sidewalk crossing the street in the foreground is at Burnside Street. (Courtesy of Watrousville-Caro Historical Society.)

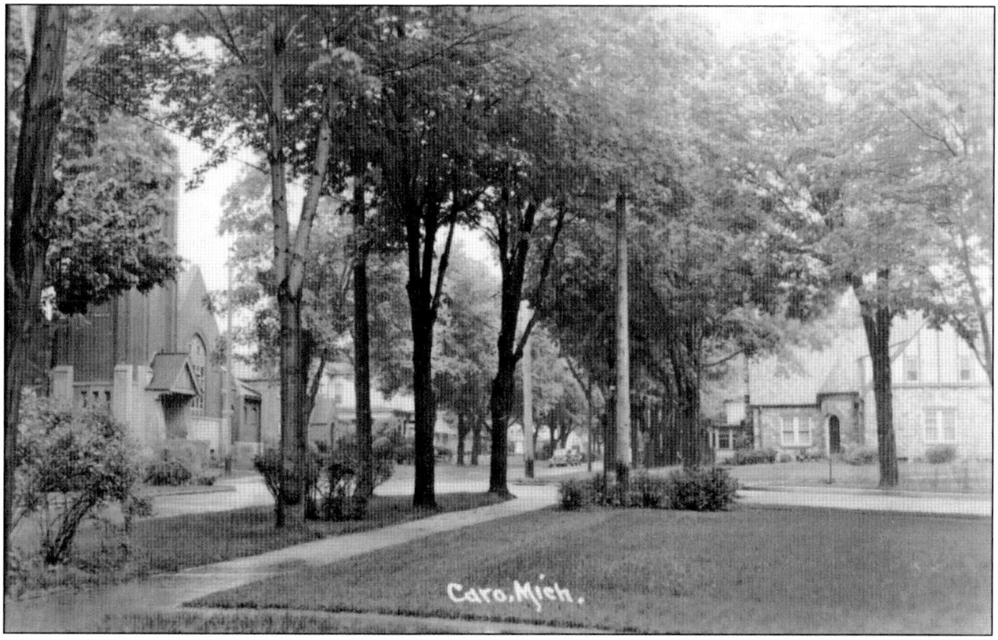

FIRST PRESBYTERIAN CHURCH. This beautiful view of the Presbyterian Church is from the lawn of the First Baptist Church, across Almer Street. The Presbyterian Church was built from Bedford stone and pressed brick in 1903. On the right is the home of optometrist Dr. Wendell Hartman. (Courtesy of Gloria Hall.)

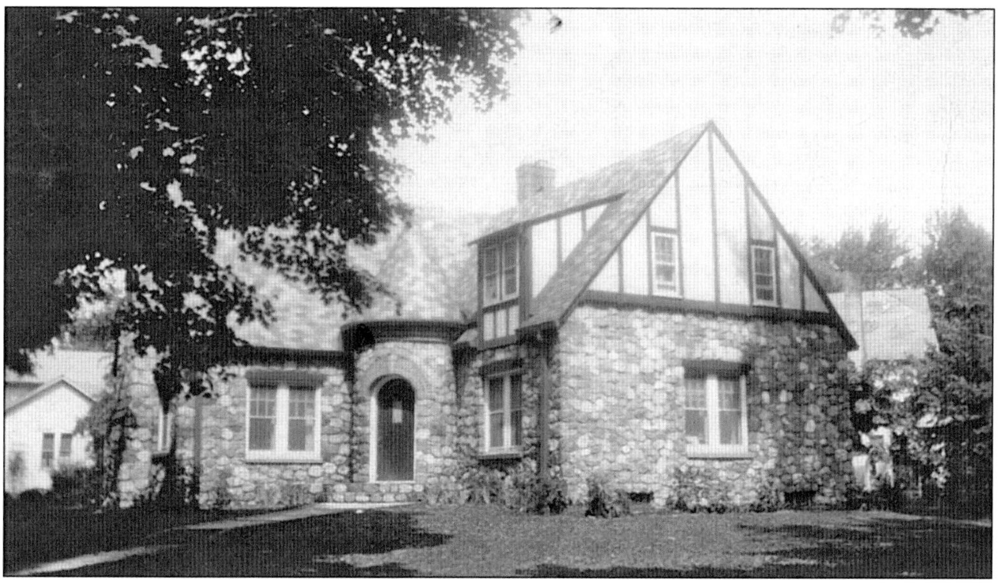

HARTMAN HOME. Originally built by blacksmith Fred McDurmon, this later became the home of Caro optometrist Dr. Wendell Hartman. It sits at the intersection of North Almer and West Lincoln Streets next to the post office. Its architecture complements that of the William J. Moore home, which stands kitty-corner to this home. (Courtesy of Watrousville-Caro Historical Society.)

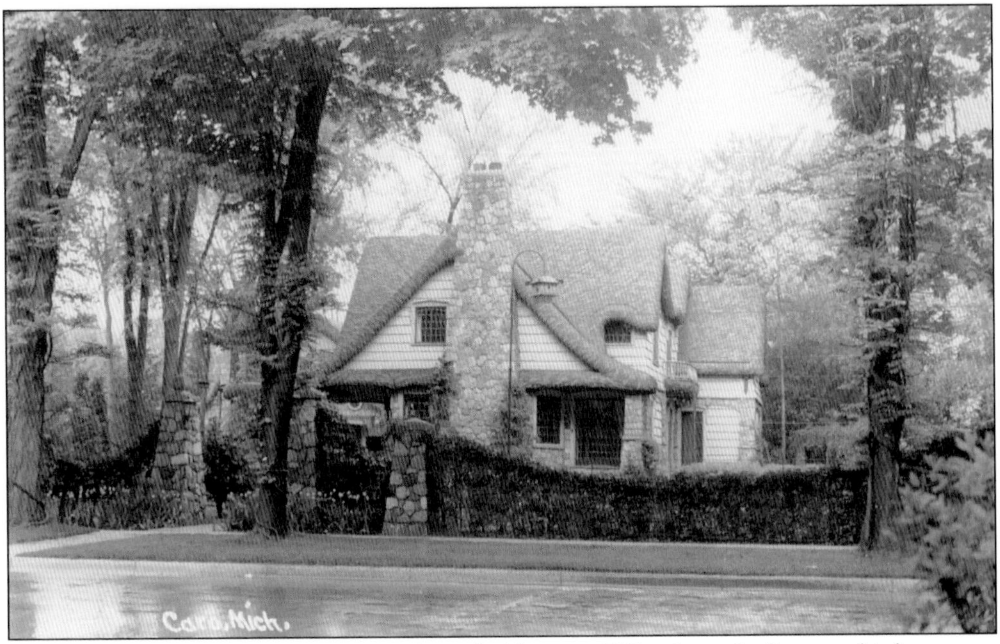

MOORE HOME. Located at the corner of North Almer and West Lincoln Streets, this home was purchased by William J. Moore in 1914. He proceeded to make this residence uniquely his own, both inside and out. The barn became a clubhouse and garage with double doors that would open at the touch of a button in his automobile (in 1914). (Courtesy of Watrousville-Caro Historical Society.)

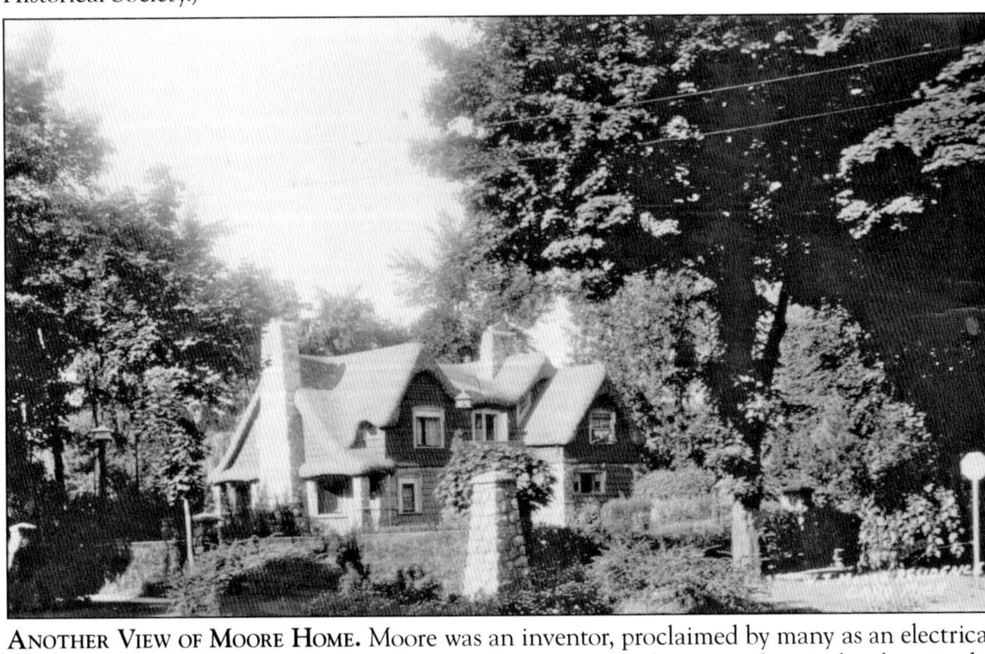

ANOTHER VIEW OF MOORE HOME. Moore was an inventor, proclaimed by many as an electrical genius, and his home had a master radio room for overseeing the many electrical gadgets in the home. There were 20 telephones, a front door that opened automatically, and an electric dishwasher in the kitchen. The home occupied four and a half city lots, and the grounds themselves were a marvel. (Courtesy of Watrousville-Caro Historical Society.)

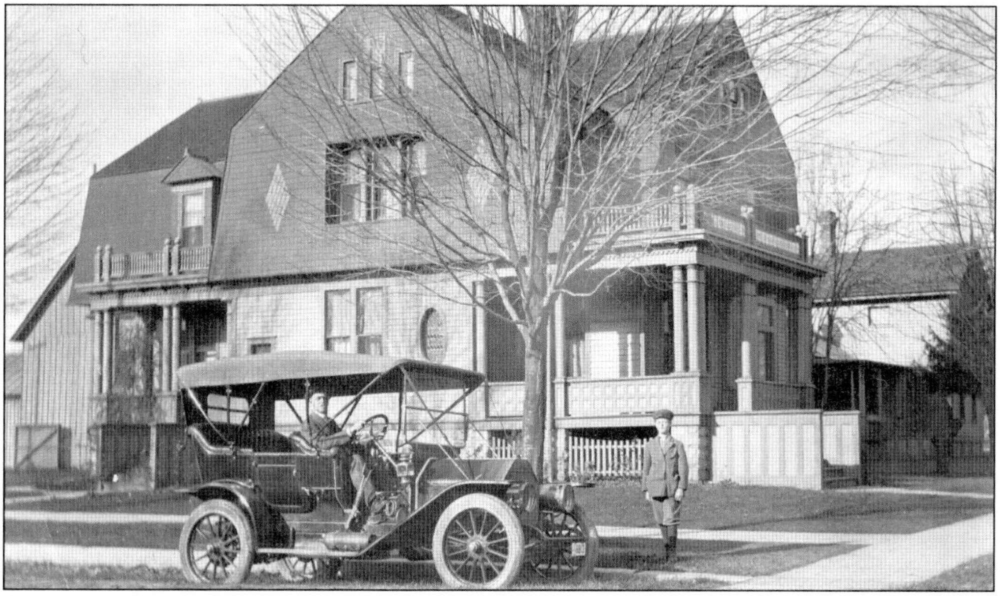

Almer and Gibbs Streets. This home on the corner of North Almer and Gibbs Streets was built by merchant Meyer Himelhoch. This photograph, taken about 1911, shows later owner H.T. Phelps and his son Raymond. Meyer and his brother Isaac Himelhoch moved to Seattle in 1905 and set up a retail business that supplied the Alaskan gold rushers. (Courtesy of Watrousville-Caro Historical Society.)

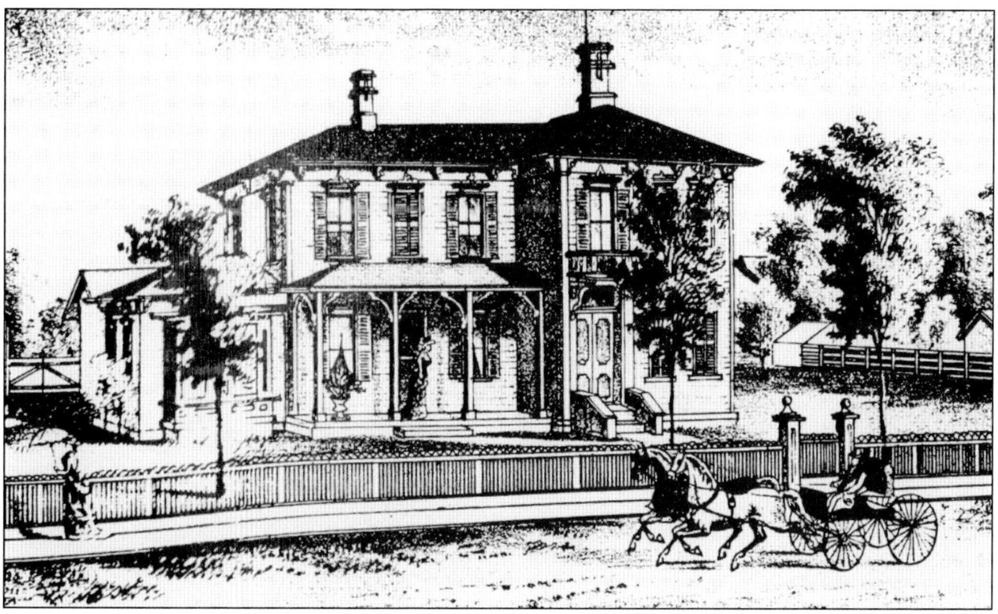

Charles Montague Home. This fine home was located on the current site of the Caro City Hall on South State Street. Montague labored tirelessly for the growth and prosperity of Caro as well as for his own success. He died at this home on January 10, 1921, at age 75. (Courtesy of Norman Dorr Wiltsie.)

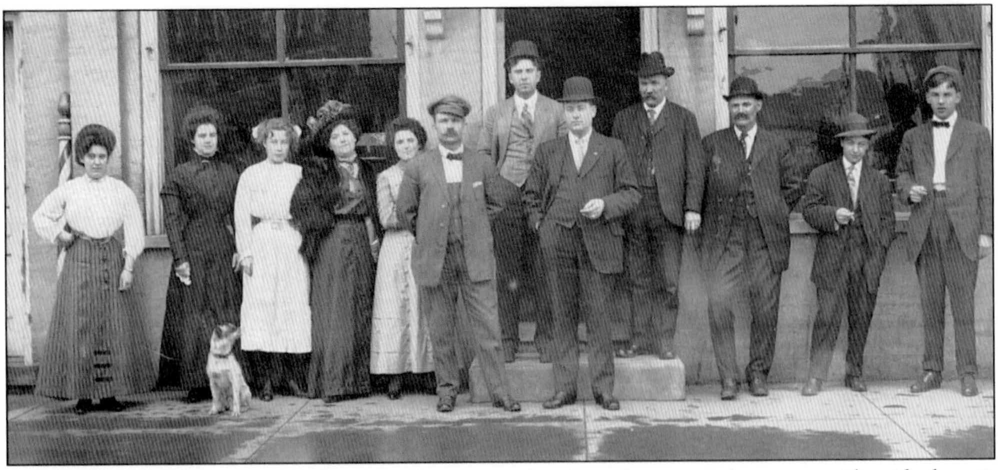

Boarders. The folks in this photograph are noted as boarders, and they are unidentified, as is the building where they are standing. It is also unclear to whom the dog actually belongs. The photograph inspires many questions, but it also shows a cross section of Caro inhabitants. (Courtesy of Watrousville-Caro Historical Society.)

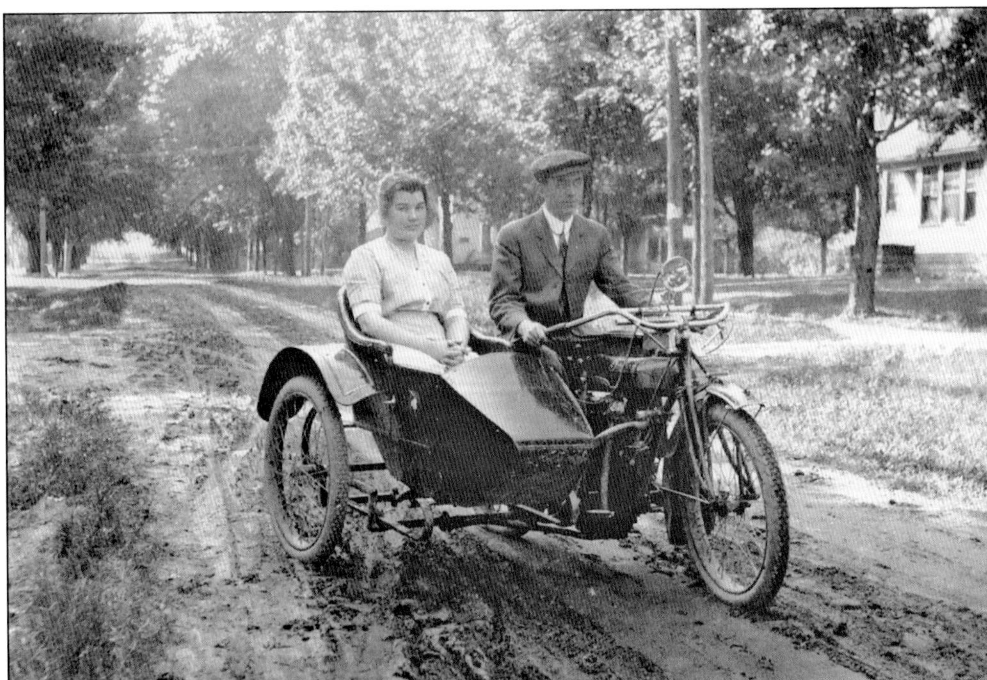

Motorcycle and Sidecar. An unidentified young couple takes a muddy ride down what is possibly West Frank Street before it was paved. Perhaps the motorcycle and sidecar were purchased from Louie Luder's shop on State Street. (Courtesy of Tim Romain/Cope collection.)

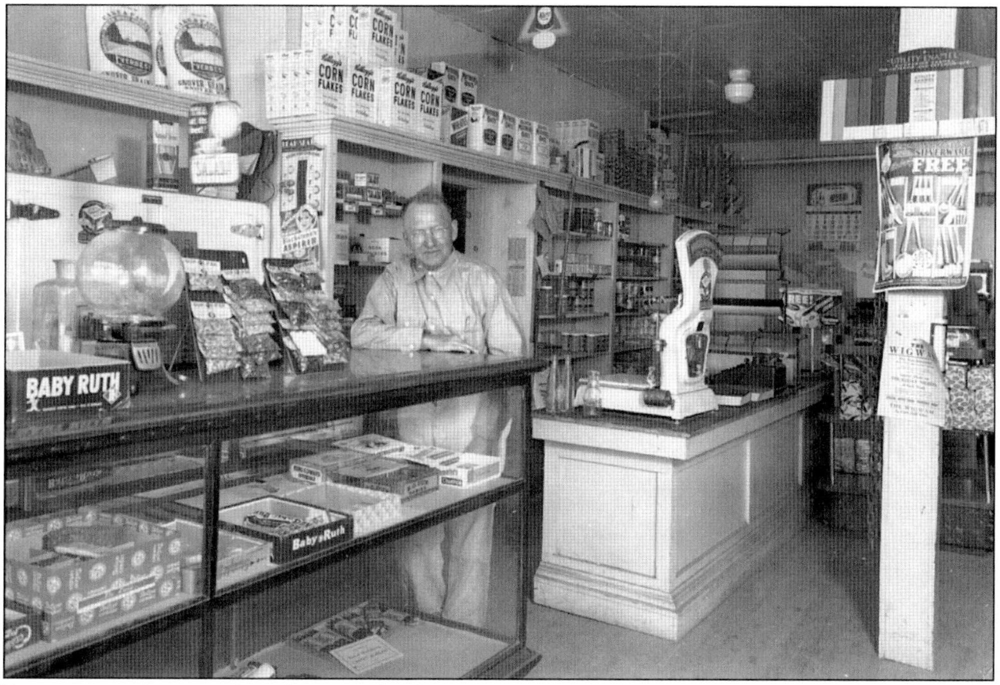

INTERIOR OF STORE. This photograph of a Caro-area general store was taken in 1940, according to the Taystee Bread calendar on the wall. Some of the goods available include Kelloggs cereals, Oxydol detergent, Salada tea, Blackstone's aspirin, and Everbest cake and pastry flour from Snover, Michigan. A poster from the Wigwam advertises special music each week on Thursday night. (Courtesy of Watrousville-Caro Historical Society.)

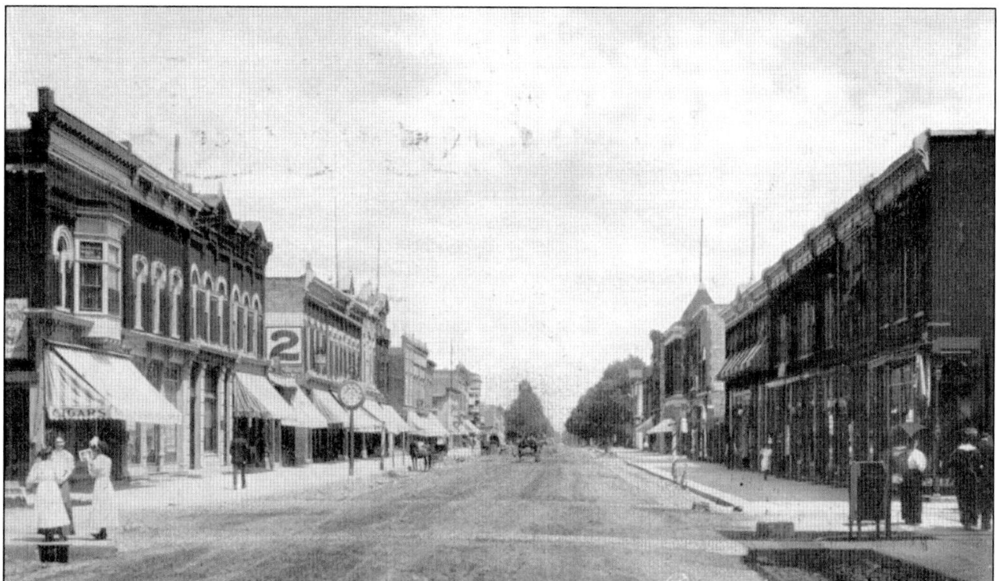

MOORE'S DRUG STORE, STATE STREET. Looking northeast from Lincoln Street in abut 1910, Moore's Drug Store is on the far left. The first drug store at this location was owned by William O. Luce, who was assisted by George Moore. Moore went on to run the Moore Drug Store for many years. (Courtesy of Gloria Hall.)

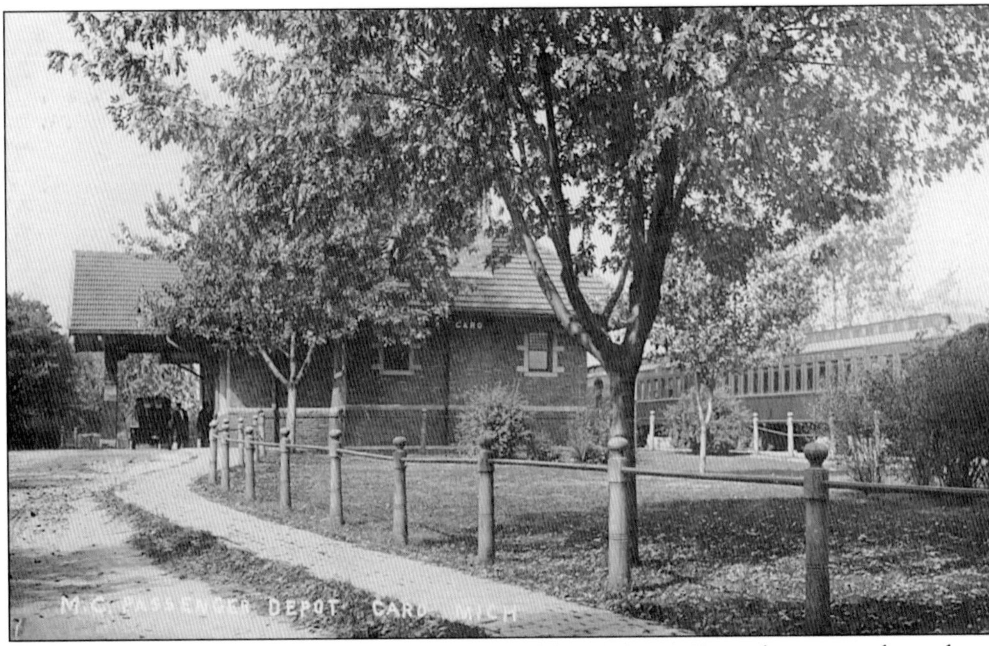

MICHIGAN CENTRAL DEPOT. This lovely 1917 view of the Michigan Central passenger depot shows the passage of time. The trees have grown around the brick depot, and the horse and wagon of the 1905 photograph have been replaced by an automobile. (Courtesy of Gloria Hall.)

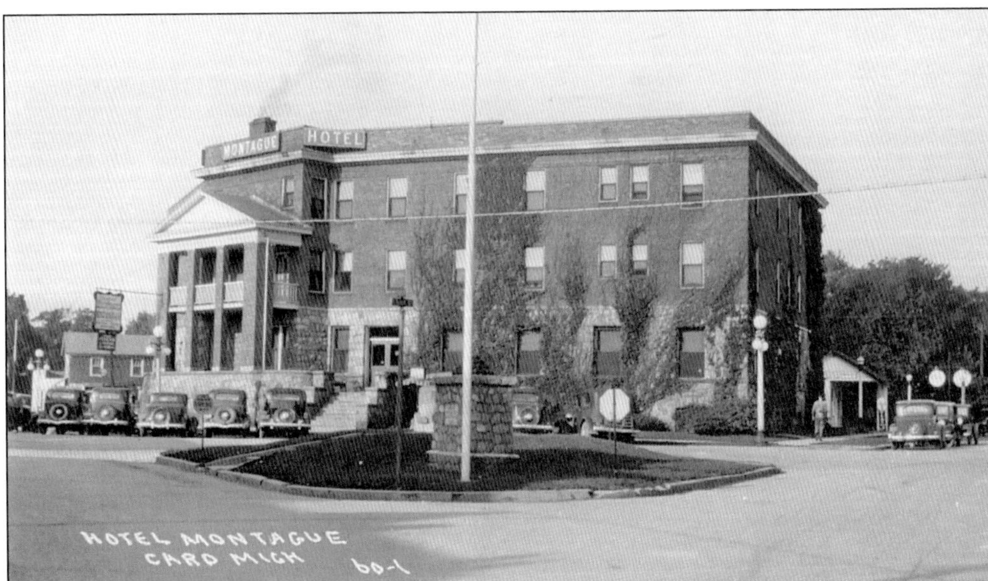

HOTEL MONTAGUE, 1940. The Civil War Memorial dedicated in 1926 (shown on page 82) is visible in the village triangle in this 1940 view of the Hotel Montague. The hotel was advertised as "the largest and finest in the Thumb, conveniently located, and with fine food and a modern taproom." (Courtesy of Gloria Hall.)

Five

Rural Life

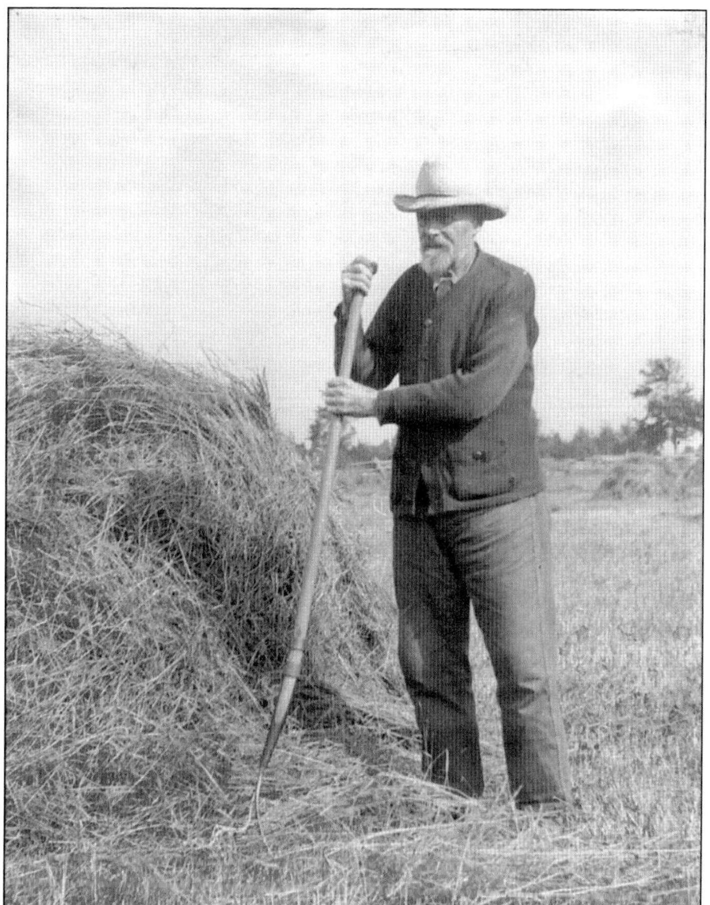

Alfred Edward Hunt. Hunt was the grandfather of Carolyn Hunt Ayre, who donated this photograph to the Watrousville-Caro Historical Society. Calloused hands, strong backs, and delineated tan lines from the hat band down to the collar were trademarks of early farmers and, indeed, of farmers today. Hunt remains forever frozen, leaning on his pitchfork in a reflective time-out from pitching hay. (Courtesy of Watrousville-Caro Historical Society.)

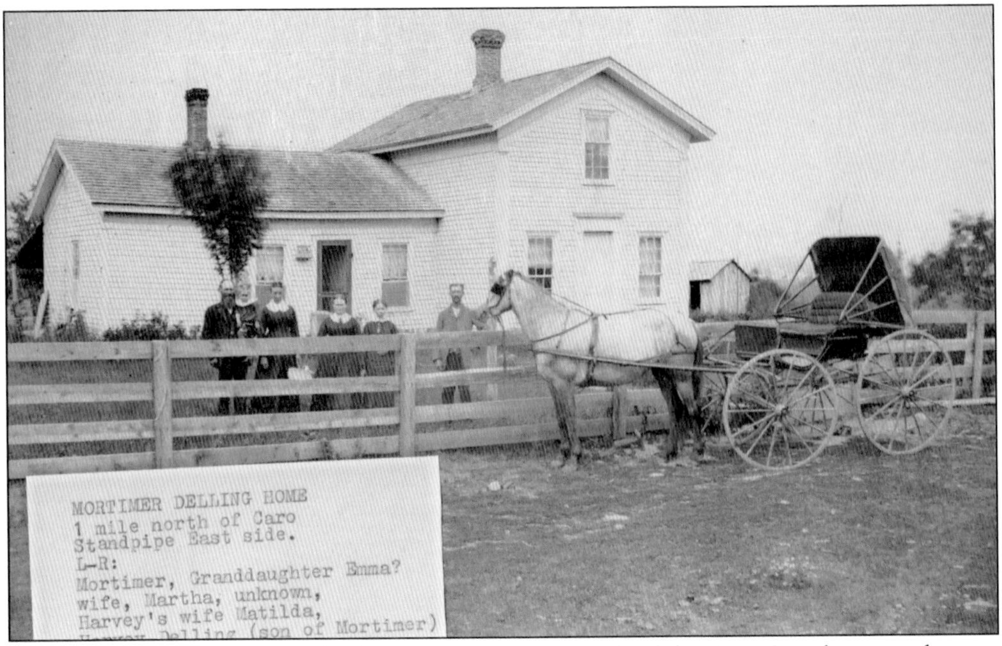

MORTIMER DELLING HOME. This home was one mile north of the Caro Standpipe on the east side of North Colling Road. The photograph appears to have been taken in the 1870s or 1880s. From left to right are Mortimer Delling, believed to be holding his granddaughter Emma, wife Martha, unidentified, daughter-in-law Matilda, and son Harvey Delling. (Courtesy of Clara Korte/ Watrousville-Caro Historical Society.)

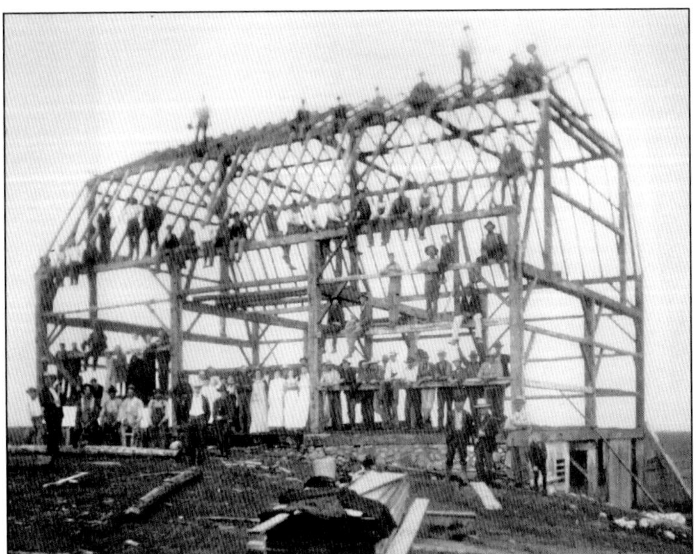

OLD-FASHIONED BARN RAISING. A barn was so important that it was often the first structure built by a family settling a new farm. Another indication of a barn's importance was that participation in the barn raising was mandatory for all able community members. This activity was a visible symbol of the need for rural community members to stand together and help each other. (Courtesy of Tim Romain/ Cope collection.)

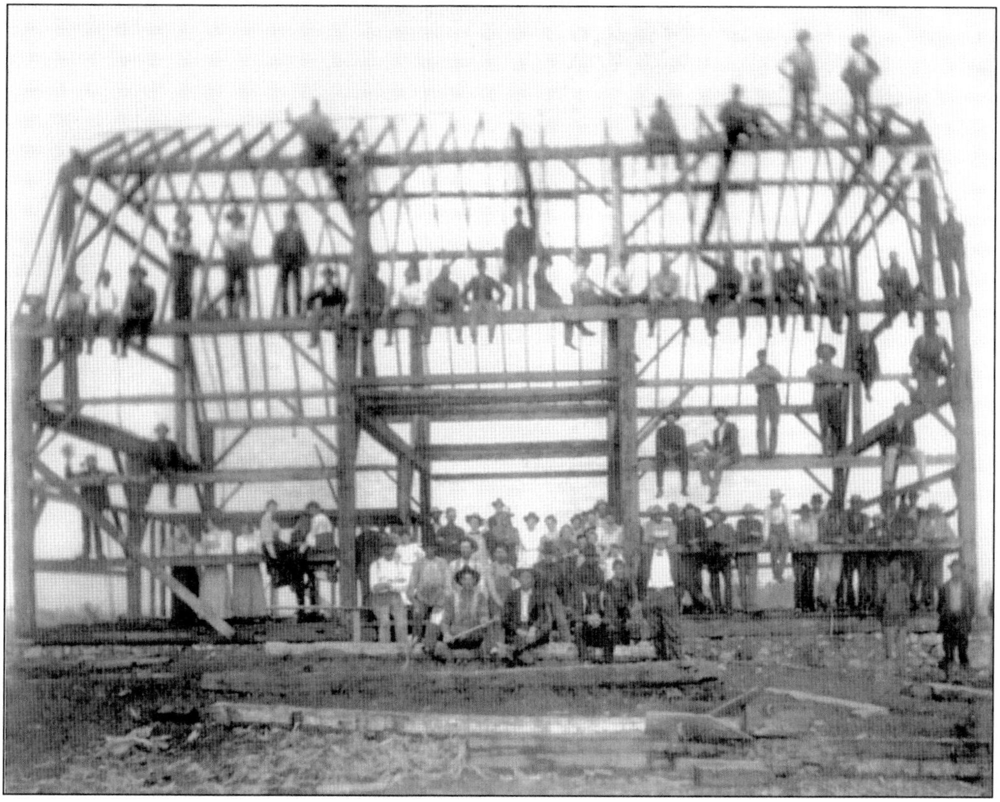

Another View. By the end of the 19th century, barn raising was increasingly rare, and most barns were constructed by hired labor. This photograph, like the previous one, shows a barn raising. This well-organized activity was done in a day or two, after lumber and hardware were brought in, ground was cleared, and plans made. (Courtesy of Tim Romain/Cope collection.)

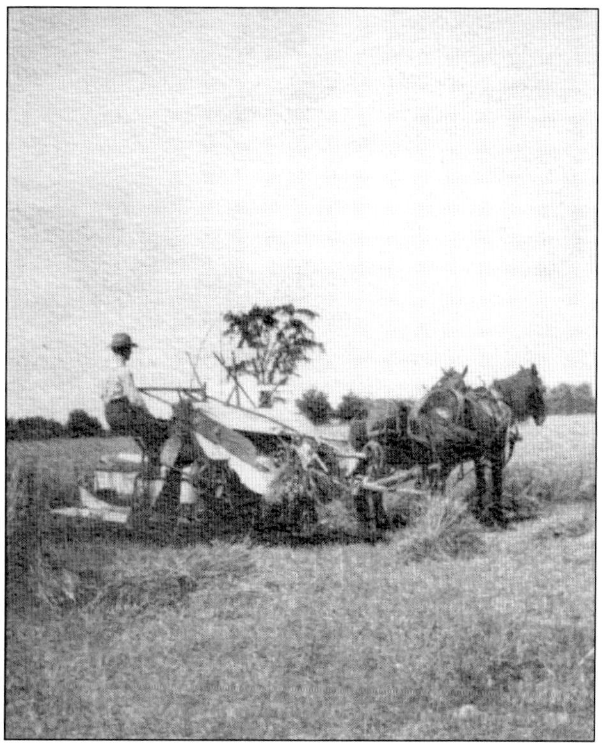

Grain Binder. The grain binder was an intermediary step between the hand-held grain cradle, or a sickle, and the combine. Developed in the 1870s, the binder cuts the standing grain and conveys it up to the driver, where it is bundled. The bundles are arranged together in the field to form small shocks to allow for further drying of the unripe grain. (Courtesy of Watrousville-Caro Historical Society.)

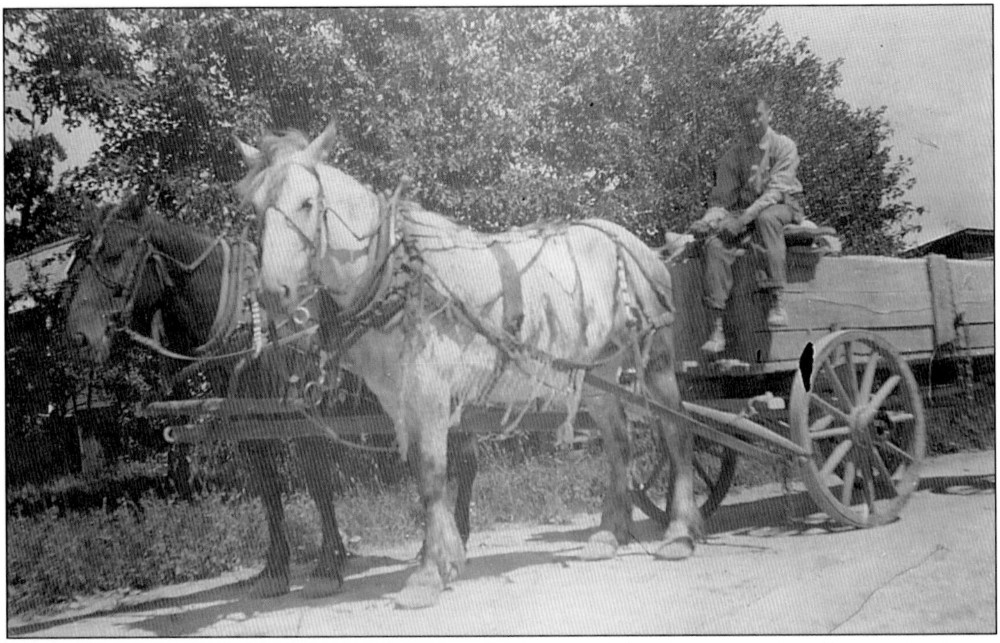

Mighty Horses. The quality of its horses and teams could make or break a farm or business. This photograph, from about 1900, is labeled simply, "Uncle Ernie," and shows business as usual in the streets, fields, and woods of the area. Even with the advent of the automobile, for many years, horses, teams with wagons, and buggies continued to be the transportation of choice. (Courtesy of Laureen Joslin.)

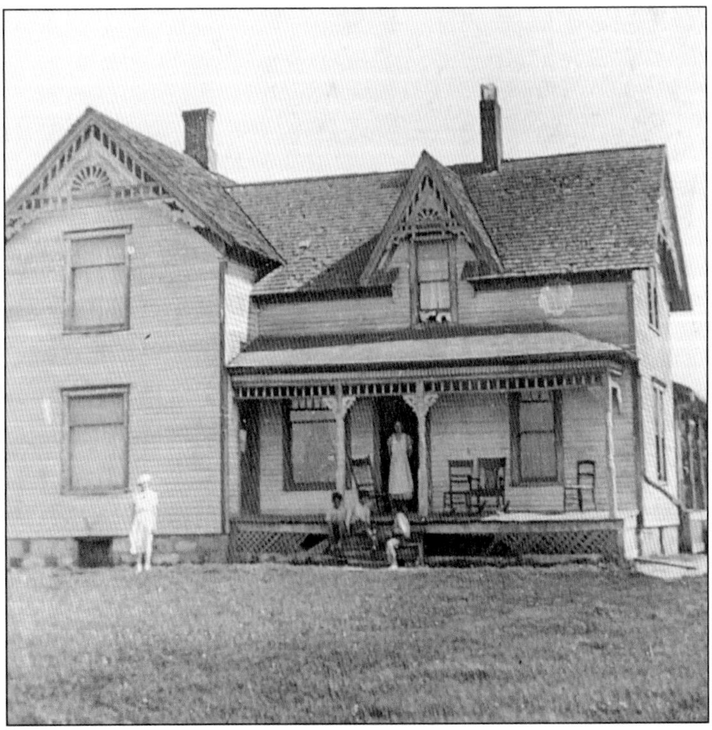

The Jacques Home. The Jacques farm was established by Victoria and Jerome Jacques. This house and land on West Dutcher Road have remained in the same family through five generations. From left to right are Madeline Jacques Marker (standing), Martin LaPratt, Francis LaPratt, Otto Jacques (sitting on the porch), and Alice Jacques (in doorway). (Courtesy of Gail Lesoski.)

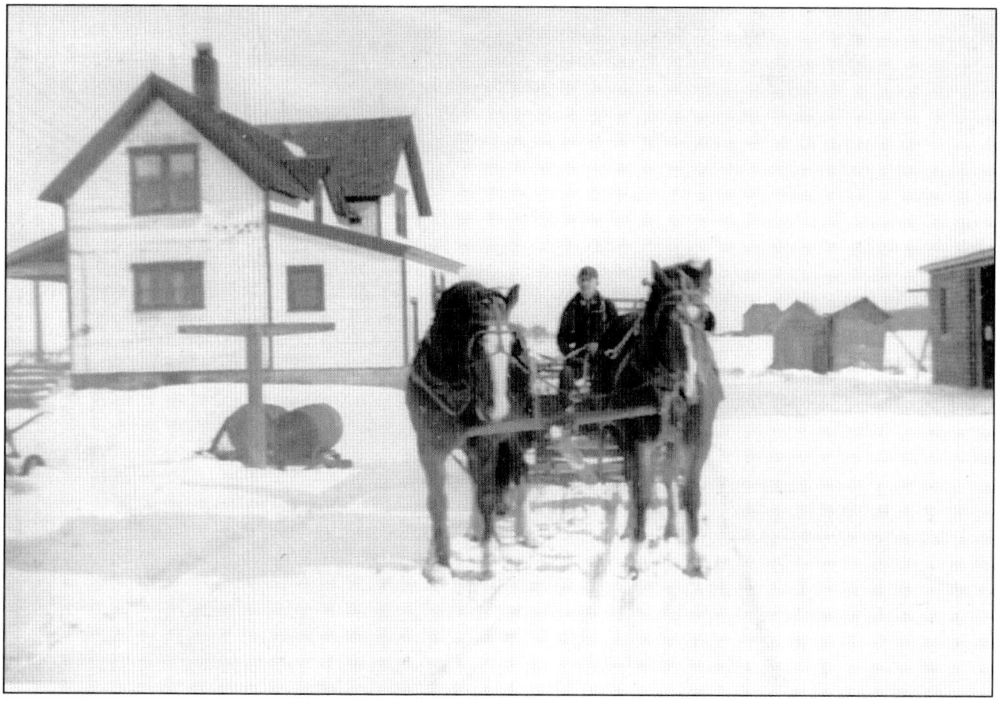

Jaques Farm, c. 1940. This photograph is a glimpse back into the 1940s, with Jerome Jaques and his team Daisy and Molly tending to winter chores at their farm on West Dutcher Road. This Jerome Jaques dropped the "c" from his family name. (Courtesy of Gail Lesoski.)

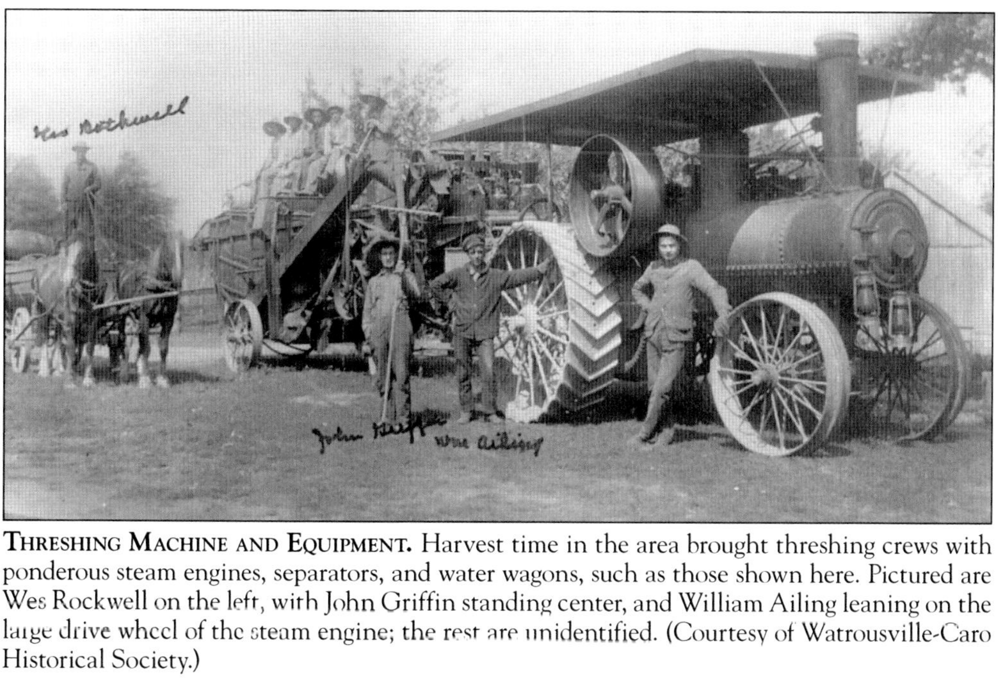

Threshing Machine and Equipment. Harvest time in the area brought threshing crews with ponderous steam engines, separators, and water wagons, such as those shown here. Pictured are Wes Rockwell on the left, with John Griffin standing center, and William Ailing leaning on the large drive wheel of the steam engine; the rest are unidentified. (Courtesy of Watrousville-Caro Historical Society.)

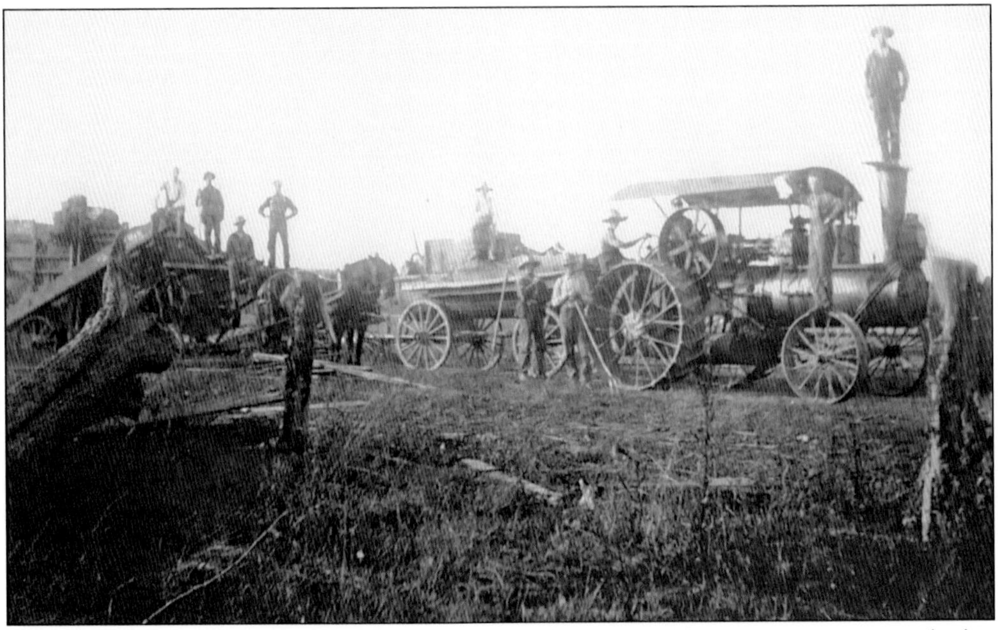

THRESHING. This is a standard threshing crew from about 1900. The steam engine is attached to a water wagon. A team of horses is pulling the thresher. On site, the thresher would be hooked to the small upper pulley on the engine via a drive belt. The shocks of wheat or oats were thrown into the thresher, which separated out the grain into a hopper for bagging. (Courtesy of Tim Romain/Cope collection.)

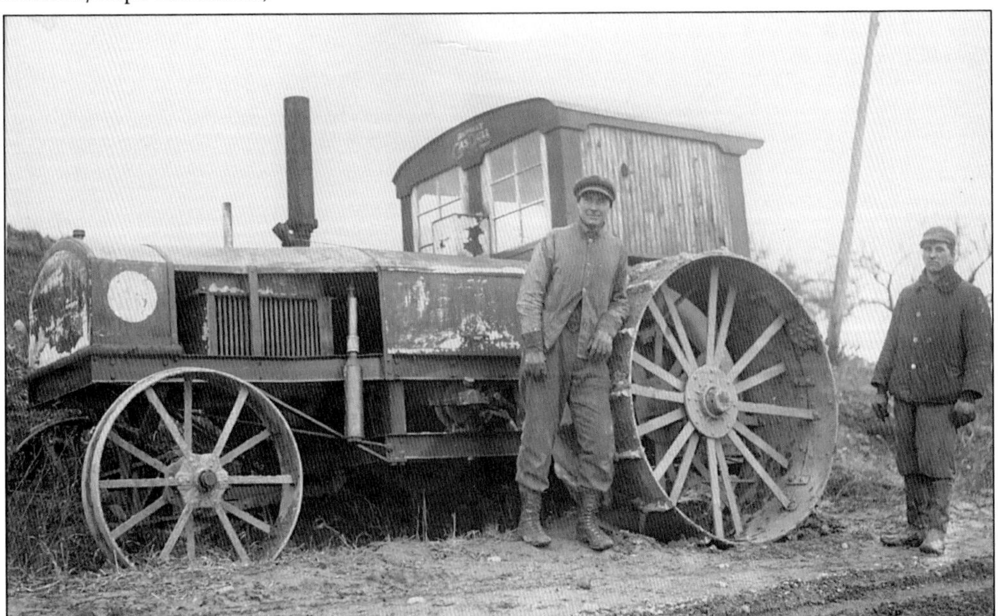

TRACTOR, 1915. This tractor was state-of-the-art in 1915, demonstrated by the early incarnation of an enclosed cab. The tractor operator is identified as H.V. Gekeler (possibly Herbert) but no further information is given. The photograph was taken by well-known Caro photographer Earl Beyette, whose photography studio was at 120 West Lincoln Street. (Courtesy of Watrousville-Caro Historical Society.)

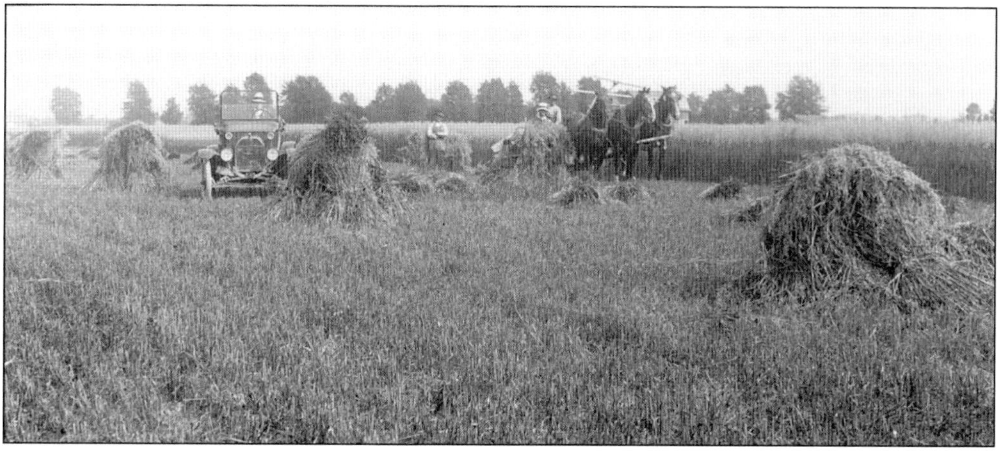

Old Meets New. An automobile and a horse team share the oat field in 1917 at the R.P. Reavey farm north of Caro. The team is pulling a grain binder that cuts the oats, pushes them through the binder, and stacks them until the platform is full. They are then pushed off in spaced piles. The workers gather the bundles, leaning them against one another into shocks. (Courtesy of Watrousville-Caro Historical Society.)

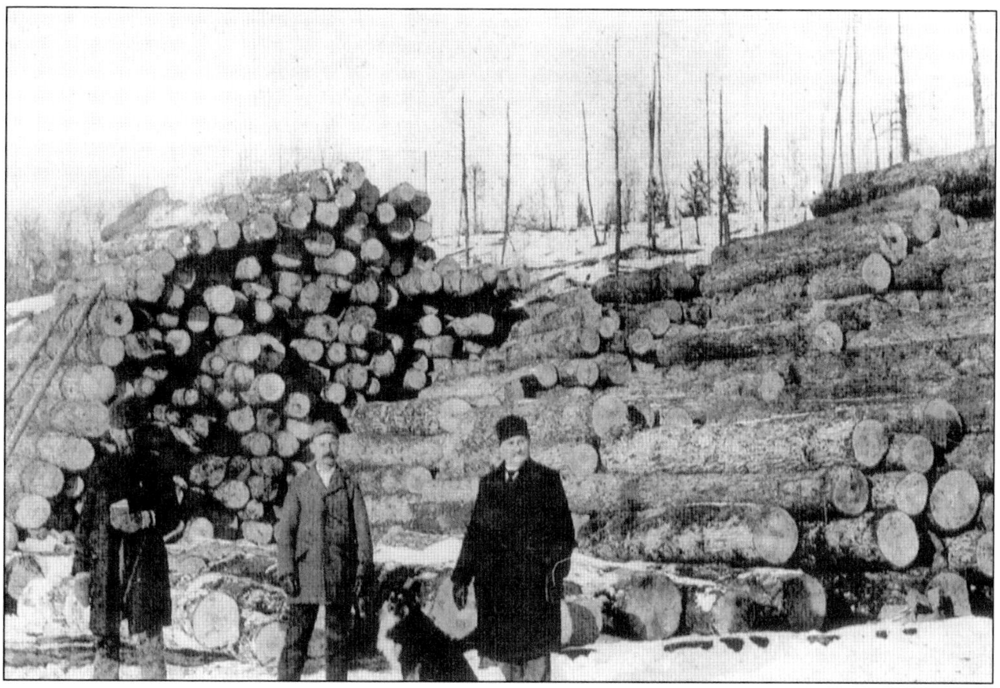

Winter Work. Lumbering continued to provide much needed income for farmers, and some villagers who kept their hand in the lucrative business, through the 1870s. This was winter work, and these logs were definitely smaller than the logs harvested in the beginning of the logging era in the Caro area. (Courtesy of Laureen Joslin.)

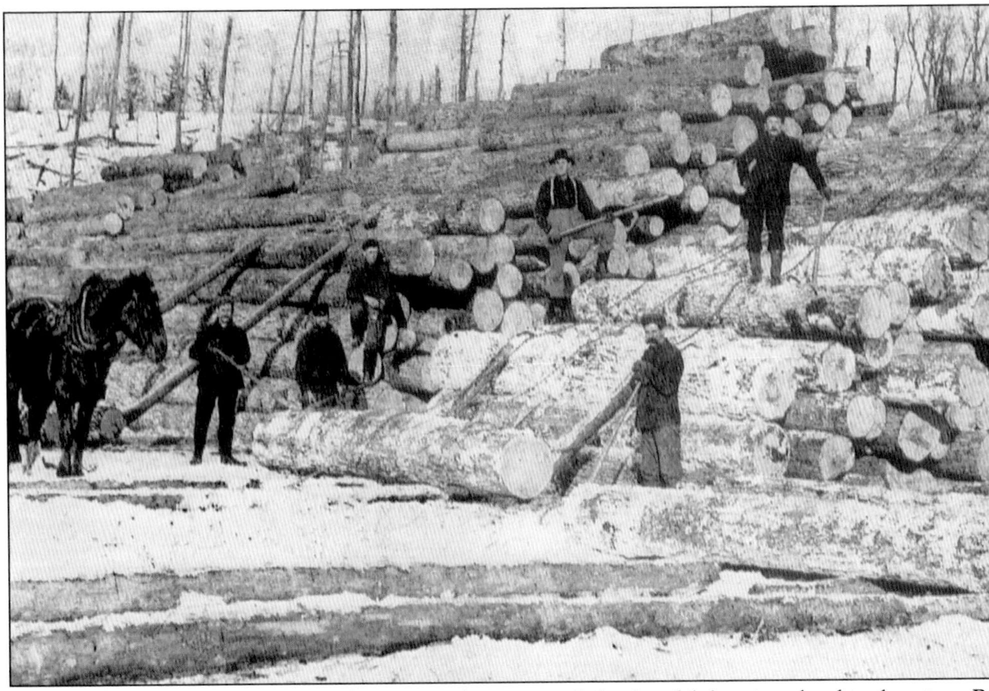

Another View of Logging. This is another view of the hard labor involved in logging. By the 1880s, lumbering had ceased for the most part. The great forest fires of 1871 and 1881 had aided in clearing the forests and set up farming as the next economic engine. (Courtesy of Laureen Joslin.)

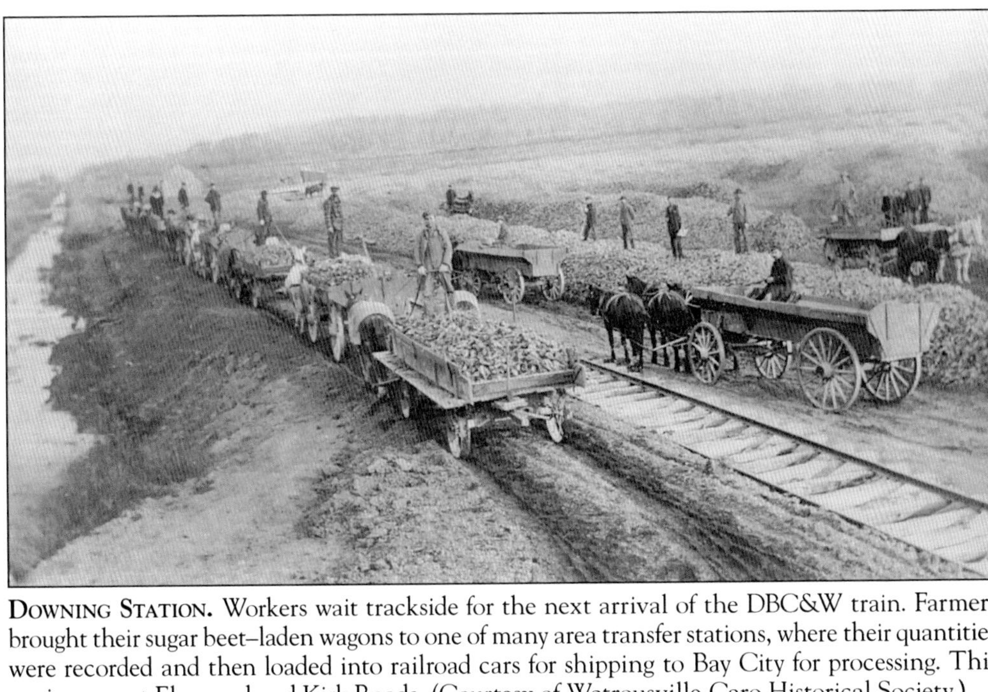

Downing Station. Workers wait trackside for the next arrival of the DBC&W train. Farmers brought their sugar beet–laden wagons to one of many area transfer stations, where their quantities were recorded and then loaded into railroad cars for shipping to Bay City for processing. This station was at Elmwood and Kirk Roads. (Courtesy of Watrousville-Caro Historical Society.)

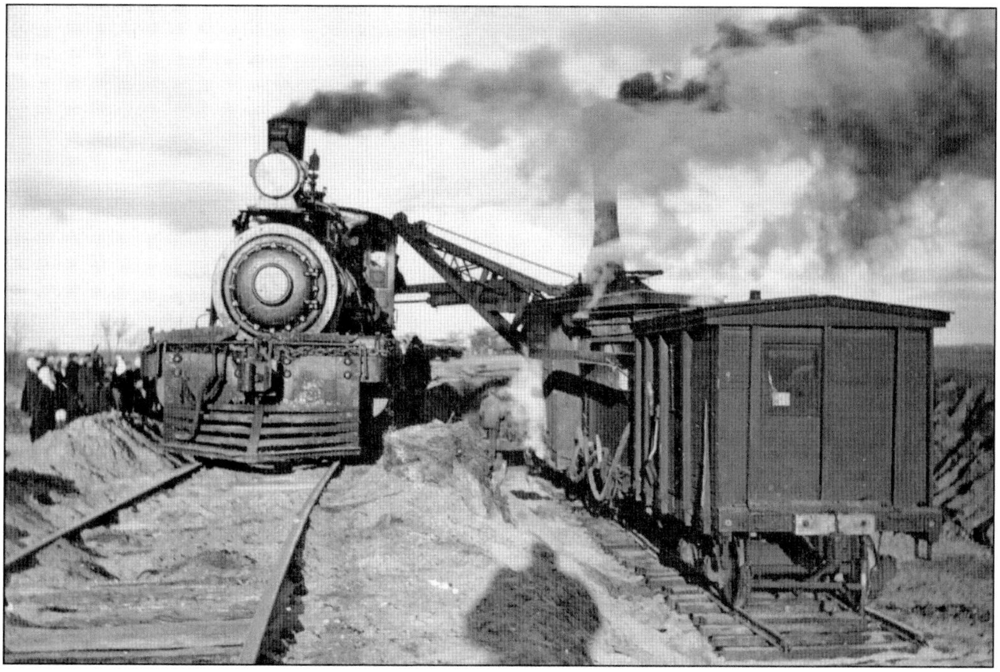

TRACKSIDE, 1908. A steam locomotive and crew work trackside to repair washout damage to the track bed (lower left corner) as unidentified onlookers watch. A steam crane with its tender car has been brought in, possibly, to right the tipping locomotive. The engine has a large spotlight on top and a steam whistle next to it. (Courtesy of Watrousville-Caro Historical Society.)

COUNTRY STORE. This unidentified store interior is representative of country stores of the late 19th and early 20th centuries. The store is packed from floor to ceiling with goods of all sorts. Considering the goods displayed, the establishment could have quite possibly been a hardware store. (Courtesy of Watrousville-Caro Historical Society.)

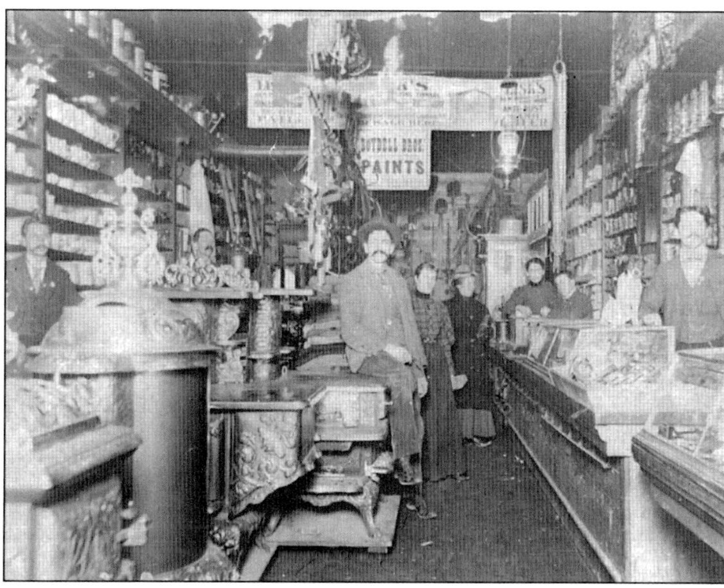

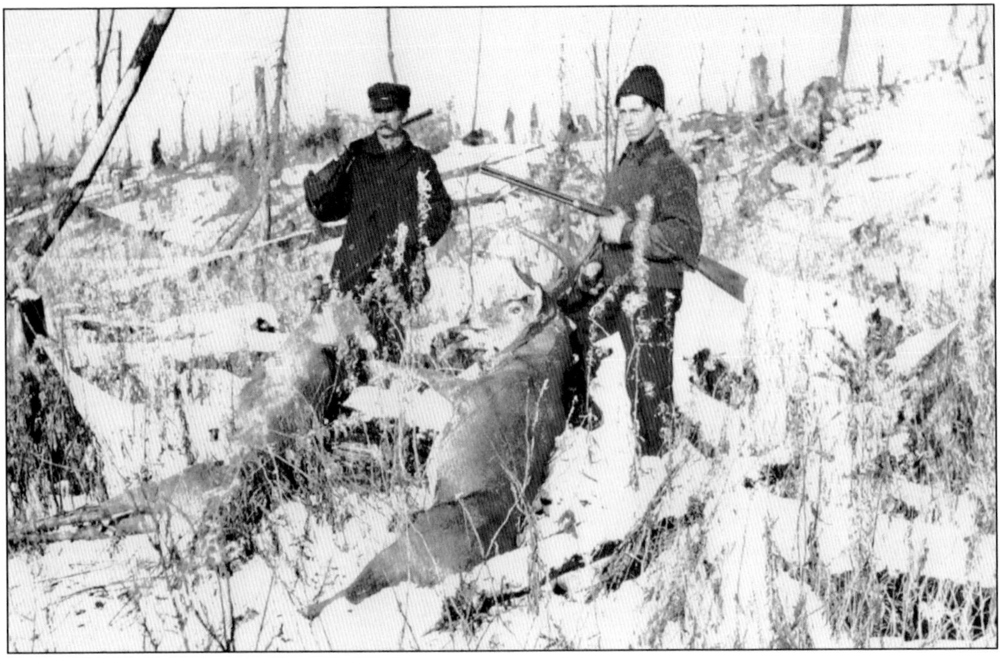

Hunting Deer. These unidentified hunters show off their day's take. The spot where they are posed shows evidence of lumbering and/or fire. Burnt trees and charred wood appear to be beneath the snow. Fire was an ever present danger to both the rural dweller and the villager. (Courtesy of Tim Romain/Cope collection.)

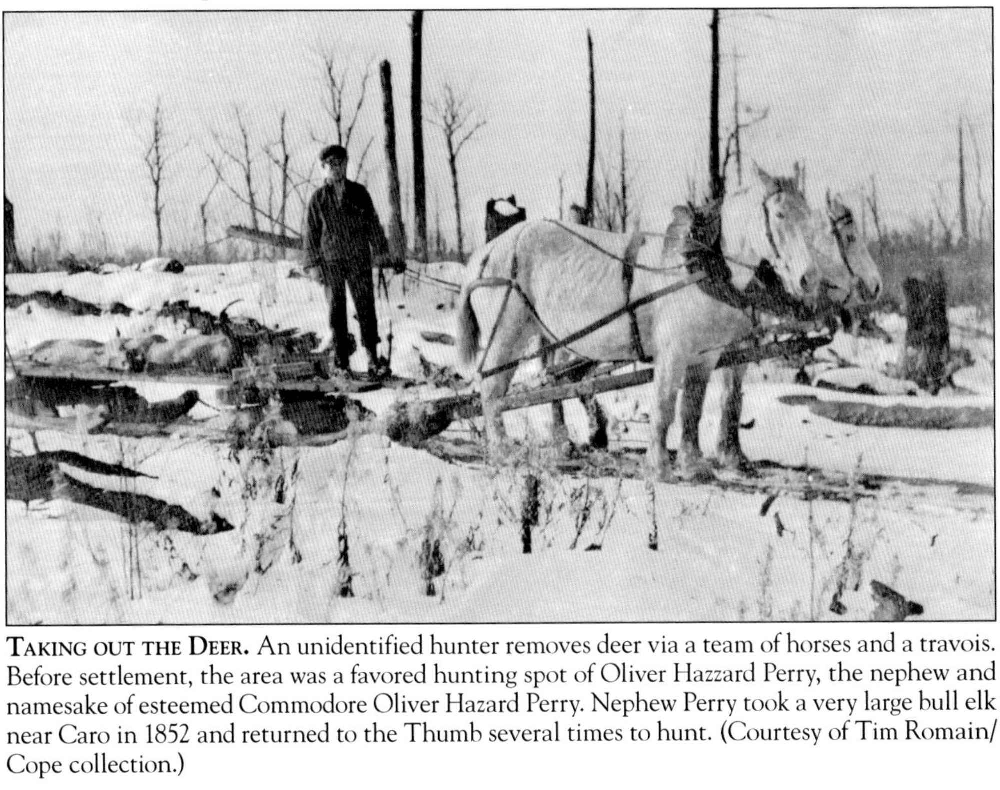

Taking out the Deer. An unidentified hunter removes deer via a team of horses and a travois. Before settlement, the area was a favored hunting spot of Oliver Hazzard Perry, the nephew and namesake of esteemed Commodore Oliver Hazard Perry. Nephew Perry took a very large bull elk near Caro in 1852 and returned to the Thumb several times to hunt. (Courtesy of Tim Romain/Cope collection.)

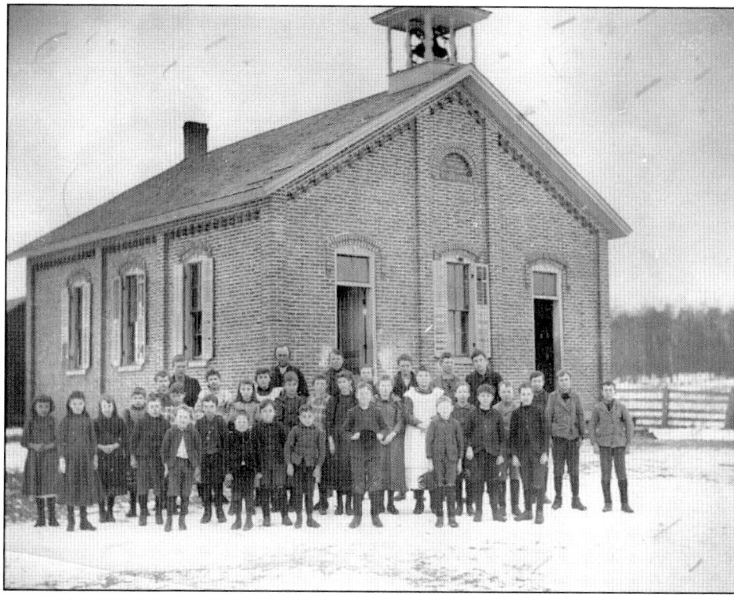

Rural School. This wintery photograph, taken about 1915, is an example of the rural schools built throughout the area. Education was a primary concern, starting with the first settlers. The two entrances include one for the girls and one for the boys. (Courtesy of Watrousville-Caro Historical Society.)

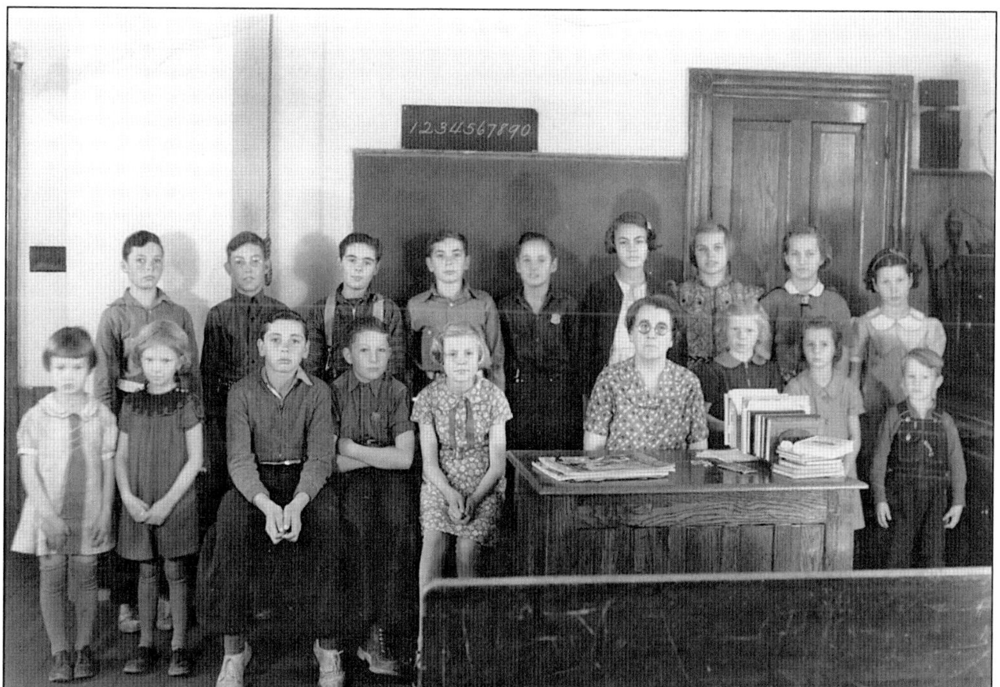

Rural School Classroom. Pictured is a typical interior of a one-room schoolhouse with the blackboard and the teacher's desk in front. This teacher is identified as Maude Allard. From 1908 through 1951, rural schoolteachers trained at the Tuscola County Normal School. (Courtesy of Watrousville-Caro Historical Society.)

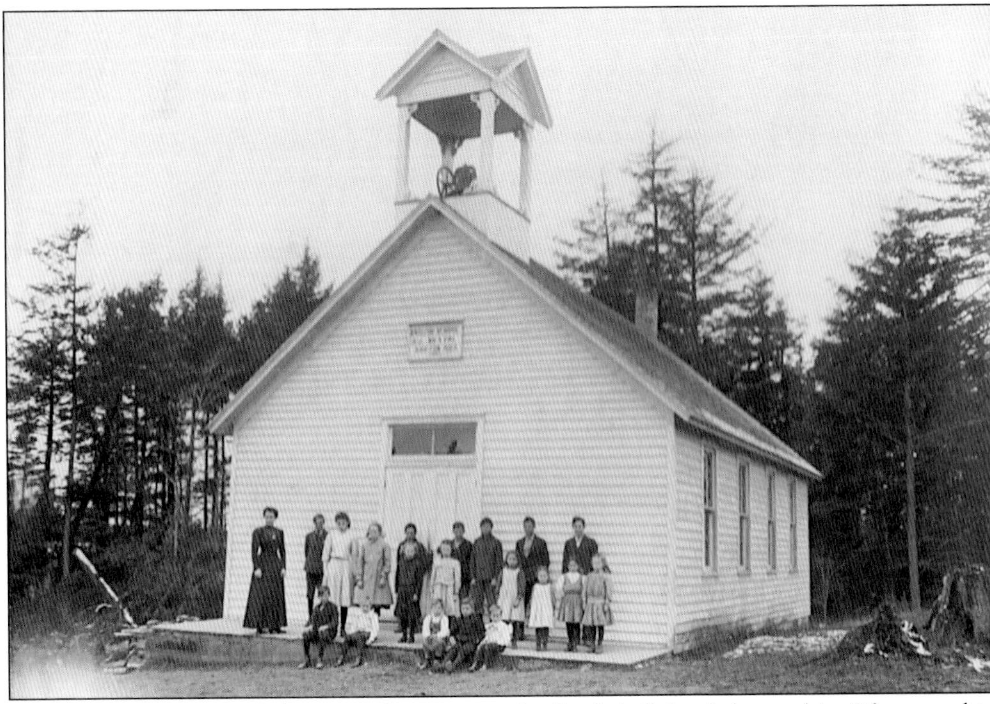

English School. Nestled among the pines is the English School, located in Silverwood in Dayton Township. Isabelle J. Gulliver is the teacher on the far left. There were numerous schools in every township and village in the county. Some of these buildings still stand today. (Courtesy of Gloria Hall.)

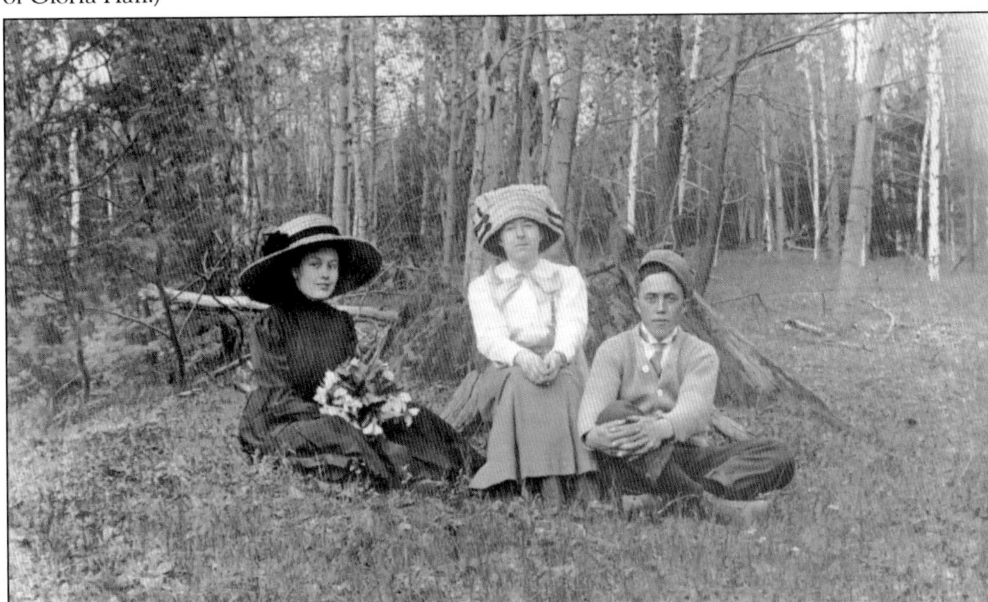

Country Day. Margaret Lawrence Gunsell (left), Analena Lethbridge (center), and Roy Lawrence enjoy what may be a spring day. Perhaps Gunsell has picked a spring bouquet. Their appearance is a reminder of how formal the necessary public attire once was. (Courtesy of Clara Korte/Watrousville-Caro Historical Society.)

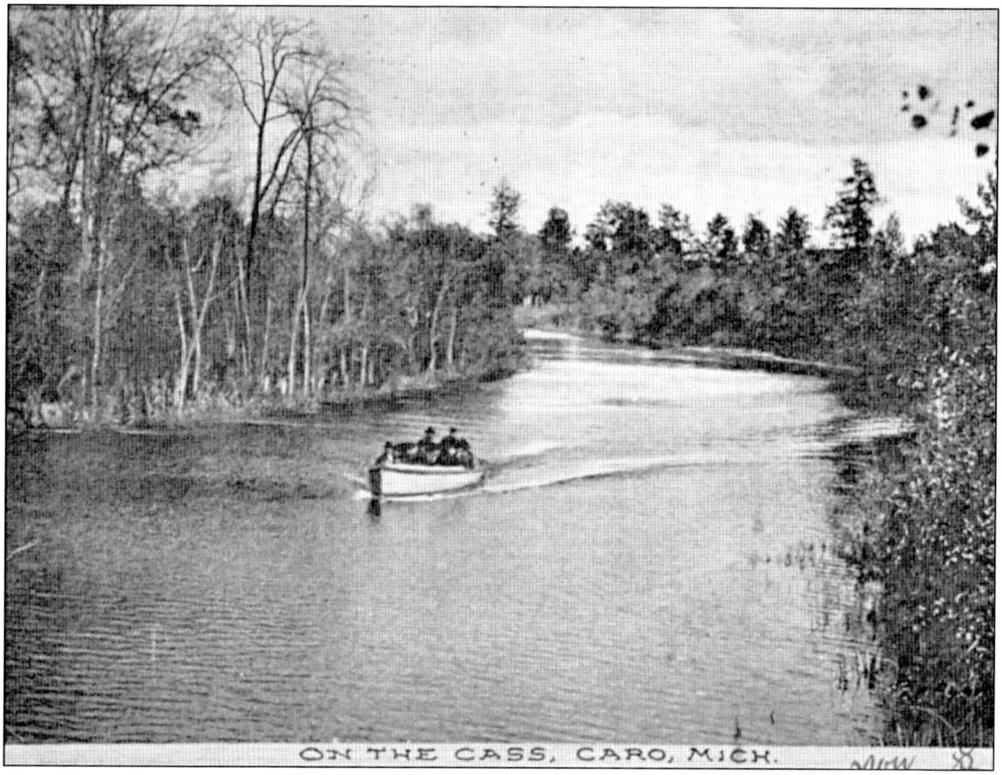

CASS RIVER RECREATION. When the power dam was built at the Ox Bow, the Cass River became a large body of placid water, which supported the quickly popular sport of recreational boating. Private as well as commercial recreational boating flourished, and attempts were made to build business for Caro as a summer resort area. (Courtesy of Gloria Hall.)

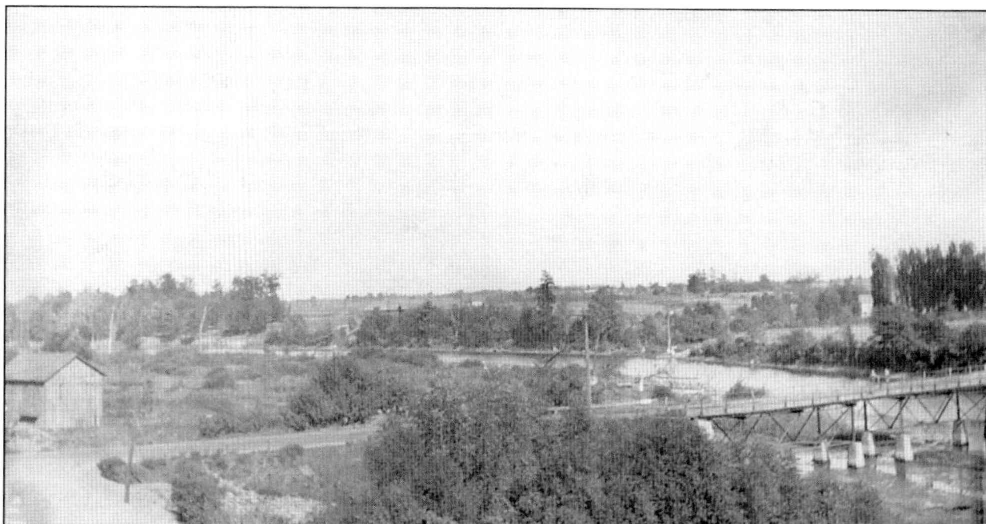

LONG VIEW. This unidentified view of the Cass River and bridge shows the bucolic nature of the area. The photograph is from about 1911 and very likely shows the lower bridge, as an excursion launch is barely visible at the shore just above the bridge; such an enterprise existed at the lower bridge at that time. (Courtesy of Gloria Hall.)

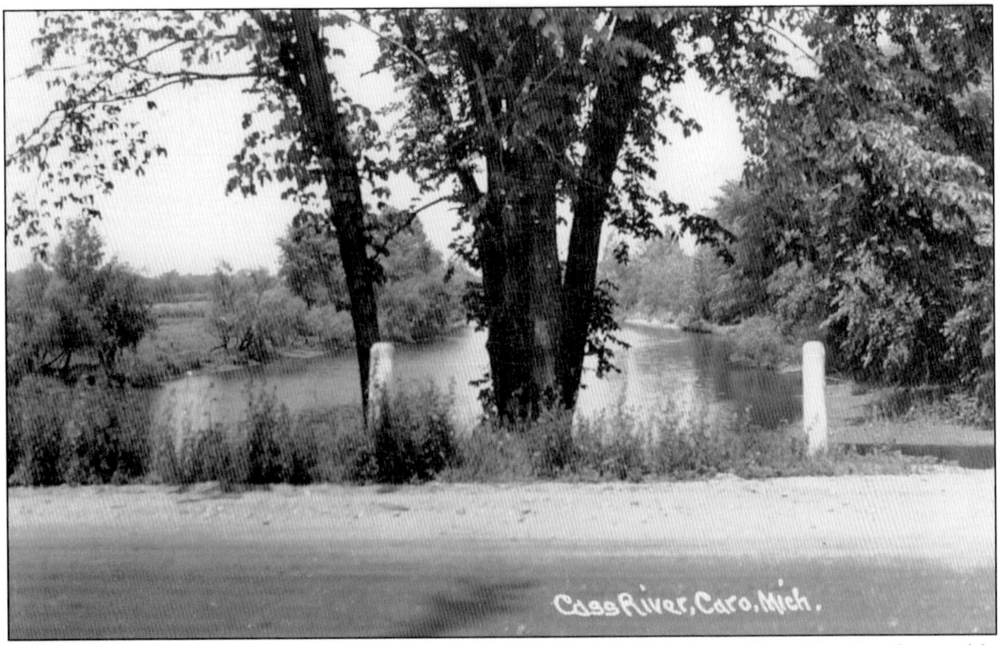

COUNTRY VIEW. In this beautiful summer view, the Cass River is seen from Orr Road, possibly at the intersection with East Dayton Road. Once heavily utilized for logging and dammed for power, the Cass River is now mostly used for recreation and as a wildlife habitat. (Courtesy of Gloria Hall.)

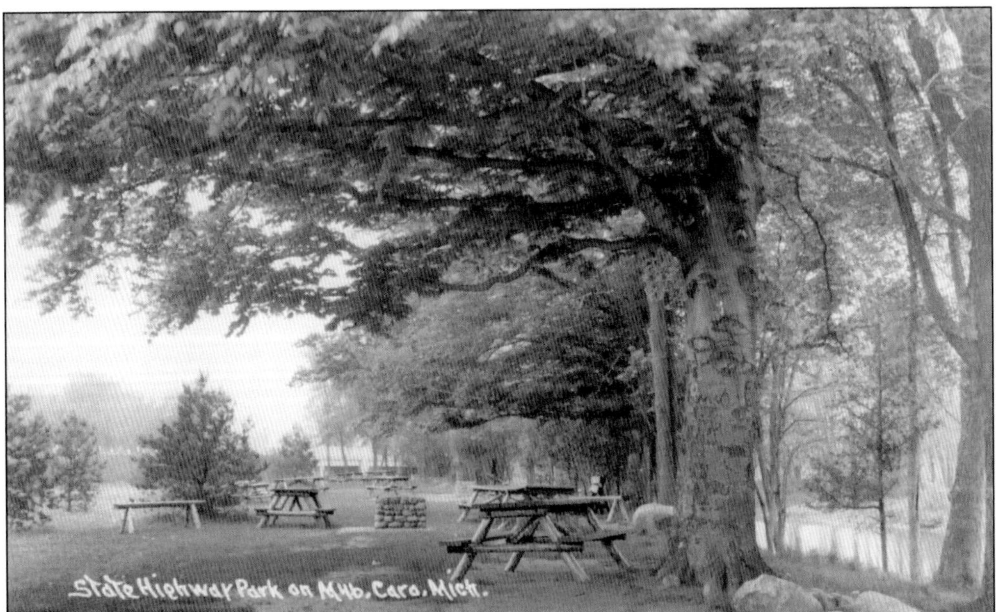

ROADSIDE PARK. Situated on M-46 and beside the Cass River, this state highway roadside park is south of Caro. The Main Branch of the Cass is formed by the merging of the North and South Branches at a point just south of Cass City. It flows into the Shiawassee River, close to the confluence of the Shiawassee and the Tittabawassee Rivers that forms the Saginaw River. (Courtesy of Gloria Hall.)

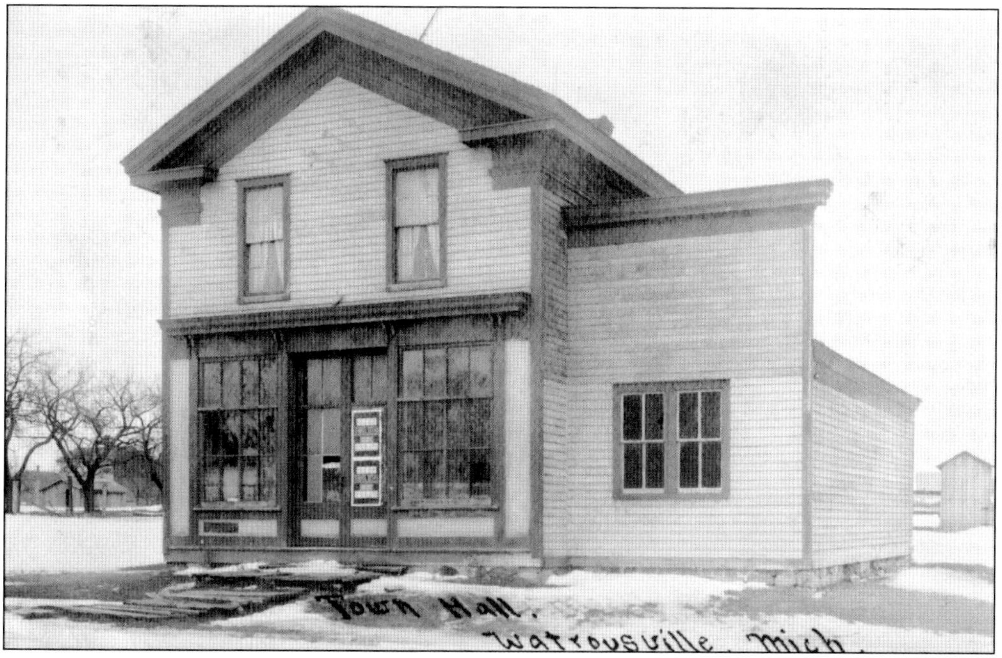

Town Hall. Watrousville was first settled in 1851 by Patrick McGlone, whose log home on the path travelled by lumbermen and settlers became a tavern. Aaron Watrous had settled here by 1853 and established a sawmill, a gristmill, and a store. He was remembered as a kind man who helped many a struggling settler. (Courtesy of Gloria Hall.)

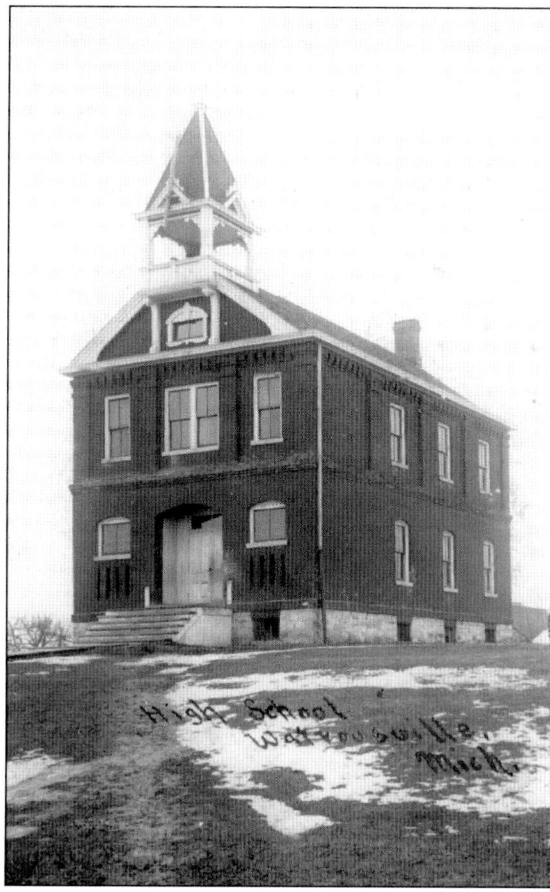

Watrousville School. The two-story brick building pictured was erected in 1889 for kindergarten through 10th grade. In the early 1940s, the upper grades started going to the Caro School. The second story was removed in 1944, resulting in a school that went only to the sixth grade. The school closed in 1960, and the Juniata Township offices are now located in the building. (Courtesy of Gloria Hall.)

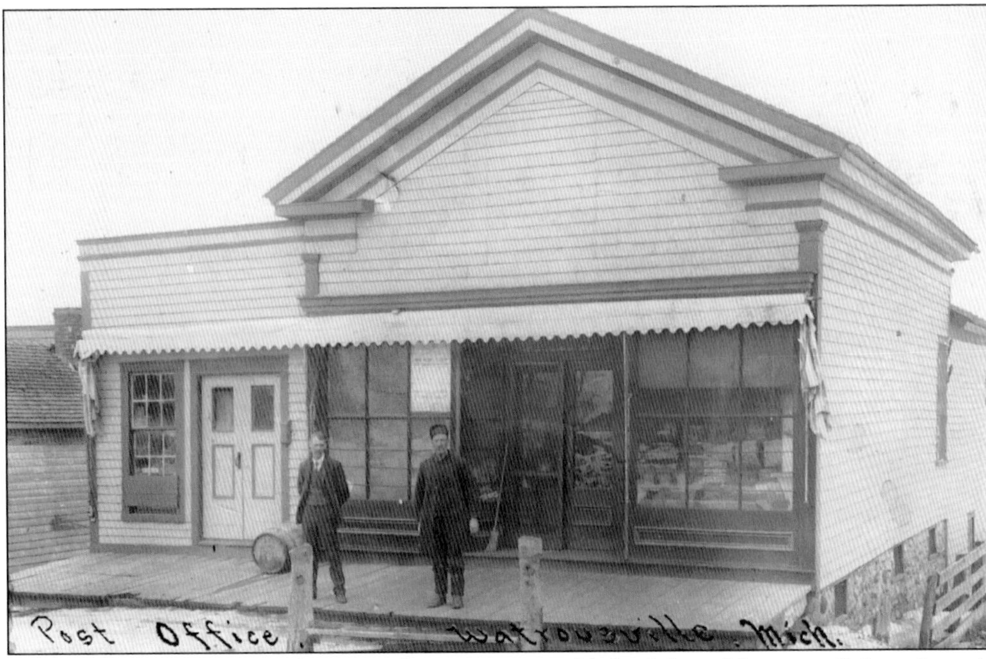

Post Office, c. 1908. After a mail route was established from Vassar to Sebewaing via Watrousville, a post office was located in Watrousville in 1856, with Aaron Watrous as postmaster. Prior to that, mail was brought in on foot or by horseback once a week from Vassar. (Courtesy of Gloria Hall.)

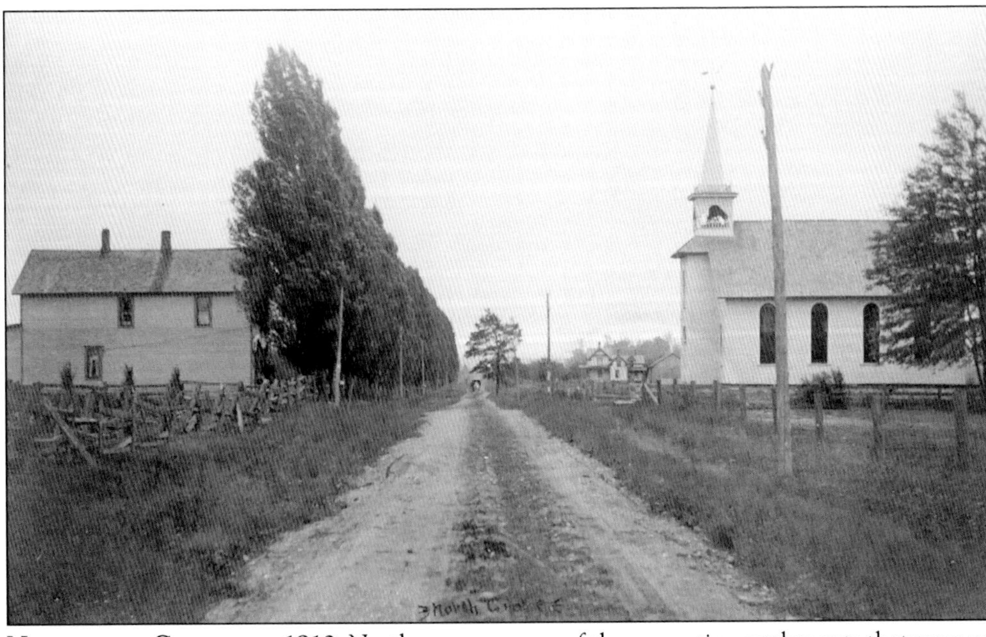

Northgrove Church, c. 1910. Northgrove was one of the many tiny settlements that grew up around the area in the latter part of the 19th century. It was located approximately seven miles southeast of Caro, then west off M-24. Northgrove had a church, a school, and a loose collection of houses with a dirt-track main street. (Courtesy of Gloria Hall.)

Bibliography

Centennial Committee. *Caro Centennial Souvenir Booklet*. 1952.

Doying, Howard P. and Joseph W. Braun. *Caro Illustrated 1905*. Saginaw, MI: Saginaw Printing and Publishing, 1905.

Gallery, Douglas C. *Early Days in Caro*. Caro, MI: *Tuscola County Advertiser*, 1957–1959.

History of Tuscola and Bay Counties, Michigan: With Illustrations and Biographical Sketches of Some of Their Prominent Men and Pioneers. Chicago: H.R. Page, 1883.

Wiltse, Dorr Norman. *A Look in Your Own Backyard or Tales of Caro and Nearby Places*. Caro, MI: self-published, 1983.